The Essence of OLE with ActiveX

A Programmer's Workbook

David S. Platt, M.E.

President, Rolling Thunder Computing, Inc.

**Instructor in Computer Science,
Harvard University Extension School**

To join a Prentice Hall P T R
Internet mailing list, point to
http://www.prenhall.com/register

Prentice Hall P T R, Upper Saddle River, New Jersey 07458

Library of Congress Cataloging-in-Publication Data

Platt, David S.
  The essence of OLE with ActiveX: a programmer's workbook / David S. Platt.
    p.   cm.
  Includes index.
  ISBN 0-13-570862-1
    1. Object-oriented programming (Computer science) 2. OLE
(Computer file)   I. Title
QA76.64.P62   1996
005.7--dc20   96-43584
                                                           CIP

Editorial Production: bookworks
Acquisitions Editor: Michael Meehan
Manufacturing Buyer: Alexis R. Heydt
Cover Designer: Design Source

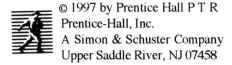 © 1997 by Prentice Hall P T R
Prentice-Hall, Inc.
A Simon & Schuster Company
Upper Saddle River, NJ 07458

The publisher offers discounts on this book when ordered in bulk quantities.
For more information, contact:

Corporate Sales Department
Prentice Hall P T R
1 Lake Street
Upper Saddle River, NJ 07458
Phone: 800-382-3419
FAX: 201-236-7141
E-mail: corpsales@prenhall.com

Printed in the United States of America

10 9 8 7 6 5 4 3 2

ISBN 0-13-570862-1

Prentice-Hall International (UK) Limited, *London*
Prentice-Hall of Australia Pty. Limited, *Sydney*
Prentice-Hall Canada Inc., *Toronto*
Prentice-Hall Hispanoamericana S.A., *Mexico*
Prentice-Hall of India Private Limited, *New Delhi*
Prentice-Hall of Japan, Inc., *Tokyo*
Simon & Schuster Asia Pte. Ltd., *Singapore*
Editora Prentice-Hall do Brasil, Ltda., *Rio de Janeiro*

To my parents, Ellen and Ben Platt

Table of Contents

This page intentionally contains no text other than this sentence.

Preface

On the Teaching and Learning of OLE

WHY I WROTE THIS BOOK

OLE has a reputation for being hard to learn. A client once told me that he knew of only two programmers in the entire world who understood it, both of whom worked for Microsoft and spent their days writing puzzles for each other. But really, nothing could be further from the truth. OLE has an elegant simplicity to its architecture and an internal self-consistency that the Windows API lacks. It's just a different way of looking at the world. This book is an attempt to clear things up, to present in a simple and easily digested fashion the stuff I had to learn the hard way.

As I hope to demonstrate in this book, learning OLE isn't that hard. It may take you a little while to get the basic concepts, though I've done my best to build easily accessible ramps into it. But once the light bulb goes off, probably after about two weeks, you have the keys to all of OLE. Learning the Windows API was largely a matter of memorizing arbitrary function calls without any central organizing principle, sort of like memorizing all those boring equations in college organic chemistry. Learning OLE as presented in this book is more like learning the basic principles that cause the entire universe to operate. Remember college physics? The simplest equations, such as $F = MA$, describe all macroscopic motion, from the falling of a feather to the collision of galaxies.

HOW TO TEACH OLE AND HOW NOT TO

Part of OLE's nasty rap results from its debut at a Microsoft professional developers' conference in Seattle in May 1993. It was a disaster. Never in my life had I seen so many people scratching their heads in the same place at the same time, myself included. Microsoft technical evangelists wear red shirts at these affairs so attendees can identify them and ask questions. At this conference the students were so annoyed that the evangelists changed into camouflage. The organizers made every mistake it was possible to make in the transfer of technical information. None of the attendees thought they had learned anything, except maybe to examine their options for career changes.

At the time I was hopping mad, as I had paid my own money to attend. But my teaching practice was starting to take off and I soon realized that I had really learned much more about instruction from the conference's abject failure to communicate anything useful than I would have had it actually taught me something about OLE. Thinking about how OLE should have been explained led me to the classes that I teach at Harvard, and to writing this book.

The first big mistake that the conference made was trying to explain OLE from the top down, a good approach for application development but not for instruction. OLE is so big that the first problem is figuring out where to grab it. This book starts with the simplest example I could think of, pasting text from the Clipboard into your app by means of OLE. It takes exactly 12 lines of code from start to finish. When you understand that, the chapter moves on to explain transferring text via drag and drop, which uses exactly the same mechanism for transferring the data but adds some support for the user interface. In the next chapter, you write your own object for placing data onto the Clipboard, and so on until you've digested all of OLE.

The second big mistake the conference organizers made was that they didn't even attempt to distill the important points from the sea of documentation. For example, when discussing an interface (a set of related functions, see Chapter 1), the presenter would simply list the functions in arbitrary order and discuss each one. The signal-to-noise ratio approached zero. In real life, an interface's functionality usually depends on and is best illustrated by one or two key functions. For example, in Chapter 2, when you write an object interface to put text into the Clipboard, you only have to write code for three of the interface's nine functions, and only one of these takes much work. The other six don't do anything useful in this instance and can be stubbed out to empty shells. If you ever need them, you can easily pick them up using the principles you learned while implementing the three important functions. I've done my best to concentrate my explanations on the important pieces and distill this sour mash into high-test moonshine.

The conference made many other small mistakes as well, which I have done my best to fix. They showed not a single code example, just neat little slides with bullet charts – a complete waste of time, the bandwidth of the medium is far too narrow to communicate anything useful. Programmers think in code, not bullets. Almost every page in this book has a code example on it. The conference presenters never told us where objects came from. "Assume you have an object," they would say, "and you want to do this or that with it. Never mind where it came from, just assume you have one." It made me very disoriented. Every chapter of this book starts by explaining where the objects that it deals with came from. The conference didn't have Kraig Brockschmidt's book to refer to. Whenever there is a topic that I thought some readers might want explained in more detail, I placed a reference to the exact page numbers in the second edition of *Inside OLE* by Kraig Brockschmidt (Microsoft Press, ISBN 1-55615-843-2) on which that topic is discussed.

THE MFC OR NOT THE MFC

This book covers both the API and the MFC implementation of OLE. The MFC prefabricates a lot of the plumbing between apps, allowing you to concentrate on the faucets on either end. The more complex the objects you are writing, the more useful this becomes. For simple text data transfer, it doesn't buy you much. For ActiveX controls, it's indispensable.

The problem with the MFC is that it's frequently marketed by people who ought to know better as a replacement for knowledge of the underlying API. It isn't; instead, it's a tool that amplifies your API knowledge or the lack thereof. If you simply use the MFC without any knowledge of what it's really doing, it's like not knowing how to swim, but using an inner tube to paddle into the middle of Boston Harbor. It's great until you spring a leak, then you are, as we say in Boston, "scrod." The MFC frequently doesn't work as advertised, or you need to do something different than what the MFC designers thought you would. Then you need to take it apart and see what it's really doing in its heart of hearts, possibly changing it, and you can only do that if you know the foundation on which it's built. In the Clipboard example in Chapter 1, the MFC expects the Clipboard to behave in a certain way. Unfortunately, the Clipboard doesn't work the way the MFC thinks it ought to. The workaround is fairly simple but it isn't documented anywhere. Unless you knew enough about the API to step into the MFC and decipher the source code, see what it was saying to the Clipboard and see what the Clipboard was saying back to it, you'd be scrod. So use the MFC, but learn what it's doing.

HOW TO USE THIS BOOK

If you are new to OLE, **READ CHAPTERS 1 AND 2 FIRST!!** Do not attempt to jump to other chapters until you feel comfortable with these. In these chapters I introduce the new programming model and vocabulary of OLE without which subsequent chapters will make no sense. I hate the term "paradigm shift;" it's been so badly overused as to have lost all meaning, but OLE does turn your head around.

You don't really own your knowledge of software until you've written some yourself. The end of each chapter contains self-study programming exercises with detailed instructions. The prepackaged labs pretty much follow the text, so they aren't hard. The extra credit sections at the end of each lab are designed to stretch your mind a bit more.

When you are actually writing your programs, keep this book handy on your desk. My students tell me that it is the first source they refer to, because it's easy to find what they want and easy to absorb it when they do find it. They only go off to a thicker book when they can't find what they want in this book. One student even has two copies, one at home and one at work.

WHY ALL THE EMPTY PAGES?

The reason I have them is to align the two-page sound bites over a spread of two facing pages. When a topic doesn't fit on a single page, such as the explanation of IDataObject::GetData( ) on pages 34 and 35, my experience has shown that students find the material much easier to absorb if it is spread across two facing pages. But the explanation of IDataObject::QueryGetData( ) on page 33 occupies only a single page. So page 32 has no point on it, so QueryGetData( ) goes on an odd-numbered page, so the following section properly spreads across two facing pages.

By the way, I can't stand pages that say "This page intentionally left blank." Does it never occur to anybody that this statement is self-negating? THE %$#^$@ PAGE ISN'T BLANK, IT CONTAINS THAT ONE LYING SENTENCE!! If the author can't even get that dinky little piece right, how can I believe anything else he says? Instead, my empty pages truthfully say, "This page intentionally contains no text other than this sentence." Call me a curmudgeon.

SEND ME FEEDBACK

I'd love to hear from readers, to find out which parts of the book were most useful. Also, I guarantee that, despite my best efforts and those of my reviewers, that some errors remain in this book, and I'd sure appreciate it if you'd tell me about them so they can be fixed in the next edition. My e-mail address is dplatt@rollthunder.com. You can also reach me via CompuServe at 73540,3430. By the time this book goes on sale, I ought to also have a Web page at http://www.rollthunder.com.

PROGRAMMING CLASSES AVAILABLE

A self-study guide like this one is great (I hope), but the fastest way to get going in programming is to have an in-house hands-on class. I'll come to your company and teach the subjects that you care about. In addition to OLE, I also teach the MFC and the Win32 API. Look for my other book, *The Win32 API from Scratch* (Prentice-Hall, ISBN 0-13-121484-5). Contact me by e-mail at the addresses in the preceding paragraph.

ACKNOWLEDGMENTS

I need to thank the following people, without whom this book would never have been completed. Mehrdad Givechi, who did a great job reading the book and finding errors. If he ever gets sick of programming, he's got a great future as a technical editor. Pat Duggan, who found so many typos in my previous book that he earned a free copy of this one. Kraig Brockschmidt, for discussions on the philosophy of OLE and of life in general. My wife Linda, for being there. And Mike Meehan, my editor at Prentice Hall, whom I have now forgiven for talking me into writing it.

— David S. Platt

This page intentionally contains no text other than this sentence.

Chapter 1

Introduction
Using Data Objects

A. CONCEPTS AND DEFINITIONS

1. COM, the *Component Object Model*, is Microsoft's top-level, all-encompassing binary and wire specification for the interoperation of one app with another, across multiple applications, machines, and hardware types. It provides the following features that are of interest to developers:

Single programming model
Binary compatibility
Uniform data transfer
Structured storage
Component software, reusable functionality
Macro programmability
Programming language independence
Distributed operation

2. OLE is a collection of higher-level functionality, primarily related to the user interface, that is built on top of the COM platform. It provides the following features which users like to have:

Compound documents
In-place activation
Drag and drop
Enhanced linking

It is not always clear exactly where COM stops and OLE begins. Philosophical debate on the topic is about as productive as debating how many pinheads can dance on an angel. In this book, the two terms will be used more or less interchangeably.

3. When you start an app that uses OLE, you must first call the function **OleInitialize( )** to initialize the OLE libraries for the app. The include files for all OLE functions are supplied via the header file "windows.h", and the import library is "ole32.lib".

If and only if this call succeeds, as shown below, should your app uninitialize the OLE libraries via the function **OleUninitialize( )** when it shuts down. The return type of OleInitialize( ), and of almost every other OLE-related function, is of type HRESULT, which is typedefed as a LONG. The high bit of the long is cleared if the call succeeded, set if the call failed. The macro SUCCEEDED( ) tests this bit and returns TRUE if the call was successful. Thus:

```
#include <windows.h>              // includes all OLE and COM files

int WINAPI WinMain(HINSTANCE hInstance, HINSTANCE hPrevInstance,
    LPSTR lpCmdLine, int nCmdShow)
{
    MSG msg;

/*
Initialize OLE Libraries.
*/

    HRESULT hr = OleInitialize (NULL) ;

/*
Run the app.
*/

    <all the other WinMain stuff>



/*
If they were initialized successfully, shut down the OLE Libraries.
*/
    if (SUCCEEDED(hr))
    {
      OleUninitialize ( ) ;
    }

    return (msg.wParam);

}
```

B. COMPONENT-OBJECT MODEL

1. OLE uses the *Component-Object Model*, switching from a function-oriented view of the world to an object-oriented view. In this model, an app does not manipulate the world via API functions, such as ShowWindow( ). Rather, the universe consists of *objects*, which expose one or more *interfaces* to the world. An interface is a group of related functions which operate on the object that exposes them. Some interfaces are standard, others are defined by the programmer. You cannot access an object's data directly, but only through the functions of the object's interface(s). This model is conceptually somewhat similar to C++ classes with all member variables private.

2. You will frequently hear the term "pointer to an object." Although the term gets used a lot as a convenient shorthand, it is really a misnomer. In COM, there ain't no such thing as a pointer to an object. What you have is *a pointer to an interface on the object*. In physical binary terms, you have a pointer to another pointer. This second pointer points to a table of pointers to the interface's member functions. This table of functions is known as a VTBL ("Vee-table"). One of the main advantages to implementing your objects in the C++ language is that the compiler will automatically set up the VTBL for you. However, when you have a pointer to an interface on someone else's object, you cannot assume anything at all about the internal organization of the object. It may well have been written in COBOL. In the following diagram, the location of the VTBL pointer and the object's private data are both shown amorphously, to re-emphasize the fact **that you cannot assume anything at all about the internal organization of an object. When you have a pointer to an interface on an object, you can call that interface's methods. That's all.** You cannot manipulate the internal reference count m_RefCount directly, but only by calling the IUnknown interface methods AddRef( ) and Release( ).

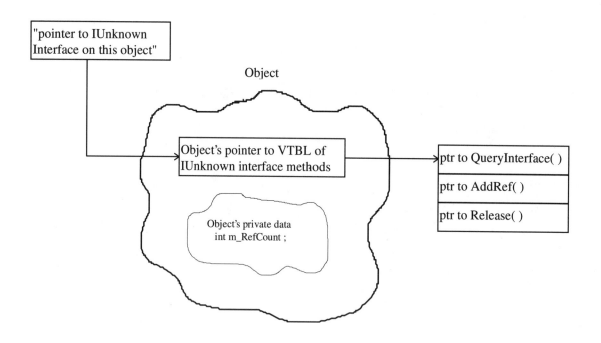

3. Once you have a pointer to an object (remember, this is shorthand for having a pointer to some interface on the object), you communicate with the object directly by calling the interface's member functions. But how do you get the first pointer to an object? There are several different ways. You might call an COM/OLE API function that returns a pointer to an object, such as the following:

CoCreateInstance( )   *// look in registry, launch COM server and get object from it*
OleLoad( )   *// read embedded or linked object from a document file*
OleGetClipboard( )   *// return an IDataObject interface pointer to the clipboard's contents*

Some interfaces have methods that create new objects and return pointers to them. If you have an object of one of these types, you can call the object's method, for example:

IDataObject::EnumFormatEtc( )   *// return an object that enumerates the format the data object has*

IClassFactory::CreateInstance( )   *// create a new object of the class manufactured by the factory*

You might register a callback object whose methods OLE will call and pass you a pointer to an object that OLE has created, for example:

RegisterDragDrop( )   *// register callback functions for drag-and-drop operations*

Or you might instantiate a C++ object whose VTBL conforms to the requirements of an OLE interface, for example:

new CSomeClass( )   *// instantiate an object that implements a COM interface*

C. IUNKNOWN INTERFACE

1. Every OLE and COM object, without exception, exposes an interface called *IUnknown* which contains the methods **AddRef( )**, **Release( )**, and **QueryInterface( )**. Each and every interface, without exception, is derived from IUnknown and has pointers to these functions as the first three entries in its VTBL. No matter which interface pointer you have, no matter how you got it, you can always call these three methods, and you frequently will.

The first two methods manipulate an internal reference count that controls an object's lifetime. When an object is first created, its creator must call the object's AddRef( ) method to increment the count. Whenever another user is given a pointer to the object, the object's AddRef( ) method must be called again. When the user is finished with the object, he calls that object's Release( ) method, thereby decrementing the reference count. When the last user calls the object's Release( ) method, the count will reach 0, causing the object to destroy itself. A simple implementation of the methods IUnknown::AddRef( ) and IUnknown::Release( ) might look like this:

```
/*
Increment member variable containing reference count.
*/

ULONG CUnknown::AddRef(void)
{
    return ++m_RefCount ;
}

/*
Decrement member variable containing reference count.  If 0, destroy
object.
*/

ULONG CUnknown::Release(void)
{
    --m_RefCount ;
    if (m_RefCount == 0)
    {
      delete this ;
      return 0 ;
    }
    return m_RefCount ;
}
```

2. Who is responsible for calling AddRef( ) and Release( )? There are two simple rules:

A. Whenever YOU CALL any function or method that returns a pointer to an object, such as OleGetClipboard() or any object's QueryInterface( ) method, the object's AddRef( ) method has already been called for you by the code that supplies the pointer. You must call that object's Release( ) method when you are finished with the object even if you don't do anything with it. It is the object's responsibility to make sure that it continues to exist until you do so.

B. When SOMEONE CALLS YOU and passes an object pointer as a parameter to one of your own callback functions, for example, in drag-and-drop operations, the object's AddRef( ) method has not been called for you. You must call the object's AddRef( ) if you want to use the object, and Release( ) it only if you have done so.

3. When you get a pointer to an object, what you really have is a pointer to one of its interfaces. Which interface you have depends on how you got the pointer. The object might or might not support other interfaces that interest you; there's no way of telling *a priori*. But since every object is guaranteed to support the IUnknown interface, you can ask the object if it supports some other interface that you care about via the method **IUnknown::QueryInterface( )**.

Interfaces are identified by means of *Interface ID's* 16-byte constants. Standard interfaces have their own IID's defined in the system header files, such as IID_IUnknown for the IUnknown interface. When you call QueryInterface( ), you pass it the IID of the interface that you want, and a pointer to an output parameter. If the object supports the requested interface, it will return the success code S_OK (defined as 0) and fill the supplied output parameter with a pointer to the requested interface. If the object does not support the requested interface, it will return a nonzero error code and set the output parameter to NULL. A simple implementation of IUnknown::QueryInterface( ) might look like this:

```
HRESULT CUnknown::QueryInterface(REFIID riid, LPVOID *ppv)
{

/*
Check the IID to see if we support the requested interface.  If we do,
increment the reference count, fill the supplied output variable with a
pointer to the interface, and return the success code.
*/

    if (riid == IID_IUnknown)
    {
        *ppv = (LPVOID)this;
        AddRef();
        return S_OK ;          // success code is 0, repeat zero
    }

/*
We don't support the interface.  Set the supplied output variable to
NULL and return an informative error code.
*/

    else
    {
      *ppv = NULL;
      return  E_NOINTERFACE ; // failure codes are nonzero
    }
}
```

D. DATA TRANSFER

1. Data transfer in OLE is handled by means of *data objects*, which are objects that support the *IDataObject* interface. A data source application creates a data object and makes it available to the consumer via drag-and-drop, the Clipboard, or other channels. In addition to the IUnknown methods supported by every object, the IDataObject interface contains the following methods:

IDataObject::GetData	*// Get object's data in callee-supplied medium*
IDataObject::GetDataHere	*// Get object's data in caller-supplied medium*
IDataObject::QueryGetData	*// Can data be rendered in specified format?*
IDataObject::GetCanonicalFormatEtc	*// Get formats that produce identical data*
IDataObject::SetData	*// Set object's data*
IDataObject::EnumFormatEtc	*// Get enumerator of object's supported data formats*
IDataObject::DAdvise	*// Establish advise loop on this data object*
IDataObject::DUnadvise	*// Unestablish advise loop on this data object*
IDataObject::EnumDAdvise	*// Get enumerator of advise loops on this data objects*

2. Data objects are conceptually similar to individual moveable Clipboards that use delayed rendering and have taken steroids. The single integer that identified a data format in the Clipboard API has been expanded into a FORMATETC structure, allowing the requester of data to be much more specific in indicating its desires. In addition to the original Clipboard format, the caller may specify the type of medium through which the data is to be transferred (global memory, file, metafile, structured storage, etc.), the aspect (level of detail) of the data representation transferred (iconic, thumbnail sketch, or full content), and the output device for which the transferred data is to be formatted.

For the purposes of this book, we will always be using the aspect level DVASPECT_CONTENT, which means "all the data." We will also set the target device to be NULL, which specifies the object's default rendition. For more detailed discussion of the options available in a FORMATETC structure, see Brockschmidt, pp. 497-501. The example on the facing page uses a FORMATETC structure to transfer simple text through an HGLOBAL.

```
typedef struct FARSTRUCT tagFORMATETC
{
    CLIPFORMAT          cfFormat;    // Clipboard format, same as CB API
    DVTARGETDEVICE FAR* ptd;         // target device to format data for
    DWORD               dwAspect;    // level of detail for data
    LONG                lindex;      // reserved, must be -1
    DWORD               tymed;       // type of medium for transfer
} FORMATETC ;
```

3. One potential source of a data object is the existing Windows Clipboard. If your app already handles data objects, it is probably easiest to use the same code for handling data from the Clipboard, rather than write a separate handler using the Clipboard API. The OLE API function **OleGetClipboard( )** synthesizes a data object containing the current contents of the Clipboard, whether or not they were put there by an OLE-aware app. The method **IDataObject::QueryGetData( )** interrogates the data object to see if it can supply data in a specified format and medium, conceptually similar to the API function IsClipboardFormatAvailable( ). Finally we release the object by calling its **Release( )** method.

In the following example, we use OLE to check the Clipboard's contents before displaying the app's menu. If the Clipboard contains text, we enable the "Paste Text" menu item; otherwise we gray it out. The working app may be found in the sample app \CHAPTER1\DONE\DATA1.EXE. Thus:

```
case WM_INITMENU:
{

/*
Get a data object pointer to the current Clipboard contents.
*/
    LPDATAOBJECT lpd ;
    HRESULT hr ;

    hr = OleGetClipboard (&lpd) ;

/*
Fill out a FORMATETC structure, see if the Clipboard data object
contains text.  Gray out EDIT-PASTE menu item if it doesn't, or if
Clipboard is empty (returned data object pointer is NULL).  Otherwise
enable menu item.
*/
    FORMATETC fe ;

    fe.cfFormat = CF_TEXT ;
    fe.ptd = NULL ;
    fe.tymed = TYMED_HGLOBAL ;
    fe.dwAspect = DVASPECT_CONTENT ;
    fe.lindex = -1 ;

    if (!lpd || lpd->QueryGetData (&fe) != S_OK)
    {
      EnableMenuItem ((HMENU)wParam, ID_DEMO_PASTETEXT, MF_GRAYED) ;
    }
    else
    {
      EnableMenuItem ((HMENU)wParam, ID_DEMO_PASTETEXT, MF_ENABLED) ;
    }

/*
Release Clipboard data object.
*/
    if (lpd) lpd->Release( ) ;

    return 0 ;
}
```

4. Actually fetching the object's data is done via the methods **IDataObject::GetData( )** and **IDataObject::GetDataHere( )**. They are conceptually identical, except that in the former, the callee both provides and fills the transfer medium, whereas in the latter, the caller provides the transfer medium and the callee fills it. The former is more common; the latter is used primarily in embedding and linking situations. The example on the facing page shows the use of the former in the DATA1.EXE example when the user picks "Paste Text" from the menu.

Transferred data is held in a structure of type STGMEDIUM. This contains space for the supplier of data to specify and supply the storage medium through which the data is being transferred. Since there are several types of storage media with different rules for their release, the function **ReleaseStgMedium( )** is provided, which is guaranteed to properly dispose of a used STGMEDIUM, no matter what its contents. Thus:

```
typedef struct tagSTGMEDIUM {
    DWORD               tymed;              // flags for self-description

// actual data storage

    union {
    HBITMAP         hBitmap;            // Bitmap
    HMETAFILEPICT   hMetaFilePict;      // METAFILEPICT structure
    HENHMETAFILE    hEnhMetaFile;       // 32-bit enhanced Metafile
    HGLOBAL         hGlobal;            // Global memory
    LPOLESTR        lpszFileName;       // File name
    ISTREAM         *pstm;              // OLE stream  (see chapter 3)
    ISTORAGE        *pstg;              // OLE storage (see chapter 3)
    };

    IUNKNOWN        *pUnkForRelease;    // IUnknown for release of data
} STGMEDIUM;
```

NOTE: In the example on the facing page, it is still necessary to call GlobalLock( ) and GlobalUnlock( ) as shown on the HGLOBAL returned by the method IDataObject::GetData( ). This is because the Clipboard data object's implementation of this method returns a handle to moveable memory rather than fixed memory. This means that the returned handle is actual an index in a table rather than a pointer, and the function GlobalLock( ) is necessary to fetch the actual memory pointer to which the handle refers. I think this is a hangover from Win16, but it exists and must be dealt with nonetheless.

```
/*
User has picked the EDIT-PASTE command off the menu.  Get data object
from Clipboard and paste its text into our app.
*/

char DisplayText [128] ;

case ID_EDIT_PASTE:
{

/*
Get Clipboard's current contents wrapped in an OLE data object.
*/
    LPDATAOBJECT lpd ;

    OleGetClipboard (&lpd) ;

/*
Get data in text format, transferred in an HGLOBAL.
*/

    STGMEDIUM stg ; FORMATETC fe ;

    fe.cfFormat = CF_TEXT ;
    fe.ptd = NULL ;
    fe.tymed = TYMED_HGLOBAL ;
    fe.dwAspect = DVASPECT_CONTENT ;
    fe.lindex = -1 ;

    lpd->GetData (&fe, &stg) ;

/*
Paste data into our app.  GlobalLock( ) and GlobalUnlock( ) are required
because the handle supplied by the data object is to moveable memory.
*/

    LPSTR cp = (LPSTR) GlobalLock (stg.hGlobal) ;
    lstrcpyn (DisplayText, cp, sizeof(DisplayText)) ;
    GlobalUnlock (stg.hGlobal) ;
    InvalidateRect (hWnd, NULL, TRUE) ;

/*
Release storage medium and data object.
*/

    ReleaseStgMedium (&stg) ;
    lpd->Release( ) ;

    return 0 ;
}
```

E. DRAG AND DROP

    1. To accept data via OLE's drag-and-drop mechanism, an app must provide the operating system with a *Drop Target Object*. This is a C++ object that supports OLE's *IDropTarget* interface, providing methods that OLE will call for different situations during a drag-and-drop operation. You must write the code for this object's methods yourself. The object must be created, AddRef( )'d, locked in memory via the function **CoLockObjectExternal( )**, and registered with OLE via the function **RegisterDragDrop( )**. Thus:

```
#include "cdroptgt.h"

CDropTarget *lpDropTarget ;

case WM_CREATE:
{

/*
Set up a drop target.  Instantiate a CDropTarget object and CoLock it
to keep it in memory.  Register it with OLE.
*/

    lpDropTarget = new CDropTarget ( ) ;

    CoLockObjectExternal (lpDropTarget, TRUE, FALSE) ;
    RegisterDragDrop (hWnd, lpDropTarget) ;

    return 0 ;

}
```

    When the app no longer wishes to be a drop target, it revokes its drop registration via the function **RevokeDragDrop( )**, unlocks it from memory via the function **CoLockObjectExternal( )**, and releases it with its own Release( ) method, thus:

```
case WM_CLOSE:
{
    RevokeDragDrop (hWnd) ;
    CoLockObjectExternal (lpDropTarget, FALSE, TRUE) ;
    lpDropTarget->Release ( ) ;

    DestroyWindow (hWnd) ;
    return 0 ;
}
```

    Note: The function CoLockObjectExternal is nonintuitive but necessary. If you leave it out, your drop target will work correctly the first time, but not on subsequent drag operations. You can just put it in as shown and stop worrying about it. Or, for a detailed discussion of the reasons it is needed, see Brockschmidt, pp. 298-300.

2. The drop target object belongs to a class that you have to write yourself. If you write in C++, inheriting from the public Microsoft-supplied class IDropTarget defined in the system header files, the compiler will properly set up all your VTBLs and your life will be relatively simple. All of IDropTarget's methods (and those of all the other standard interfaces) are defined as pure virtual, which means that you have to implement all of them yourself and you can't change any parameters or leave anything out. Your header file CDROPTGT.H will look something like this:

```
class CDropTarget : public IDropTarget
{

    protected:
        ULONG               m_RefCount ;
        LPDATAOBJECT        m_pIDataSource ;

    public:

        CDropTarget(void);
        ~CDropTarget(void);

//IUnknown interface members

        STDMETHODIMP        QueryInterface(REFIID, LPVOID FAR *);
        STDMETHODIMP_(ULONG)    AddRef(void);
        STDMETHODIMP_(ULONG)    Release(void);

//IDropTarget interface members

        STDMETHODIMP DragEnter(LPDATAOBJECT, DWORD, POINTL, LPDWORD);
        STDMETHODIMP DragOver(DWORD, POINTL, LPDWORD);
        STDMETHODIMP DragLeave(void);
        STDMETHODIMP Drop(LPDATAOBJECT, DWORD, POINTL, LPDWORD);

};
```

The class constructor and destructor will look like this:

```
CDropTarget::CDropTarget(void)
{
    m_RefCount = 1 ;            // calling constructor implies AddRef( )
    return;
}

CDropTarget::~CDropTarget(void)
{
    return;
}
```

Note: I like to set my objects' reference counts to 1 in my class constructors. My reasoning is that the constructor is a function that returns a pointer to an object, and any time you call a function that returns a pointer to an object, the pointer has already been AddRef( )'d for your convenience. This is an implementation detail that you can choose to follow or not. If I didn't do it this way, I would have to AddRef( ) my object on the preceding page immediately after constructing it.

3. The IDropTarget interface contains four methods in addition to the standard IUnknown. The first is **IDropTarget::DragEnter( )**, which is called only once when the mouse first enters the target window with a drag operation in progress. You can use this to examine the offered data object and decide if it contains a data format that your app knows how to handle. Note the similarity of this code to that used in the Clipboard data object example on page 9. The main difference is that in the DragEnter( ) method, since OLE called us, we have to AddRef( ) the data object pointer if we want to keep it. This drop target accepts only plain text and doesn't do anything clever with it.

Your drop target signals the result that would happen if the object was dropped by setting the value pointed to by the last parameter, *pdwEffect*. Since this operation is performed in the DragOver( ) method on the facing page, the DragEnter( ) method simply calls DragOver( ) instead of duplicating its code. Thus:

```
STDMETHODIMP CDropTarget::DragEnter(LPDATAOBJECT pIDataSource,
    DWORD grfKeyState, POINTL pt, LPDWORD pdwEffect)
{

/*
Check to see if the data is in a format we can handle (in this case,
only text).  If so, keep a copy of the data object pointer, which means
that we must AddRef( ) it. Note similarity to Clipboard example.
*/

    FORMATETC fe ;

    fe.cfFormat = CF_TEXT ;
    fe.ptd = NULL ;
    fe.tymed = TYMED_HGLOBAL ;
    fe.dwAspect = DVASPECT_CONTENT ;
    fe.lindex = -1 ;

    if (pIDataSource->QueryGetData (&fe) == S_OK)
    {
      m_pIDataSource = pIDataSource ;
      m_pIDataSource->AddRef( ) ;
    }
    else
    {
      m_pIDataSource = NULL ;
    }

/*
Call our own DragOver( ) method to set the effect code.
*/

    DragOver(grfKeyState, pt, pdwEffect) ;

    return S_OK ;
}
```

14

4. The method **IDropTarget::DragOver( )** is called every time the mouse is moved in the target window during a drag operation, similar to a WM_MOUSEMOVE message. The target's job is to signal back to the source the operation (move, copy, link, nothing, etc.) that would take place if the user dropped the data object at the current mouse location. The target does this by setting the output variable pointed to by the parameter pdwEffect to a specified flag as shown below. On input, this parameter contains flags describing the actions that the source will allow. For example, Winhlp32.exe, being a read-only app, allows a copy operation but not a move. Winword.exe allows copy and move operations, but not link. The state of the mouse, CTRL, and SHIFT keys are provided to the drop target in the parameter grfKeyState.

This method is called frequently, so you want to make it as fast and efficient as possible. You don't have to check if the data is acceptable; you did that when it first entered. DragOver( ) is always called, regardless of the effect code returned from your DragEnter( ) method. Thus:

```
STDMETHODIMP CDropTarget::DragOver(DWORD grfKeyState, POINTL pt,
    LPDWORD pdwEffect)
{

/*
If data is in a format we couldn't handle, then set effect code to
indicate nothing would happen if data was dropped here.
*/
    if (m_pIDataSource == NULL)
    {
      *pdwEffect = DROPEFFECT_NONE ;
    }
/*
Otherwise, if CTRL key is up and permitted effects (supplied by drop
source) allow a move, set the effect code to indicate a move.
*/
    else if (!(grfKeyState&MK_CONTROL) && (*pdwEffect&DROPEFFECT_MOVE))
    {
      *pdwEffect = DROPEFFECT_MOVE ;
    }


/*
Otherwise, if effect permits a copy, set effect code to indicate that.
*/
    else if (*pdwEffect & DROPEFFECT_COPY)
    {
      *pdwEffect = DROPEFFECT_COPY ;
    }
/*
Otherwise, even though the data is in a format that we could accept, the
effect code isn't. Set the effect code to indicate that nothing would
happen if data was dropped here.  Unlikely to actually get here in real
life.
*/
    else
    {
      *pdwEffect = DROPEFFECT_NONE ;
    }
    return S_OK;
}
```

5.   The user may drop the data object on the target, which will cause the method **IDropTarget::Drop( )** to be called. Your app takes the data object and does whatever it wants with its data. This signals the end of a drag operation, so you also have to undo any initialization here. Note the similarity of the pasting code to that used in the Clipboard data object operation on page 11. Thus:

```
extern int xText, yText ;
extern char DisplayText[ ] ;
extern HWND hMainWnd ;

STDMETHODIMP CDropTarget::Drop(LPDATAOBJECT pIDataSource,
    DWORD grfKeyState,  POINTL pt, LPDWORD pdwEffect)
{
    if (m_pIDataSource)
    {

/*
Get point on screen where data was dropped.  Convert to client
coordinates, store in global variables xText and yText, which will cause
main window to display the text where it was dropped.
*/

        ScreenToClient (hMainWnd, (POINT *)(&pt)) ;
        xText = pt.x ;
        yText = pt.y ;

/*
Fetch text from data object.
*/

        STGMEDIUM stg ; FORMATETC fe ;


        fe.cfFormat = CF_TEXT ;
        fe.ptd = NULL ;
        fe.tymed = TYMED_HGLOBAL ;
        fe.dwAspect = DVASPECT_CONTENT ;
        fe.lindex = -1 ;

        m_pIDataSource->GetData (&fe, &stg) ;


/*
Copy data into string for display in main window and Invalidate to cause
a repaint.
*/
        LPSTR cp = (LPSTR) GlobalLock (stg.hGlobal) ;
        lstrcpyn (DisplayText, cp, 127) ;
        GlobalUnlock (stg.hGlobal) ;
        InvalidateRect (hMainWnd, NULL,  FALSE) ;
```

```
/*
Release data object and storage medium.
*/

        ReleaseStgMedium (&stg) ;
        m_pIDataSource->Release( );


    }

/*
Call our own DragOver( ) method to set the effect code.
*/

    DragOver(grfKeyState, pt, pdwEffect) ;
    return NOERROR;
}
```

6.   When the mouse leaves the target window without dropping, your app's **IDropTarget::DragLeave( )** method is called. You use this to undo any initialization that you had done during the DragEnter( ) method. Thus:

```
STDMETHODIMP CDropTarget::DragLeave(void)
{
    if (m_pIDataSource)
    {
      m_pIDataSource->Release();
    }

    return NOERROR;
}
```

F. Using Data Objects in the MFC

1.   The Microsoft Foundation Classes provide an implementation of the IDataObject and IDropTarget interfaces that we need to make an MFC version of our simple text client app. To use data objects alone in an MFC app, do not select any of the OLE options in App Wizard; they will pull in many large pieces of the MFC that you don't care about, making your app bigger and slower. Instead, simply add the header file "**afxole.h**" to your "stdafx.h" file. You must also call the function **AfxOleInit( )**, which calls OleInitialize( ) and sets up the MFC's own internal OLE bookkeeping, in your app's CWinApp::InitInstance( ) method. Thus:

```
<file stdafx.h>

// stdafx.h : include file for standard system include files,
//  or project-specific include files that are used frequently, but
//      are changed infrequently
//

#define VC_EXTRALEAN

#include <afxwin.h>          // MFC core and standard components
#include <afxext.h>          // MFC extensions
#include <afxole.h>          // MFC OLE stuff

#ifndef _AFX_NO_AFXCMN_SUPPORT
#include <afxcmn.h>
#endif // _AFX_NO_AFXCMN_SUPPORT


<file mfcdata1.cpp>

BOOL CMfcdata1App::InitInstance()
{

/*
Add this function to initialize OLE in the MFC.
*/

    AfxOleInit ( ) ;

    <rest of InitInstance( ) method>
}
```

WARNING: If you have not already read the cautionary note in the preface about dependency on the MFC, go back and do it now.

2. The client side of a data object in the MFC is represented by the class *COleDataObject*, an MFC wrapper that encapsulates an IDataObject pointer. To obtain a COleDataObject that represents the current contents of the Clipboard, you instantiate an object of this class and call its **AttachClipboard( )** method. The method **COleDataObject::IsDataAvailable( )** is the wrapper for the IDataObject::QueryGetData( ) method, asking the object whether or not it could render the data in a specified format. We turn the sample app's "Paste Text" menu item on or off based on the object's reply.

```
/*
Called when the app's menu is about to be shown.
*/


void CMfcdata1View::OnUpdateDataobjectPastetext(CCmdUI* pCmdUI)
{

/*
Instantiate  a  COleDataObject.   Tell  it  to  attach  itself  to  the
Clipboard.
*/
    COleDataObject dataobj ;

    dataobj.AttachClipboard ( ) ;

/*
Ask the COleDataObject attached to the Clipboard if it could supply us
with text.  Turn the "Paste Text" menu item on or off accordingly.
*/

    pCmdUI->Enable (dataobj.IsDataAvailable (CF_TEXT)) ;

/*
The COleDataObject is automatically detached from the Clipboard by its
destructor as it goes out of scope.
*/


}
```

3. We obtain data from a COleDataObject via its **GetData( )** method. When the user selects "Paste Text" from the sample app's menu, the command handler shown below is executed. We instantiate a COleDataObject, attach it to the Clipboard, and paste the text from it into our document. Because the drag-and-drop operation supplies us with the same object, I have placed the pasting code in a separate method of my CView class to be called from both Clipboard and drag-and-drop operations.

```
void CMfcdata1View::OnDataobjectPastetext()
{
    COleDataObject dataobj ;

    dataobj.AttachClipboard ( ) ;

    PasteTextIntoMyDocument (&dataobj) ;
}
```

The code for the pasting operation is shown on the facing page. It illustrates the fact that data transfer using OLE is identical no matter where the data object comes from. It also illustrates the fact that the MFC sometimes gets too clever for its own good, and that you will not, repeat NOT, be able to ship a working app without understanding what OLE is doing in its heart of hearts. (You may be able to make plenty of money from half-working apps, but that's another issue.)

Why do I need to fill out a FORMATETC structure when I call COleDataObject::GetData( )? Why can't I just say :

```
pData->GetData (CF_TEXT, &stg) ;
```

and use the default FORMATETC supplied by the MFC ? If you do this in Windows NT version 3.51, your sample app will not paste text from the Clipboard. It will accept text via drag-and-drop from WinWord, but not from WinHelp. (Try this on the sample app.) Why is this, and what do I do to fix it?

If you use the debugger to step down into the COleDataObject::GetData( ) source code, you will find that when it fills out its default FORMATETC, it sets the `tymed` element to 0xFFFFFFFF. If you look in the documentation for IDataObject::GetData( ), you will find that this is allowed, in fact, encouraged; the caller is saying that it will accept any tymed that the object is able to render and that the object should choose the most appropriate tymed for the requested format and aspect. OK, sounds fine, but the data objects provided by the Clipboard and WinHelp do not support this feature even though the docs say they are supposed to and the data objects supplied by WinWord do. When presented with a choice of tymed, they will choke and supply nothing. As a guess, I'd say they are using the == operator to check the requested tymed rather than the & operator (see page 33). This is the kind of bug that you see in OLE all the time. No matter what the docs say an object ought to do, objects do whatever their programmers wrote code to make them do.

But we checked the object first! Why did the default work in the IsDataAvailable( ) method but not in the GetData( ) method? It's because the MFC got a little too clever. If you use the debugger to step down into the IsDataAvailable( ) method, you will see that if the COleDataObject is connected to the Clipboard, the MFC uses the Clipboard API to check for format availability instead of going through OLE, presumably for speed. That's fine, but the GetData( ) method does not use the Clipboard API, it always uses OLE even to access the Clipboard. The channel the MFC checked for availability is not the channel used for transfer, and the results are different.

How do we fix it? Once we figure out what's happening, it's quite simple; just explicitly provide a FORMATETC requiring the data to be transferred through an HGLOBAL, which is all our sample app knows how to use anyway. But it shows that the MFC is not a magic bullet, there ain't no such thing as a magic bullet in software. It is a very powerful tool, but like all powerful tools, it is double-edged and you need to understand fully what it's really doing before you can make a profit wielding it.

```
/*
Pasting function.  Default values are provided for last two parameters;
see header file on next page.
*/


BOOL CMfcdata1View::PasteTextIntoMyDocument(COleDataObject *pData,
    DROPEFFECT de, CPoint point)
{
    STGMEDIUM stg ;

/*
Fill  out  a  FORMATETC  structure  describing  how  we  want  the  data
transferred.
*/
    FORMATETC fe ;
    fe.cfFormat  = CF_TEXT ;
    fe.tymed = TYMED_HGLOBAL ;
    fe.lindex = -1 ;
    fe.dwAspect = DVASPECT_CONTENT ;
    fe.ptd = NULL ;

/*
Attempt to get the data from the COleDataObject.
*/
    if (pData->GetData (CF_TEXT, &stg, &fe))
    {
/*
Copy data from STGMEDIUM into document's CString.
*/
        CMfcdata1Doc* pDoc = GetDocument();
        pDoc->m_String = (char *) GlobalLock (stg.hGlobal) ;
        GlobalUnlock (stg.hGlobal) ;
/*
Copy supplied point into member variable used by OnDraw( ).  Invalidate
to force a repaint.
*/
        m_DropPoint = point ;
        Invalidate ( ) ;

/*
Return success or failure code as appropriate.
*/
        return TRUE ;
    }
    else
    {
      return FALSE ;
    }
}
```

4. Now we want to make our app accept text by means of drag-and-drop as well as the Clipboard. From reading the first part of this chapter, you know that we need a drop target. The MFC has provided a default implementation of the IDropTarget interface in the class *COleDropTarget*. We add a member variable of this class to our view. Then in the view's OnCreate( ) handler, call the method **COleDropTarget::Register**( ), passing it a pointer to the view, which causes the drop target to register and lock itself. Thus:

```
class CMfcdata1View : public CView
{
    COleDropTarget m_DropTarget ;
    BOOL m_bCanDrop ;
    CPoint m_DropPoint ;

    BOOL PasteTextIntoMyDocument (COleDataObject *,
      DROPEFFECT de = DROPEFFECT_COPY, CPoint point = CPoint(0,0));

    < rest of view header file >
} ;



/*
When the view is created, register the drop target.
*/

int CMfcdata1View::OnCreate(LPCREATESTRUCT lpCreateStruct)
{
    if (CView::OnCreate(lpCreateStruct) == -1)
      return -1;

    m_DropTarget.Register (this) ;

    return 0;
}
```

5. The base class CView contains the methods **OnDragEnter( )**, **OnDragOver( )**, and **OnDrop( )** that are called from the registered COleDropTarget when these events happen. The default implementations don't do anything. We use Class Wizard to override them in our view, supplying our own version of what ought to happen when these take place. Thus:

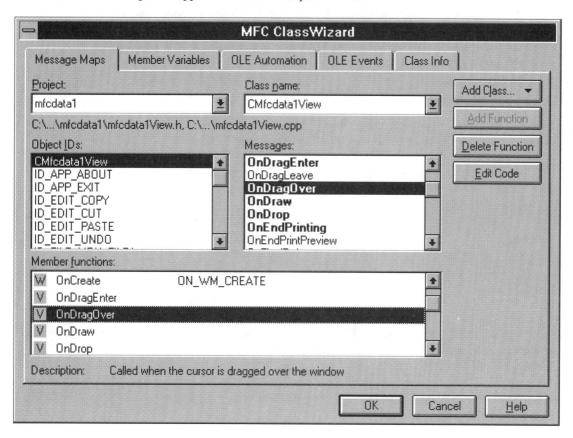

6. Our view's **OnDragEnter( )** method is called once, when the drag operation first enters our view. The COleDataObject that represents the data being dragged is supplied to us as the first parameter. As in the API, we check the data object to see if it contains a format that our view knows how to use, in this case, only text. We signal the effect that would take place if the drop occurred here by returning a DROPEFFECT, the code for determining which lives in our OnDragOver( ) method. Thus:

```
DROPEFFECT CMfcdata1View::OnDragEnter(COleDataObject* pDataObject,
    DWORD dwKeyState, CPoint point)
{

/*
Check to see if the offered data object is capable of supplying text.
Remember its capability in a BOOL member variable.
*/
    if (pDataObject->IsDataAvailable(CF_TEXT))
    {
      m_bCanDrop = TRUE ;
    }
    else
    {
      m_bCanDrop = FALSE ;
    }

/*
Rather than duplicate code for determining drop effects, call our own
OnDragOver( ) method and return its result.
*/

    return OnDragOver (pDataObject, dwKeyState, point) ;

}
```

7. Our view's **OnDragOver( )** method gets called every time the mouse moves in our view while a drag operation is in progress. We determine what operation would take place if the drop took place at the specified point with the specified state of the keys and return a DROPEFFECT code to signal this back to the drop source app.

```
DROPEFFECT CMfcdata1View::OnDragOver(COleDataObject* pDataObject,
    DWORD dwKeyState, CPoint point)
{
/*
If data object contains a format we can use, as determined previously in
OnDragEnter( ), check to see if the control key is down.  If so, return
effect code to signal copy operation, otherwise return effect code to
signal move operation. We don't bother looking at the drop location; our
view does the same thing at every point.
*/
    if (m_bCanDrop)
    {
      if (!(dwKeyState & MK_CONTROL))
      {
            return DROPEFFECT_MOVE ;
      }
      else
      {
            return DROPEFFECT_COPY ;
      }
    }
/*
Data object does not contain a format we can use; return the DROPEFFECT
code that signals this.
*/
    return DROPEFFECT_NONE ;
}
```

8. In our view's **OnDrop( )** method, we copy the data out of the supplied object and make use of it. We already have a helper function in our view class that does this. Thus:

```
BOOL CMfcdata1View::OnDrop(COleDataObject* pDataObject,
    DROPEFFECT dropEffect, CPoint point)
{
    return PasteTextIntoMyDocument (pDataObject, dropEffect, point) ;
}
```

Lab Exercises
Chapter 1
Data Transfer Object Consumer

Directory: \EssenceofOLE\chap01\data1\templ

This lab creates an app that accepts simple text data from the Clipboard by means of a data object. It also implements a drop target object that accepts simple text via drag and drop. A skeleton app is supplied for you in the directory listed above; you may want to build it and run it first (it won't do much) to make sure that your development environment is properly configured.

1. Your app must first initialize the OLE libraries. In the file WINMAIN.CPP, add a call to OleInitialize( ) at the start of the function WinMain( ). Add a call to OleUninitialize( ) at the end of WinMain( ).

2. The Demo-Paste Text menu item starts out grayed. We would like to make it respond to the contents of the Clipboard, enabling the menu item if the Clipboard contains text and disabling it otherwise. In the file MAINWIND.CPP, in the WM_INITMENU message handler, add the following code: Call the function OleGetClipboard( ) to get a data object that encapsulates the current contents of the Clipboard. Allocate a FORMATETC structure and fill its fields with the correct parameters for requesting data in the CF_TEXT format via an HGLOBAL transfer medium. Use the data object's QueryGetData( ) method to ask the object if it can supply data in this manner. If it can, enable the menu item, otherwise gray it out. The menu modification code has been supplied for you. Release the Clipboard data object when you are finished.

3. When the user chooses the Demo-Paste Text menu item, we need to get the text from the Clipboard and paste it into the app. In the file MAINWIND.CPP, in the ID_DEMO_PASTETEXT case of the WM_COMMAND message handler, use the function OleGetClipboard( ) to get the Clipboard's contents wrapped in a data object. Allocate a FORMATETC structure and also an STGMEDIUM structure; fill out the fields of the former. This time, use the object's GetData( ) method to actually retrieve the data in text format. Copy the new data from the STGMEDIUM structure into the global string array named DisplayText[ ], which is provided for you. Finally, release the storage medium via the function ReleaseStgMedium( ) and release the Clipboard data object via its own Release( ) method. Your app should now properly paste text from the Clipboard into the upper left corner of its window.

4. Our app now supports the Clipboard, we would like to make it do the same thing via drag-and-drop. A skeleton of a drop target class, called CDropTarget, has been provided for you in the file CDROPTGT.CPP. Examine this file and its header file CDROPTGT.H. You will find the IUnknown methods have been written for you, but the other four methods are empty shells. In the file MAINWIND.CPP, in the WM_CREATE message handler, instantiate a CDropTarget object and use the function CoLockObjectExternal( ) to lock it into memory. Use the function RegisterDragDrop( ) to notify OLE that your app will accept drop operations. In the WM_CLOSE message handler, use the function RevokeDragDrop( ) to notify OLE that your window will no longer accept drop operations, unlock it from memory via the function CoLockObjectExternal( ), then free it with its own Release( ) method.

5. Our drop target is connected. Its methods will be called when a drag operation takes place over our window, but so far they don't do anything. Now we have to start implementing the code to make it do what we want. The first method, CDropTarget::DragEnter( ), is called when the mouse first enters the target window. What we need to do here is to check if the data object that the operation contains (passed as the first parameter) can supply the data in the format that we need. Use the object's QueryGetData( ) method to ask the object if it can render its data in CF_TEXT via an HGLOBAL medium. This code will bear an uncanny resemblance to what you did in step 2 above. If the data can be so rendered, save the data pointer in the member variable m_pIDataSource and AddRef( ) it to make sure it will stay valid until

we need it. Otherwise, set the member variable to NULL. You can set the effect code yourself, or, to save duplication, call your own DragOver( ) method described in the next paragraph.

6.   The next method is CDropTarget::DragOver( ), which is conceptually similar to the WM_MOUSEMOVE message. In this case, simply check the value of the data pointer m_pIDataSource. If it is NULL, then our DragEnter( ) method initially decided that the object couldn't supply the data in a format that we wanted, so set the effect to DROPEFFECT_NONE. If it is non-NULL, then we can accept the data. Check the state of the control key, passed in the first parameter. If it's up, and the source permits a move (check the last parameter), then set the effect code to DROPEFFECT_MOVE. Otherwise, if the source permits a copy, then set it to DROPEFFECT_COPY.

7.   The DragLeave( ) method is trivial. If the m_pIDataSource pointer is valid, release the object via its Release( ) method. That's all.

8.   Now we are left with the Drop( ) method. First, convert the point from the screen coordinates it comes in to the client coordinates that your window wants via the API function ScreenToClient( ). The main window's handle is supplied for you in the global variable hMainWnd. Set the drop point's X value into the global variable xText and its Y value into the global yText. This will cause the WM_PAINT message handler to draw it at the place on the screen where it was dropped. Next, use the data object pointer to get the data from the object in the CF_TEXT format. This will be very similar to step 3 above, including the release of both data object and storage medium. Finally, call your own DragOver( ) method to set the effect code.

EXTRA CREDIT: When dragging text inside your window, use a focus rectangle to show the size of the string being dragged. In your DragEnter( ) method, get the data from the dragged object via its GetData( ) method, then use the function DrawText( ) with the flag DT_CALCRECT to calculate the rectangle that the text would occupy if drawn. Store the rectangle in a member variable. Then in your DragOver( ) method, use the function DrawFocusRect( ) to put a focus rectangle on the screen at the point where the mouse is, showing the rectangle that the text would occupy. You will also have to add another member variable to your drop target for storing the point at which you drew the last focus rectangle, so you can remove it before you draw the new one.

Lab Exercises
Chapter 1
MFC Data Transfer Object Consumer

Directory: \EssenceofOLE\chap01\mfcdata1\templ

This lab uses the MFC to do the same thing as the data1 lab did in the API. It creates an app that accepts simple text data from the Clipboard by means of a data object. It also implements a drop target object that accepts simple text via drag and drop. A skeleton app is supplied for you in the directory listed above; you may want to build it and run it first (it won't do much) to make sure that your development environment is properly configured.

1. First, we need to include the necessary header files and initialize OLE. Add the header file "afxole.h" to the other #include files in your "stdafx.h" master header file. In the function CMfcdata1App::InitInstance( ), add a call to AfxOleInit( ).

2. We want to turn the "Paste Text" menu item on and off to indicate whether the Clipboard contains text, and we want to implement this feature using OLE. In the UpdateCommandUI handler CMfcdata1View::OnUpdateDataobjectPastetext( ) supplied for you, instantiate a COleDataObject and attach it to the Clipboard via its AttachClipboard( ) method. Use the data object's IsDataAvailable( ) method to find out if it can supply us with text or not. Use the pCmdUI->Enable( ) method to turn the menu item on or off based on this result.

3. Now we want to paste data into our app from the Clipboard using the COleDataObject. In the command handler CMfcdata1View::OnDataobjectPastetext( ), instantiate a COleDataObject and attach it to the Clipboard. A function CMfcdata1View::PasteTextIntoMyDocument( ) is supplied for you; pass it a pointer to the Clipboard data object. Only the skeleton of this function is supplied for you, you have to provide the guts of the function yourself. Instantiating and setting the necessary structures, call the data object's GetData( ) method to retrieve the text. Your document contains a CString member variable called "m_String", the contents of which are drawn by the supplied CMfcdata1View::OnDraw( ) method. Copy the data from the STGMEDIUM in which the data object supplies it into this variable and invalidate( ) to force a repaint.

4. Now we want to make our app accept text via drag and drop. In the header file "mfcdata1view.h", add a member variable of class COleDropTarget to your view class. In the handler function CMfcdata1View::OnCreate( ), call the drop target's Register( ) method to register it with OLE.

5. We now need to override the OnDragEnter( ), OnDragOver( ), and OnDrop( ) methods of our view class in order to add our own handling for these events. Use Class Wizard to override these member functions.

6. In your view's OnDragEnter( ) member function, use the method COleDataObject::IsDataAvailable( ) to see if the object is capable (or thinks it is capable) of rendering its data in text format. Remember its response in a BOOLean member variable. Call your own OnDragOver( ) member function to get the DROPEFFECT code to return.

7. In your view's OnDragOver( ) member function, check to see what the effect would be if the user dropped the data object in your view. If the object contains a format you can use, then return DROPEFFECT_COPY if the control key is down and DROPEFFECT_MOVE if it is up. Otherwise, return DROPEFFECT_NONE.

8. In your view's OnDrop( ) member function, use the helper function that you added in step 3 to paste the dropped text into your app's window.

Chapter 2

Sourcing Data Objects

A. Data Objects, Part 2: Sourcing Data

1. To make your app a source of data objects, you must derive a class from the public class *IDataObject*, the definition of which is found in the system header files. The methods of a data object are conceptually similar to the code that you would have to write for an app that used delayed rendering on the Clipboard. You header file might look like this:

```
class CTextData : public IDataObject
{

    private:
      ULONG        m_RefCount ;
      UINT         m_length ;
      LPSTR        m_cp ;

    public:

      CTextData(LPSTR);           // constructor needs text pointer
      ~CTextData(void);

// IUnknown methods

      STDMETHODIMP        QueryInterface(REFIID, LPVOID *);
      STDMETHODIMP_(ULONG)    AddRef(void);
      STDMETHODIMP_(ULONG)    Release(void);

// IDataObject methods

      STDMETHODIMP GetData (LPFORMATETC, LPSTGMEDIUM) ;
      STDMETHODIMP GetDataHere (LPFORMATETC, LPSTGMEDIUM) ;
      STDMETHODIMP QueryGetData (LPFORMATETC) ;
      STDMETHODIMP GetCanonicalFormatEtc (LPFORMATETC, LPFORMATETC) ;
      STDMETHODIMP SetData (LPFORMATETC, STGMEDIUM *, BOOL) ;
      STDMETHODIMP EnumFormatEtc (DWORD, LPENUMFORMATETC *) ;

      STDMETHODIMP DAdvise (FORMATETC *, DWORD, LPADVISESINK, DWORD*) ;
      STDMETHODIMP DUnadvise  (DWORD) ;
      STDMETHODIMP EnumDAdvise  (LPENUMSTATDATA *);

};
```

Of the nine methods required by the IDataObject interface, only the three shown in bold above are required for a simple one-way data transfer object of the type used for drag-and-drop or the Clipboard. The remainder can be stubbed out, as described on page 37.

2. Consider the case of a data object that encapsulates text data, but offers it to the consumer in either text or metafile format. This is the object provided by the sample app in the directory \chap02\data2. You instantiate such an object by passing the desired text string to the class constructor, thus:

```
#include "ctxtdata.h"
extern char DisplayText[ ] ;

case ID_DEMO_COPYTEXT:
{
    LPCTEXTDATA lpd = new CTextData (DisplayText) ;
    etc...
```

The class constructor allocates a piece of global memory in which to store the text data. This is the object's own internal storage, represented by the inner amorphous figure on page 4. It has nothing to do with how the object does or doesn't render the data to a consumer. The class destructor frees the memory. Thus:

```
/*
Constructor -- allocate global memory to hold text string.   Initialize
other member variables.
*/


CTextData::CTextData(LPSTR lpString)
{
    m_RefCount = 1 ;
    m_length = lstrlen (lpString) + 1;
    m_cp = (LPSTR) GlobalAlloc (GMEM_FIXED, m_length) ;
    lstrcpy (m_cp, lpString) ;
}


/*
Class destructor -- free internal storage to avoid a memory leak.
*/


CTextData::~CTextData(void)
{
    GlobalFree (m_cp) ;
}
```

This page intentionally contains no text other than this sentence.

3. The simplest method of a data object is **IDataObject::QueryGetData( )**, which specifies whether the object can or cannot be rendered in the format specified by FORMATETC structure supplied by the caller. It is conceptually similar to the API function IsClipboardFormatAvailable( ). You look at the contents of the FORMATETC, and if your object is smart enough to supply its data in the requested format, you return the success code S_OK. If not, you return the error code DATA_E_FORMATETC.

Note that the TYMED enumeration may contain more than one flag ORed together. In this case, the client is saying that it can accept any of the specified TYMED choices, and the object should pick whichever it thinks is most appropriate. Because of this, we need to use the **&** operator as shown below. Our class which can render both CF_TEXT and CF_METAFILEPICT implements this method thus:

```
STDMETHODIMP CTextData::QueryGetData (LPFORMATETC lpfe)
{

/*
We'll give you text, transferred through a global, with aspect
content.  If the user is asking for this, return success code.
*/
    if (lpfe->cfFormat == CF_TEXT
      && (lpfe->tymed & TYMED_HGLOBAL)
      && lpfe->dwAspect == DVASPECT_CONTENT)
    {
      return S_OK ;
    }


/*
Or we'll give the same text drawn in a metafile, also with aspect
content.  Return success code.
*/

    else if (lpfe->cfFormat == CF_METAFILEPICT
      && (lpfe->tymed & TYMED_MFPICT)
      && lpfe->dwAspect == DVASPECT_CONTENT)
    {
      return S_OK ;
    }

/*
But we won't give you anything else
*/

    return DATA_E_FORMATETC ;

}
```

4. The primary method used for actually transferring data is **IDataObject::GetData( )**. In this method, the object itself allocates the medium through which the data is transferred. The recipient is responsible for freeing the transfer medium by calling the function ReleaseStgMedium( ). Our text/metafile object implements it thus:

```
/*
GetData Method.  Caller demanding that we supply data in a given
format and medium.
*/

STDMETHODIMP CTextData::GetData (LPFORMATETC lpfe, LPSTGMEDIUM lpstg)
{

/*
We support text format, transferred through a global, with aspect
content. Allocate a new global, copy our text into it.
*/
    if (lpfe->cfFormat == CF_TEXT
      && (lpfe->tymed & TYMED_HGLOBAL)
      && lpfe->dwAspect == DVASPECT_CONTENT)
    {
      LPSTR cpout ;

      cpout = (LPSTR) GlobalAlloc(GMEM_FIXED, m_length);
      if (!cpout)
      {
            return E_OUTOFMEMORY ;
      }

      lstrcpy (cpout, m_cp) ;

/*
Fill in the elements of the STGMEDIUM structure that we were passed.
*/
      lpstg->tymed = TYMED_HGLOBAL ;       // flag specifying data type
      lpstg->hGlobal = (HGLOBAL) cpout ;   // HGLOBAL containing data
      lpstg->pUnkForRelease = NULL ;       // caller must free memory

      return S_OK ;

    }
```

```
/*
We also support the metafile format (in tasteful colors of yellow on
green).
*/

    else if (lpfe->cfFormat == CF_METAFILEPICT
       && (lpfe->tymed & TYMED_MFPICT)
       && lpfe->dwAspect == DVASPECT_CONTENT)
    {
      HMETAFILE hMF ; HDC hDC ;

/*
Create a DC mapped to a metafile, draw our text on the DC, then close
the DC to convert it into a memory metafile.
*/
      hDC = CreateMetaFile (NULL) ;

      SetBkColor (hDC, RGB (0, 255, 0)) ;
      SetTextColor (hDC, RGB (255, 255, 0)) ;
      TextOut (hDC, 0, 0, m_cp, m_length) ;

      hMF = CloseMetaFile (hDC) ;

/*
Allocate a METAFILEPICT structure to describe the picture. Fill in its
elements.
*/
      METAFILEPICT *pMF = (METAFILEPICT *) GlobalAlloc (GPTR,
            sizeof (METAFILEPICT));

      pMF->hMF = hMF ;
      pMF->mm = MM_TEXT ;
      pMF->xExt = 100 ;
      pMF->yExt = 100 ;

/*
Fill in the elements of STGMEDIUM structure to return data to caller.
*/
      lpstg->tymed = TYMED_MFPICT ;          // flag specifying data type
      lpstg->hMetaFilePict = (HMETAFILEPICT) pMF ;    // data itself
      lpstg->pUnkForRelease = NULL ;         // caller must free memory

      return S_OK ;

    }

/*
User asked for a format that we couldn't supply.  Return error code.
*/

    return DATA_E_FORMATETC ;
}
```

5. Your data object must also support the method **IDataObject::EnumFormatEtc( )**, which is conceptually similar to the API function EnumClipboardFormats( ). Your data object must create and return an *Enumerator Object*, which is an object that supports the following methods for iterating along a list of FORMATETC structures:

IEnumFORMATETC::Next
IEnumFORMATETC::Skip
IEnumFORMATETC::Reset
IEnumFORMATETC::Clone

The easiest thing to do is to swipe an already written format enumerator from the sample code supplied with this book. I have written a generic enumerator object which works with any structure. You will find it in the files cenum.cpp and cenum.h in the data2 sample. You simply instantiate an object of the supplied class CEnumerator, passing the constructor an array of the FORMATETC structures that your object supports along with other necessary administrative information. You may use this code freely in your products provided you tell everyone who asks about the cool book from which you shamelessly pirated it. Anyone interested in more information about format enumerators may find it in Brockschmidt, pp. 508-511. The caller is responsible for releasing the enumerator object when finished with it. Thus:

```
#include "cenum.h"

FORMATETC feArray []= {
      { CF_TEXT, NULL, DVASPECT_CONTENT,  -1, TYMED_HGLOBAL },
      { CF_METAFILEPICT, NULL, DVASPECT_CONTENT,  -1, TYMED_MFPICT }
     };


STDMETHODIMP CTextData::EnumFormatEtc (DWORD dwDir,
    LPENUMFORMATETC * lpEnum)
{

/*
Create format enumerator object from providentially supplied sample
code, and store a pointer to it in the supplied output variable. We must
make sure that the enumerator's AddRef( ) method is called before we
give the pointer back to the caller.  This is done for us automatically
in the CEnumerator's constructor.
*/

    *lpEnum = (LPENUMFORMATETC) new CEnumerator (
      this,                 // object whose formats the enumerator describes
      feArray,              // array of FORMATETC structures
      2,                    // number of structures in array
      sizeof (FORMATETC),    // size of each structure
      IID_IEnumFORMATETC) ;   //interface supported by enumerator obj

    if (*lpEnum == NULL)
    {
      return E_FAIL ;
    }

    return S_OK ;
}
```

6. The IDataObject interface contains six other methods that this particular object chooses not to support. It is entirely up to the provider of the object to decide which methods it will or won't support.

Not implementing a method means that the object will be somewhat less useful. For example, an object that doesn't implement the IDataObject::SetData( ) method will be able to transfer data in only one direction. This is frequently all the functionality you need.

We have to provide entries in the VTBL for all methods in the interface specification, whether or not our object does anything useful with them, as the user of this object has no idea which methods the object does and doesn't support. The unimplemented methods can be empty shells that return only an error code, but the user has to be able to call all the methods without crashing. As my old rabbi used to say, "God answers all prayers, but sometimes the answer is 'No'." Thus:

```
STDMETHODIMP CTextData::GetDataHere (LPFORMATETC lpfe, LPSTGMEDIUM lpst)
{
    return E_NOTIMPL ;
}


STDMETHODIMP CTextData::SetData (LPFORMATETC lpfe, STGMEDIUM * lpst,
    BOOL fRelease)
{
    return E_NOTIMPL ;
}


STDMETHODIMP CTextData::GetCanonicalFormatEtc (LPFORMATETC lpout,
    LPFORMATETC lpin)
{
    return E_NOTIMPL ;
}


STDMETHODIMP CTextData::DAdvise (FORMATETC *lpfe, DWORD dw,
    LPADVISESINK lpas, DWORD * lpdw)
{
    return E_NOTIMPL ;
}


STDMETHODIMP CTextData::DUnadvise  (DWORD dw)
{
    return E_NOTIMPL ;
}


STDMETHODIMP CTextData::EnumDAdvise  (LPENUMSTATDATA * lpen)
{
    *lpen = NULL ;
    return E_NOTIMPL ;
}
```

NOTE: Methods whose parameter lists contain output parameters for returning pointers to objects must set the pointer value to NULL in addition to returning the error code, as shown in the method IDataObject::EnumDAdvise( ) above. The specifications call for this, and a number of consumer apps depend on it and will croak if you fail to do it. Consult the documentation for the stubbed method to be sure.

B. Setting the Clipboard with Data Objects

1. Once you have a data object, you can make it available to other apps by placing it on the Clipboard via the function **OleSetClipboard( )**. The Clipboard will enumerate the formats from your object and make an entry for each of them, thereby making your data available to other apps that do not necessarily support OLE. Thus:

```
#include "ctxtdata.h"

extern char DisplayText [ ] ;

/*
User picked EDIT--COPY from the menu.  The Clipboard itself will be
responsible for releasing it.   Thus:
*/

case ID_DEMO_COPYTEXT:
{

/*
Create a new data object encapsulating the current display text and
place it on the Clipboard. The Clipboard is responsible for calling the
object's AddRef( ) method if it wants to retain the object's pointer
longer than the duration of this call.
*/

    LPCTEXTDATA lpd = new CTextData (DisplayText) ;
    OleSetClipboard (lpd) ;

/*
We have no further use for this object, so we release our pointer on it.
When the Clipboard is also finished and releases all of its pointers,
the reference count will drop to zero and the object will destroy
itself. We can't delete the object ourselves because we don't know how
long the Clipboard needs to keep it.
*/

    lpd->Release( ) ;
    return 0 ;
}
```

C. Drop Sourcing

1. Sourcing a drag-and-drop operation is controlled by the *IDropSource* interface. When an app wants to begin a drag operation, it calls the API function **DoDragDrop( )**, passing a pointer to an IDropSource object to control the operation, and also a data object which contains the data being offered. This function causes OLE to capture the mouse and begin the drag operation. It does not return until the drag operation completes. Its return code indicates whether the user has dropped the data on a willing target, and the output parameter indicates the effect code set by the target. Thus:

```
#include "ctxtdata.h"
#include "cdropsrc.h"

case WM_LBUTTONDOWN:
{
    DWORD dwEffect ;

/*
Create a data object encapsulating the currently displayed text, and
also a drop source object.
*/

    LPCTEXTDATA lpd = new CTextData (DisplayText) ;
    LPDROPSOURCE lps = new CDropSource ( ) ;

/*
Perform the drag operation.  If the return code indicates a successful
drop and the output effect code indicates that the user said to move the
text (DROPEFFECT_MOVE) as opposed to copying it, then remove the text
from our window.
*/
    if (DoDragDrop (lpd,        //data object containing offered data
        lps,                    //drop source object controlling operation
        DROPEFFECT_COPY | DROPEFFECT_MOVE,   // permitted effect codes
        &dwEffect)              // effect code output parameter
        == DRAGDROP_S_DROP)
    {
        if (dwEffect & DROPEFFECT_MOVE)
        {
            DisplayText [0] = 0x00 ;
            InvalidateRect (hWnd, NULL, TRUE) ;
        }
    }

/*
Release data object and drop source object.
*/

    lpd->Release( ) ;
    lps->Release( ) ;
    return 0 ;
}
```

2. The IDropSource interface has only two methods, and they're both pretty simple. Since DoDragDrop( ) doesn't return until the drag operation is finished, your app will not be processing messages during this time. The method **IDropSource::QueryContinueDrag( )** is your app's chance to control the drag operation while it is in progress. OLE will call this method in response to each WM_MOUSEMOVE message that it receives while dragging.

If the user presses the escape key, or your app detects other cancellation criteria (not shown), returning the value DRAGDROP_S_CANCEL causes the operation to be canceled. If the left mouse button has been released, then returning DRAGDROP_S_DROP causes the drop operation to take place. Otherwise, returning S_OK allows the operation to continue unchanged. Thus:

```
STDMETHODIMP CDropSource::QueryContinueDrag(BOOL fEsc,
    DWORD grfKeyState)
{

/*
Escape key pressed, cancel drag operation.
*/
    if (fEsc)
    {
        return DRAGDROP_S_CANCEL ;
    }

/*
Left mouse button released, perform drop operation.
*/

    if (!(grfKeyState & MK_LBUTTON))
    {
        return DRAGDROP_S_DROP ;
    }

    return NOERROR;
}
```

3. The method **IDropSource::GiveFeedback( )** allows you to examine the effect code returned by the drop target's methods. If you want to show your own cursors you can do so here, otherwise returning the value DRAGDROP_S_USEDEFAULTCURSORS causes OLE to use the standard ones. In a real-life app, this method frequently contains only the last line. Thus:

```
extern HWND hMainWnd ;

STDMETHODIMP CDropSource::GiveFeedback(DWORD dwEffect)
{
    POINT p ;

/*
If the cursor is over our own window, show a different cursor.
*/

    GetCursorPos (&p) ;
    if (WindowFromPoint (p) == hMainWnd)
    {
      SetCursor (LoadCursor (NULL, IDC_SIZE)) ;
      return S_OK ;
    }

/*
Cursor is not over our own window, so show default cursor.
*/

    return  DRAGDROP_S_USEDEFAULTCURSORS ;
}
```

D. DATA OBJECT SERVERS

1. A data object server does not have to be running for you to obtain its object. Via the API function **CoCreateInstance( )**, you can ask OLE to wake up a registered server app or DLL and create an object for you. You identify the object you want by means of its *globally unique ID* (GUID), also known as a *class ID* (CLSID). This is a 16-byte constant provided by the supplier of the server, who in turn created it with the utility app GUIDGEN.EXE that comes with your development environment.

When you call CoCreateInstance( ), you can specify whether you want to load the object from a *local server* (.EXE) or an *in-proc server* (.DLL). Most servers come in only one or the other flavors; it is rare to find both together. Combining the context flags as shown below causes OLE to look for an in-proc server first, and use a local server only if unable to find an in-proc server.

OLE looks in the system registry to find the server that has registered to supply this class of object. OLE then loads the server, has the server create an object of the requested class, and give you back a pointer to the requested interface on the newly created object. You will find the sample code for this app in the directory \chap02\data3. Thus:

```
/*
Globally unique ID of the object we want to create.  Supplied by the
vendor who made the server.
*/

static const GUID GUID_TimeData = { 0xe7767a70, 0xa409, 0x11ce,
    { 0xad, 0xf, 0x0, 0x60, 0x8c, 0x86, 0xb8, 0x9c } };


/*
User made menu selection telling us to create an object of the specified
type, using either an in-proc or a local server.  Tell OLE to find the
server, wake it up, make it create an object, and give us back a pointer
to its IDataObject interface.
*/

LPDATAOBJECT lpd = NULL ;

case ID_DATAOBJECT_CREATE:
{
    HRESULT hr ;

    hr = CoCreateInstance (
        GUID_TimeData,              // GUID of desired object
        NULL,                       // outer wrapper, here none
        CLSCTX_LOCAL_SERVER |       // try in-proc server first, use
          CLSCTX_INPROC_SERVER,     // local server if unavailable
        IID_IDataObject,            // interface pointer desired
        (void **) &lpd) ;           // output variable

    return 0 ;
}
```

2. Servers must make entries in the system registry so that OLE knows where to find them. This is most commonly done with a .REG file, of the type supplied with this book's sample code. You run the registry editor REGEDIT.EXE, and choose "File -- Merge Registration File..." from the main menu. When the dialog box pops up, simply type in the name of the .REG file containing the registration entries. The keys that you must set are:

HKEY_CLASSES_ROOT
   CLSID
                     <your object's class ID>
                              LocalServer32 = <full path to server .EXE>
                              InProcServer32 = <full path to server .DLL>

In the Data3 example, the entries are:

HKEY_CLASSES_ROOT
   CLSID
                     {E7767A70-A409-11ce-AD0F-00608C86B89C}
                              LocalServer32 = c:\EssenceofOLE\chap02\data3\server\data3sv.exe
                              InProcServer32 = c:\EssenceofOLE\chap02\data3\inprocsv\data3ips.dll

After all of your registration entries are made, you can view or edit them with the more sophisticated registry editor/viewer REGEDT32.EXE. Thus:

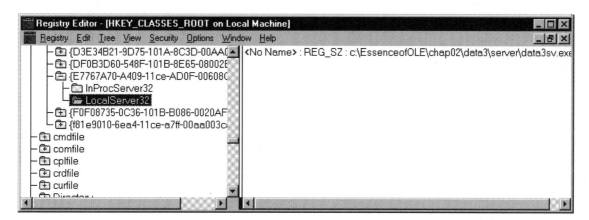

Note: Production apps these days are tending to perform self-registration. This is also done by server apps created with the MFC, and is required for OLE controls. Rather than having a separate .REG file as shown here, the app will make registry API calls to register itself every time it runs. This technique is discussed in Appendix A, and in Brockschmidt, pp. 228-229 and 268-269.

3. In addition to the required settings under the CLSID key, most servers choose to provide a human-readable name to identify the class ID. This has the form

HKEY_CLASSES_ROOT
    <your app's human-readable name>
        CLSID = <your app's class ID>

In the Data3 example, these entries are:

HKEY_CLASSES_ROOT
    EssenceofOLE.Data3
        CLSID = {E7767A70-A409-11ce-AD0F-00608C86B89C}

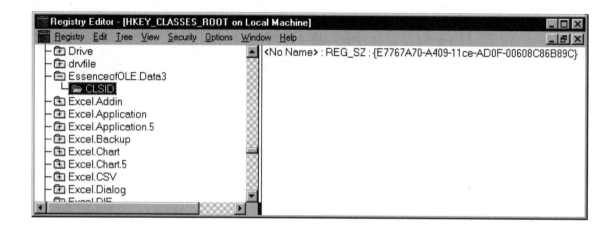

4. If you don't know the object's class ID but do know its registered name, or perhaps have the user pick it from a list, you can fetch the class ID via the function **CLSIDFromProgID( )**. This function finds the specified key under HKEY_CLASSES_ROOT, looks for the CLSID subkey, reads the string value of the subkey and converts it into a CLSID. It requires a wide character string, as do all OLE functions and interface methods that take strings as their parameters. A wide character string is a string of 16-bit characters which uses the Unicode character set. A full explanation of the Unicode/ANSI dilemma appears in Appendix A. For now, prepending the character 'L' to the string in quotes causes the compiler to treat the string as wide characters, whether the rest of your app uses wide characters or not. Thus:

```
case ID_DATAOBJECT_CREATEDLL:
{
    HRESULT hr ;

/*
Read class ID from registry key.
*/

    CLSID clsid ;
    hr = CLSIDFromProgID (L"EssenceofOLE.Data3", &clsid) ;

/*
Create object based on class ID read from registry.
*/

    hr = CoCreateInstance (clsid, ...) ;

    <rest of creation case>
}
```

5. When the client calls CoCreateInstance( ), OLE goes to the registry, finds the server for the object's class, and loads the server. OLE then gets from the server a *class factory*, an object that supports the *IClassFactory* interface. This interface is somewhat misnamed, as it manufactures objects rather than classes. Each class of object requires its own class factory object.

In addition to IUnknown, the IClassFactory interface has only two methods. The method **IClassFactory::CreateInstance( )** is called by OLE to create a new object and get a pointer to an interface on it, thus:

```
extern int LockCount, ObjectCount ;

STDMETHODIMP CClassFactory::CreateInstance(LPUNKNOWN pUnkOuter,
    REFIID riid, LPVOID* ppvObj)
{

/*
Check for aggregation request. OLE is asking us to create a new object
inside another object provided by OLE.  This simple example doesn't
support this feature, and neither do most real-world apps.
*/
    if (pUnkOuter != NULL)
    {
      *ppvObj = NULL ;
      return CLASS_E_NOAGGREGATION ;
    }

/*
Create a new data object.  Query the new object for the interface
requested by the caller.  If found, release our reference on the object
and return success code.
*/

    CTimeData * pTD = new CTimeData ( ) ;

    if (pTD->QueryInterface (riid, ppvObj) == S_OK)
    {
      pTD->Release ( ) ;
      ObjectCount ++ ;
      return NOERROR ;
    }

/*
The new object could not support the requested interface.  Delete the
newly created object and return an error code.
*/
    else
    {
      delete pTD ;
      return E_NOINTERFACE ;
    }
}
```

6. A client that creates and destroys many objects might want to keep the server running, ready for fast action, instead of frequently loading and unloading it. The client can get a pointer to the class factory itself via the API function **CoGetClassObject( )** (not shown), and call its **IClassFactory::LockServer( )** method. If your class factory implements the method, as does this one, you simply increment or decrement a lock count and refuse to shut down the server until all objects created by the server have been destroyed AND the lock count is zero. Many apps simply stub this one out. Thus:

```
extern HWND hMainWnd ;

STDMETHODIMP CClassFactory::LockServer(BOOL bLock)
{

/*
Increment or decrement the lock count, based on the parameter passed to
this method.
*/

    if (bLock == TRUE)
    {
      LockCount ++ ;
    }
    else
    {
      LockCount -- ;
    }

/*
If lock count is decremented to 0 and there are no outstanding objects,
shut down the server app.
*/
    if (LockCount == 0 && ObjectCount == 0)
    {
        PostMessage (hMainWnd, WM_CLOSE, 0, 0) ;
    }
    else
    {
        InvalidateRect (hMainWnd, NULL, TRUE) ;
    }
    }
    return NOERROR ;
}
```

7. When OLE launches a local server app, it passes the string "-Embedding" on the server's command line. When a server finds this on its command line, it must register its class factory interface with OLE via the function **CoRegisterClassObject( )**. This interface provides OLE with the methods it needs to create new objects of the specified class. When the server app shuts down, it must unregister its class factory via the function **CoRevokeClassObject( )**.   The sequence of events is shown in the block diagram below. The code executed by the local server is shown on the facing page.

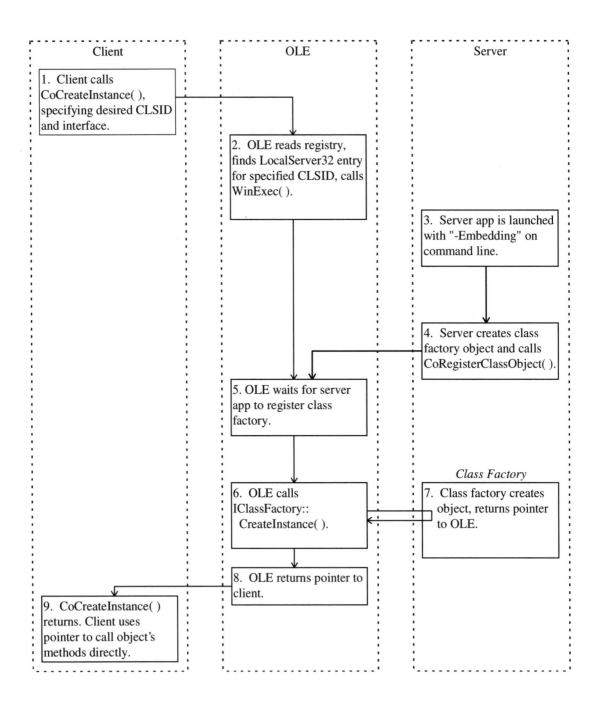

```
int WINAPI WinMain(HINSTANCE hInstance, HINSTANCE hPrevInstance,
    LPSTR lpCmdLine, int nCmdShow)
{

    <initialize, register classes, create main window>

/*
Check command line to see if launched as an OLE server.  If so, register
the class factory for this app.
*/

    DWORD dwRegister ;

    if (strstr (lpCmdLine, "-Embedding"))
    {
      LPCLASSFACTORY pCF = new CClassFactory ( ) ;

      CoRegisterClassObject(
            GUID_TimeData,          // GUID of object mfd by this fact'y
            pCF,                    // ptr to IClassFactory object
            CLSCTX_LOCAL_SERVER,    // context,here a local(.EXE) server
            REGCLS_MULTIPLEUSE,     // more flags
            &dwRegister) ;          // output variable

    }

    <standard message loop >

/*
App going down, revoke down class factory
*/

    CoRevokeClassObject (dwRegister) ;


    <standard app shutdown>
}
```

8. You may provide your server in an in-proc (.DLL) server instead of a separate .EXE program. The primary advantage of this is greater speed. Since a DLL is mapped into the address space of the process that loads it, OLE does not need to copy (marshal) the method calls and their data from the client's address space into the server's and back again. The "Data Object -- GetData Time Test" menu item on the data3cl.exe sample app's menu provides an easy way of measuring this performance advantage on your system. It's usually in the ballpark of 100 times faster in an in-proc object.

An in-proc server has two disadvantages. First, if you are adding OLE support to an existing app, it may be hard to extract server functionality from your existing .EXE into a DLL. Second, since it is mapped into the client's address space, a badly behaved in-proc server can kill a client app in a way that a local server cannot. Most vendors choose the speed. The sequence of events when an object is created from an in-proc server is shown in the following block diagram. The server's code is on the facing page.

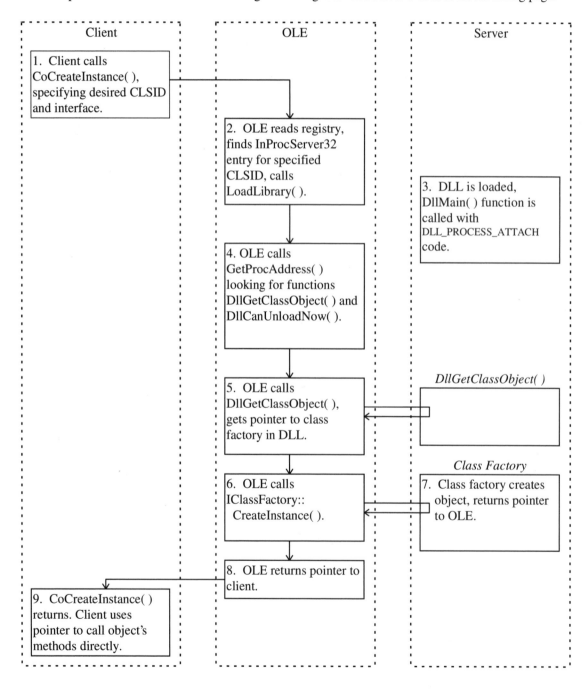

50

9. The connection between OLE and your in-proc server is made differently than for a local server. The server DLL must provide two exported functions for OLE to call. The first, **DllGetClassObject( )**, provides OLE with a pointer to the class factory object that creates objects of the server's class. This is the same class factory as we passed to CoRegisterClassObject( ) in the local server example previously shown. Thus:

```
CClassFactory cf ;          // IClassFactory interface for this server

STDAPI DllGetClassObject(REFCLSID rclsid, REFIID riid, LPVOID *ppv)
{

/*
Check to make sure that COM is asking for the CLSID that we support.
Maybe someone got the registry entry wrong.
*/

    if (rclsid !=  GUID_TimeData)
    {
      *ppv = NULL ;
      return E_FAIL ;
    }

/*
Take our hard-wired class factory and call QueryInterface( ) on it, on
behalf of the COM that called this function.
*/

    return cf.QueryInterface (riid, ppv) ;

}
```

A local server is responsible for shutting itself down, but an in-proc server will be unloaded by OLE. It must provide a function called **DllCanUnloadNow( )**, which tells OLE whether or not there are any outstanding references on this server's objects. Thus:

```
STDAPI DllCanUnloadNow(void)
{
/*
If no outstanding objects or lock counts, tell OLE that it is now safe
to unload this DLL.  Otherwise, say it isn't.
*/
    if (ObjectCount == 0 && LockCount == 0)
    {
      return S_OK ;
    }
    else
    {
      return S_FALSE ;
    }
}
```

WARNING: The examples shown here have to be exported from the DLL via a .DEF file. The combination of STDAPI and __declspec(dllexport) in the function declaration does not work. The DLL will compile and link, but the function names will not be listed in the DLL's name table. OLE's call to GetProcAddress( ) will therefore fail, and so will CoCreateInstance( ).

E. ADVISE LOOPS

1. Once you have a pointer to a data object, you can subscribe to be notified when the object's data changes, conceptually similar to a hot link in DDE. You accomplish this by calling the data object's method **IDataObject::DAdvise( )**. In this method, you specify the FORMATETC in which you want data updates rendered, and provide the data object's server an *advise sink* object. The latter is a generic callback notification object that supports the *IAdviseSink* interface discussed on the facing page. The server will call your advise sink's methods to notify you of changes to the data object. When you are finished with the advise loop, you terminate it via the method **IDataObject::DUnadvise( )**. Thus:

```
extern DWORD dwAdviseConnection ;
LPADVISESINK pAdvSink ;

/*
User has told us to start an advise loop.  Create an advise sink, and
call the method IDataObject::DAdvise( ).
*/

case ID_DATAOBJECT_DADVISE:
{
    FORMATETC fe ;
    HRESULT hr ;

    fe.cfFormat = cfTimeData ;
    fe.ptd = NULL ;
    fe.dwAspect = DVASPECT_CONTENT ;
    fe.lindex = -1 ;
    fe.tymed = TYMED_HGLOBAL ;

    pAdvSink = new CAdviseSink ( ) ;
    hr = lpd->DAdvise (&fe, 0, pAdvSink, &dwAdviseConnection) ;
    return 0 ;
}


/*
User told  us  to  stop  the  advise  loop.   Call  the  method
IDataObject::DUnadvise( ) and destroy the advise sink object.
*/

case ID_DATAOBJECT_DUNADVISE:
{
    lpd->DUnadvise (dwAdviseConnection) ;
    pAdvSink->Release ( ) ;
    return 0 ;
}
```

2. The advise sink contains methods which the server will call to tell the client that the data has changed. It is a generic object used in many different situations callback throughout OLE. In this simple data object case, you only need to implement one method, **IAdviseSink::OnDataChange( )**. The server will call this method when the data changes, passing you the FORMATETC structure describing the data's format and the STGMEDIUM structure containing the data itself. You process this in a manner similar to what you did when you got the data from calling IDataObject::GetData( ). The server won't call the other methods, and you wouldn't care if it did, so they are stubbed out. Thus:

```
/*
This method is called when the data object's data changes, with the new
data passed in its parameters.  We take the data, copy it into global
storage, and invalidate the window to force a repaint.
*/

STDMETHODIMP_(void) CAdviseSink::OnDataChange(LPFORMATETC pFEIn,
    LPSTGMEDIUM pSTM)
{

    char *cp ;
    cp = (char *)GlobalLock (pSTM->hGlobal) ;
    memmove (&st, cp, sizeof (st)) ;
    GlobalUnlock (pSTM->hGlobal) ;
    ReleaseStgMedium (pSTM) ;
    InvalidateRect (hMainWnd, NULL, TRUE) ;
    return;
}


/*
The other change methods are of no interest to us in this application.
*/

STDMETHODIMP_(void) CAdviseSink::OnViewChange(DWORD dwAspect,
    LONG lindex)
{
    return;
}


STDMETHODIMP_(void) CAdviseSink::OnRename(LPMONIKER pmk)
{
    return;
}


STDMETHODIMP_(void) CAdviseSink::OnSave(void)
{
    return;
}


STDMETHODIMP_(void) CAdviseSink::OnClose(void)
{
    return;
}
```

3. On the server side, a data object that supports advise loop connections must keep track of all the connections that it currently has open, along with their desired FORMATETC structures and advise sinks. It must add a connection to the list in response to the IDataObject::DAdvise( ) method, remove a connection from the list in response to the IDataObject::DUnadvise( ) method, and provide an enumerator object listing all current connections in response to the method IDataObject::EnumDAdvise( ).

This sounds like a pain in the ass, and it would be if we had to write all this ourselves. Fortunately, OLE provides a standard class called a *data advise holder* (an object that implements the *IDataAdviseHolder* interface) that does all of this bookkeeping for us. All we have to do is create one via the API function **CreateDataAdviseHolder( )**, and delegate calls to the data object's three advise loop methods to it. The advise holder knows how to add and remove connections and provide an enumerator. Thus:

```
/*
Create advise holder for this data object.
*/

CTimeData::CTimeData()
{
    m_RefCount = 1 ;
    CreateDataAdviseHolder (&m_pDataAdviseHolder) ;
    return;
}


/*
Delegate all advise method calls to the advise holder.  "Hey, I don't
deal with this stuff. Here, talk to my agent."
*/

STDMETHODIMP CTimeData::DAdvise (FORMATETC * lpfe, DWORD dw,
    LPADVISESINK lpas, DWORD * lpdw)
{
    return  m_pDataAdviseHolder->Advise (this, lpfe, dw, lpas, lpdw) ;
}


STDMETHODIMP CTimeData::DUnadvise  (DWORD dw)
{
    return  m_pDataAdviseHolder->Unadvise (dw) ;
}


STDMETHODIMP CTimeData::EnumDAdvise  (LPENUMSTATDATA * lpen)
{
    return  m_pDataAdviseHolder->EnumAdvise (lpen) ;
}
```

4. When the server's data changes, it needs to signal the change to any clients that have a current advise loop connection. The data advise holder contains the list of connections. Simply calling the method **IDataAdviseHolder::SendOnDataChange( )** will cause the advise holder to run through its list of current connections. For each connection, the advise holder will call the IDataObject::GetData( ) method to get the object's newly changed data in the FORMATETC specified when the connection was established. The advise holder will then call the connection's IAdviseSink::OnDataChange( ) method, passing the data to the waiting client, simply and elegantly. Thus:

```
LPDATAOBJECT lpFirstObj ;

/*
Server's data has changed.  Use the object's internal method to tell it
to send the data change to any watching client.
*/

case WM_TIMER:
{
    GetLocalTime (&lt) ;
    InvalidateRect (hWnd, NULL, FALSE) ;

    if (lpFirstObj)
    {
      lpFirstObj->SendDataChangeToClient ( )   ;
    }
    return 0 ;
}


/*
Call the data advise holder's SendOnDataChange( ) method.  This handles
all the heavy lifting of sending the newly changed data to all waiting
clients.
*/

void CTimeData::SendDataChangeToClient ( )
{
    m_pDataAdviseHolder->SendOnDataChange (this, 0, 0) ;
}
```

F. SOURCING DATA OBJECTS IN THE MFC

1. The MFC provides a prefabricated generic implementation of the IDataObject interface in its **COleDataSource** class. This class supports all of the IDataObject functionality (such as the format enumerator) except for advise loops. An example of using the MFC for data object operations is found in the directory \chap02\mfcdata2.

To use this class to place data on the Clipboard, we use the `new` operator to create a COleDataSource object and place our text data inside it via its **CacheGlobalData( )** method. The method **COleDataSource::SetClipboard( )** places the object on the Clipboard.   The object will be destroyed when the Clipboard finally releases it. Thus:

```
void CMfcdata2View::OnDataobjectCopytoclipboard()
{
    CMfcdata2Doc* pDoc = GetDocument();

/*
Create a new COleDataSource object.
*/

    COleDataSource *pds = new COleDataSource ( ) ;

/*
Cache our text string inside the data object.
*/
    char *cp = (char *) GlobalAlloc (GMEM_FIXED,
      pDoc->m_String.GetLength( )+1) ;
    lstrcpy (cp, (LPCTSTR)pDoc->m_String) ;

    pds->CacheGlobalData (CF_TEXT, cp) ;

/*
Place our data object on the Clipboard.  It will be destroyed when the
Clipboard finally releases it.
*/

    pds->SetClipboard ( ) ;
}
```

2. The COleDataSource class is also the basis for a drag operation. We construct and fill a COleDataSource as before, then call its **DoDragDrop( )** method. Internally, this causes the MFC to create a default drop source object and call the API function DoDragDrop( ) as shown previously in this chapter. The return value tells us the operation (move, copy, etc.) that the drop target wants us to perform. Since the drag operation will take place solely within the boundaries of this function, we do not allocate the COleDataSource object with new, but simply instantiate it on the stack. Thus:

```
void CMfcdata2View::OnLButtonDown(UINT nFlags, CPoint point)
{
    CMfcdata2Doc* pDoc = GetDocument();

/*
Create COleDataSource object and fill with data formats.
*/
    COleDataSource ds ;

    char *cp = (char *) GlobalAlloc (GMEM_FIXED,
      pDoc->m_String.GetLength( )+1) ;
    lstrcpy (cp, (LPCTSTR)pDoc->m_String) ;
    ds.CacheGlobalData (CF_TEXT, cp) ;

/*
Perform drag operation.  If effect code is MOVE, then erase string from
our own app.
*/
    if (ds.DoDragDrop () == DROPEFFECT_MOVE)
    {
      pDoc->m_String = "" ;
      Invalidate ( ) ;
    }
}
```

Note: The examples on these two pages do not use the IClassFactory interface. Any reader wanting to see how the MFC implements a class factory will find it in Chapter 9, "Custom Interfaces."

Directory: \EssenceofOLE\chap02\data2\templ

This lab is a continuation of the app you worked on in lesson 1. We continue working on the same app, adding code to make it be a source of data objects as well as a consumer of them. As always, a skeleton app is supplied in the above directory. The skeleton app contains a menu item called "Edit Text...", which allows you to change the app's text string from within.

1. Your app must be able to create its own data objects encapsulating its DisplayText[ ]. Your object must implement an IDataObject class that accepts text and renders it either in CF_TEXT or CF_METAFILEPICT. The files CTXTDATA.H and CTXTDATA.CPP contain a skeleton of this class. The IUnknown methods have been written for you, the rest are present but stubbed out. When your object is created, you must create a snapshot of the data which will live inside the object. The class constructor accepts a string pointer as its single parameter. In the constructor, allocate a global memory handle and store the string in it, adding member variables as necessary. Free the global memory handle in the class destructor.

2. Next, implement the QueryGetData( ) method. This takes a single parameter which is a pointer to a FORMATETC structure. Examine the structure to see if the caller is asking for renderings that we support — either CF_TEXT in a TYMED_HGLOBAL, or CF_METAFILEPICT in a TYMED_MFPICT. Return the success code if your object can support the requested rendering, otherwise return an error code.

3. The most important method of this object is GetData( ), which is the method that actually supplies the data when the caller asks for it. Check the supplied FORMATETC structure as you did in step 2. If the user is asking for data in CF_TEXT, allocate a global memory block and copy the member string contents into it. Then store the memory handle in the STGMEDIUM structure, set its other elements, and return success. If the user is asking for data in metafile format, create a metafile DC via the function CreateMetaFile( ), maybe set its colors with SetBkColor( ) and SetTextColor( ), draw the text on the DC with TextOut( ), then convert the DC into a metafile via the function CloseMetaFile( ). Allocate a structure of type METAFILEPICT and fill in its elements. Then store the METAFILEPICT structure's memory handle (not the metafile handle itself) in the STGMEDIUM structure, set its elements, and return success.

4. You must now implement the EnumFormatEtc( ) method. The file CENUM.CPP and .H have been already included in your project. Examine these files so that you understand them, then write your method to instantiate an object of this type using an array of FORMATETC structures that contain the format that your data object supports. Give the user a pointer to it, and return success.

5. You now have a data object but no real way of looking at it or using it. Implement the "Demo -- Copy Text" menu item in the WM_COMMAND case of file MAINWIND.CPP. Instantiate an object of your new data class, using as its starting parameter the global array DisplayText[ ] which contains the text string shown in your app. When you have the object created, put it onto the Clipboard via the function OleSetClipboard( ). You should now be able to use the Clipbook Viewer in your Main application folder to see the data that your app has put onto the Clipboard. You should be able to paste it into WinWord in either text or metafile format.

6. Now that we have our data object, we want to make it do drag and drop. A skeleton IDropSource object has been supplied for you in the file CDROPSRC.CPP and .H. Examine these files

until you feel comfortable with them. In file MAINWIND.C, in response to the WM_LBUTTONDOWN message, create an IDropSource object and a CTextData object. Then use the function DoDragDrop( ) to perform the drag-and-drop operation. Check the return code, and if it is DROPEFFECT_DROP, signaling a successful drop operation, check the effect code. If this is DROPEFFECT_MOVE, then rub out the data in your window by setting DisplayText[0] to 0x00 and invalidating.

7. Drag operations in your own window are often special-cased. Modify your IDropSource::GiveFeedback( ) method to check if the drag operation is over your own window (use the functions GetCursorPos( ) and WindowFromPoint( )). If it is, use the function SetCursor( ) to show a special cursor, perhaps the window moving/sizing 4-way arrow (IDC_SIZE).

EXTRA CREDIT: Add more data formats to your object.

EXTRA EXTRA CREDIT: Check whether your data transfer object will work with an Enhanced Metafile, a new type of metafile added to Win32. This behavior would seem reasonable; the Clipboard automatically synthesizes either type of metafile when the other type is placed inside it, but the behavior is not documented and might not exist. I suspect that it will work in the Clipboard but not in drag-and-drop.

EXTRA EXTRA EXTRA CREDIT: The drop source object is in charge of showing the cursor, but sometimes the drop target might want to do it instead. For example, a wastebasket program might want to show a cursor that looks like a shredder. You can't require the drop source to have specific knowledge of every other app it might want to drop on. Try to think of a way either for the drop target to signal the drop source that the former wants to show the cursor so the latter shouldn't, or for the drop target to wrest control of the cursor from the drop source so that the former can display whatever cursor it wants. Any way that works well will be featured in the next edition of this book; I'm not sure that there is one. The target app could, however, draw its own picture around the cursor location; for example a slavering, shark's mouth or a chain saw.

EXTRA EXTRA EXTRA EXTRA CREDIT: It is probably more convenient for the user if a drag operation doesn't begin exactly at the left button mouse click, but rather when the mouse has moved a small number of pixels, thereby clearly differentiating the selection operation from the start-drag operation. Save the last click position in the WM_LBUTTONDOWN message case. Then move the drag operation to the WM_MOUSEMOVE message, happening only if the left button is down and the position has moved from the location of the original click. Experiment with different numbers of pixels and see what feels good.

EXTRA EXTRA EXTRA EXTRA EXTRA CREDIT: You probably noticed that if you click the left mouse button in your app, the text string in it disappears. Why is that, and how would you fix it ? Hint: In what order are the drop source and drop target operations performed?

Lab Exercise
Lesson 2
MFC Data Transfer Object Server

Directory: \EssenceofOLE\chap02\mfcdata2\templ

This lab uses the MFC to do the same thing as the data2 lab did in the API. A skeleton app is supplied for you in the directory listed above.

1. Our app's document class contains a string member variable named CMfcdata2Doc::m_String that is initialized to a default value. When the user selects "Data Object -- Copy to Clipboard" from the main menu, we want to use OLE to place this string onto the Windows Clipboard. In the command handler method CMfcdata2View::OnDataobjectCopytoclipboard( ), which you will find near the bottom of the file mfcdata2view.cpp, use the new operator to allocate an object of class COleDataSource. Use the API function GlobalAlloc( ) to allocate a block of global memory and copy the contents of the document's m_String variable into it. Use the method COleDataSource::CacheGlobalData( ) to place the global into the data object. Then use the method COleDataSource::SetClipboard( ) to place it on the Clipboard.

2. Next, we want to offer our text string to other apps by means of drag and drop as well as the Clipboard. Create and fill a COleDataSource as described above, except this time, instantiate it on the stack instead of using new. Use the method COleDataSource::DoDragDrop( ) to perform the drag operation. If the drop target signals a drop effect code of DROPEFFECT_MOVE, then empty the document's m_String variable and invalidate your view to force a repaint that will display its new empty contents.

EXTRA CREDIT: Examine the extra credit suggestions in the API lab example and implement them in the MFC.

Chapter 3

OLE Automation

A. Concepts and Definitions

1. *OLE automation* is the process whereby one application or DLL (the *automation server*) creates and exposes *automation objects* for use by another app (the *automation controller*). It was originally conceived as a way for app writers to expose their internal macro programming languages to external programming tools. App vendors could thus have all the advantages of macro programming without having to develop and maintain the tools to do it, and customers could use whatever tools they liked and were familiar with for programming all of their applications. The architecture of OLE automation was dictated by the need to accommodate Microsoft Visual Basic (VB), the first programming environment at which it was targeted. OLE automation has since expanded into a generalized mechanism for one app to control another.

2. An automation object may expose *methods*, which are functions that optionally accept arguments and return values. An automation object may also expose *properties*, which are data values within the object that the controller may set and get. The set of methods and properties is exposed to the world as a custom interface, conceptually similar to those used in other parts of OLE. Unlike the VTBL interfaces that we have been using so far, to facilitate the runtime binding required for interpreted languages such as VB, all methods and properties of an automation object are accessed through the single, deceptively simple-looking *IDispatch* interface. Its methods are:

```
IDispatch::GetIDsOfNames    // Maps a single member name and an optional set of argument names
                            // to a set of integer DISPIDs for use by IDispatch::Invoke().
IDispatch::GetTypeInfo      // Get ITypeInfo interface describing an object.
IDispatch::GetTypeInfoCount //Get  number of ITypeInfo interfaces in an object .
IDispatch::Invoke           // Access property or method exposed by the object.
```

WARNING: If you have picked up this book for the first time and jumped straight to this chapter because OLE automation is the only piece of OLE you care about, **STOP!** Unless you are already familiar with the component-object model, including interface VTBLs and class factories, go back and read at least the first half of Chapter 1 and the second half of Chapter 2. Otherwise this chapter will make no sense, and you will only get frustrated and send me nasty e-mail, to which I will reply "RTFC1AC2."

3. Hey, wait a minute, where are the custom methods and properties in the IDispatch interface? They are all accessed through the single method IDispatch::Invoke( ). Each method or property is identified by a *dispatch ID*, an integer constant. This ID is passed to the Invoke( ) method, along with any required parameters. The server's implementation of the Invoke( ) method looks at the dispatch ID and executes the code specified by that ID. Parameters and return values are passed in VARIANT structures, self-describing structures used extensively in Visual Basic, which OLE knows how to marshal across process boundaries. When you call the method IDispatch::Invoke( ), you are in essence saying, "Hey, Mr. Object, do thing number 1 (or 2, or 3, etc.) and here's the data for it." Thus:

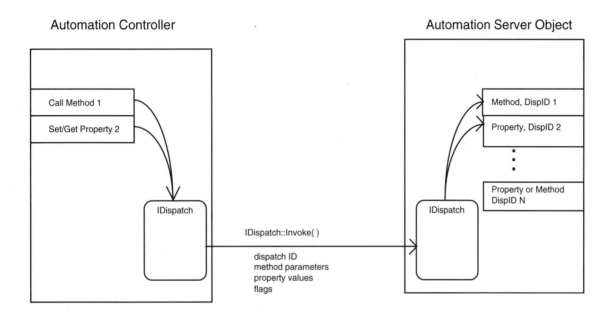

4. Although all automation objects are accessed through the same IDispatch interface, it is clear that the same dispatch ID may mean different things to different objects. A dispatch ID of 1 may instruct one object to save all of its data carefully to disk, whereas to another object, the same dispatch ID may mean to format its hard drive and everyone else's on the network without asking for confirmation. The meaning of the set of IDs accessed through an IDispatch interface to which an object responds is called a *dispinterface*. It is conceptually similar to a custom interface, except the dispinterface's VTBL does not vary from one object to another. It is the interpretation of the data supplied to the IDispatch::Invoke( ) method that makes it custom. Making sure you have the right methods and parameters for the dispinterface you are using is the primary challenge of OLE automation programming.

B. BASIC CONTROLLER FUNCTIONALITY

1. Building an automation controller is conceptually simple, although the exact syntax of the methods can be tricky. To ease the task of the application programmer, you probably want to encapsulate the controller's interface to the automation object in a C++ wrapper, in this example called CHelloDriver. This also makes it much easier to supply dummy or test data while the server is still under development. A smart component vendor would provide this class along with its server. In the following chapter, we will see how automated tools can generate this wrapper class for us.

In the following examples, we want to create a dedicated controller app that manipulates a very simple automation server. The server object displays a text string in a window on the screen. The object exposes a single method called "SayHello( )", which draws the object's current string in an edit control. It also exposes that current string as a property named "HelloMessage", whose value controllers may set and get. In this example, we pretend we knew all this from reading the documentation provided by the vendor that sold us the server. The source code for this example is in the directory \chap03\helloau\hlodrv32. The controller app's WinMain( ) looks like this:

```
extern BOOL WINAPI HelloDlgProc (HWND, UINT, WPARAM, LPARAM) ;

/*
Controller object that encapsulates the interface to the server's
automation object.
*/


CHelloDriver chd ;

int WINAPI WinMain(HINSTANCE hInst, HINSTANCE hPrevInstance,
    LPSTR lpCmdLine, int nCmdShow)
{
    MSG msg ;
    OleInitialize (NULL) ;

/*
Try to connect to the automation object.  If unsuccessful, terminate
app.
*/

    if (chd.Create( ) == FALSE)
    {
      MessageBox (NULL, "Can't hook up hellodrv", "Error", 0) ;
      return -1 ;
    }

/*
Connection made to automation object.  Pop up dialog box that will call
object's methods in response to dialog box's controls.
*/

    DialogBox (hInst, MAKEINTRESOURCE(IDD_DIALOG1), NULL, HelloDlgProc);

    OleUninitialize ( ) ;
    return msg.wParam;
}
```

2. The class *CHelloDriver* is the controller's wrapper for the exposed automation object. Its header files, constructor, and destructor will look like this:

```
/*
Wrapper class for the controller side of the Hello automation object.
*/

class CHelloDriver
{
    private:
      LPDISPATCH m_pDisp ;              // IDispatch interface from server
      DISPID m_dSayHelloId ;           // Say hello method ID
      DISPID m_dHelloPropID ;          // string set/get ID

    public:
      CHelloDriver( ) ;
      ~CHelloDriver( ) ;

      BOOL Create(LPSTR) ;              // set up dispatch with server
      HRESULT SetString (LPOLESTR) ;// tell server what string to use
      HRESULT GetString (LPOLESTR) ;// ask what string server is using
      HRESULT SayHowdy(void) ;         // tell server to output its string
      HRESULT BadSetString (void) ; // intentionally make error for demo
} ;

CHelloDriver::CHelloDriver( )
{
    return ;
}

/*
Class destructor.  If we have a pointer to an IDispatch interface,
release it.
*/

CHelloDriver::~CHelloDriver( )
{
    if (m_pDisp)
    {
      m_pDisp->Release( );
    }
    return ;
}
```

65

3. To start the automation process, the controller must first cause an automation object of the appropriate class to be created and get a pointer to the object's IDispatch interface. We do exactly the same thing as we did to get a data object in Chapter 2, call the API function **CoCreateInstance( )**. The only difference is that this time we ask for the IDispatch interface pointer. Thus:

```
BOOL CHelloDriver::Create( )
{
    HRESULT hr ;

    CLSID clsid ;

    < read class ID from the registry >


/*
Try to create an instance of the Hello object and get a pointer to its
IDispatch interface.
*/

    hr = CoCreateInstance (
        clsid,                      // class ID of object
        NULL,                       // controlling IUnknown, here standalone
        CLSCTX_LOCAL_SERVER,        // context
        IID_IDispatch,              // type of interface ptr wanted
        (LPVOID *) &m_pDisp) ;      // output variable

    if (!SUCCEEDED(hr))
    {
        return FALSE ;
    }
```

4. The IDispatch interface provides access to all the methods and properties exposed by the automation object. Each method or property is identified by a DWORD *dispatch ID*, which we will need to access via the method IDispatch::Invoke( ). The vendor might have given us a header file with those IDs predefined, but maybe was too lazy or wanted to reserve the right to change them later. Since we don't have them at compile time, we must query the object for them at run time via the method **IDispatch::GetIDsOfNames( )**. This is a somewhat misnamed method, as it provides the ID of only a single method or property at a time. The designers gave it a plural name because it can also get the IDs of any named parameters (dealt with later) that a single method might support. Note that as for all strings in OLE, the names provided to this method must always use wide (Unicode) characters, even if neither controller nor server are wide character apps. Thus:

```
/*
Get the ID numbers associated with the names in the IDispatch interface.
SayHello( ) is a method.
*/

    WCHAR *Name = L"SayHello" ;

    hr = m_pDisp->GetIDsOfNames (
       IID_NULL,                     // reserved
       &Name,                        // Array of names to get IDs for
       1,                            // # of names in the array
       LOCALE_SYSTEM_DEFAULT,        // System locale
       &m_dSayHelloId) ;             // Array of IDs to fill on output

    if (hr)
    {
       return FALSE ;
    }


/*
HelloMessage is a property.
*/
    Name = L"HelloMessage" ;

    hr = m_pDisp->GetIDsOfNames (
       IID_NULL,                     // reserved
       &Name,                        // Array of names to get IDs for
       1,                            // # of names in the array
       LOCALE_SYSTEM_DEFAULT,        // System locale
       &m_dHelloPropID) ;            // Array of IDs to fill on output

    if (hr)
    {
       return FALSE ;
    }

    return TRUE ;
}
```

This page intentionally contains no text other than this sentence.

5. A method is called in an automation object via the method **IDispatch::Invoke( )**, specifying the dispatch ID of the object's method that you want to call. We also specify a flag that tells the server that what we are doing is calling a method on the object, as opposed to getting or setting a property. The arguments required by the object's method are passed in a structure of type **DISPPARAMS**, which is defined thus:

```
typedef struct  tagDISPPARAMS
{
    VARIANTARG *rgvarg;           // array of VARIANT structs holding args
    DISPID  *rgdispidNamedArgs;    // array of DISPIDs naming args
    UINT cArgs;                   // number of VARIANTS in array
    UINT cNamedArgs;              // number of names in array
} DISPPARAMS;
```

All parameters in OLE automation are passed by means of VARIANT structures, which are described in more detail on the next page. The DISPPARAMS structure is a holder for VARIANTs and the items that describe their use, containing pointers to two arrays and the counts of the items in each array. In this example, the object's method does not require any arguments, so we set both pointers in the DISPPARAMS to NULL and both counts to zero. Thus:

```
/*
Invoke the server's SayHello( ) method.
*/

HRESULT CHelloDriver::SayHowdy(void)
{
    HRESULT hr ;
    EXCEPINFO ei ;
    UINT uiErr ;
    DISPPARAMS dispparamsNoArgs = {NULL, NULL, 0, 0};

    hr = m_pDisp->Invoke (
        m_dSayHelloId,                // ID of function to call
        IID_NULL,                     // reserved
        LOCALE_SYSTEM_DEFAULT,        // system locale
        DISPATCH_METHOD,              // we are calling a method
        &dispparamsNoArgs,            // no parameters are being passed
        NULL,                         // no return value expected
        &ei,                          // exception information
        &uiErr ) ;                    // error information

    return hr ;
}
```

6. The value of a property is fetched via the same IDispatch::Invoke( ) method with slightly different parameters. We pass the dispatch ID of the property that we want to fetch and the flag that says that what we are doing is getting the value of a property. We declare a structure of type **VARIANT** and pass it as the sixth parameter; the server will place the property's value into it.

All parameters and return values in OLE automation are passed by means of VARIANT structures, the definition of which is shown on the facing page. Used extensively throughout VB, a VARIANT is a structure containing a self-describing union supporting 13 different data types which OLE knows how to marshal both by value and by reference. You can pass essentially any type of single-variable value, including arrays (via the SAFEARRAY type). You can pass pointers to IDispatch interfaces directly, and pointers to any other interface by passing the object's root IUnknown interface and then querying it at the destination for the desired interface. A VARIANT does not support structures, so if you need to pass structures to automation objects, you will have to either write a custom interface (see Chapter 7), pack it up as a SAFEARRAY, or think of something else. See Brockschmidt, pp. 647-653 for a fuller discussion of VARIANT data types.

Strings in OLE automation are always passed in the form of a BSTR, again a structure used in VB. You can use it in C++ as if it were a regular null-terminated string, however, you must allocate it via the function SysAllocString( ) and free it via the function **SysFreeString( )**. Thus:

```
HRESULT CHelloDriver::GetString (LPOLESTR pOut)
{
    HRESULT hr ;
    VARIANT var ;          // holder for return value
    EXCEPINFO ei ;
    UINT uiErr ;
    DISPPARAMS dispparamsNoArgs = {NULL, NULL, 0, 0};

    var.vt = VT_EMPTY ;

/*
Try to get the string from the object.
*/

    hr = m_pDisp->Invoke (
      m_dHelloPropID,              // ID of property
      IID_NULL,                    // reserved
      LOCALE_SYSTEM_DEFAULT,       // system locale
      DISPATCH_PROPERTYGET,        // flag
      &dispparamsNoArgs,           // no parameters passed
      &var,                        // holder for returned value
      &ei,                         // exception info
      &uiErr ) ;                   // error info

/*
If string was successfully retrieved, it is in the buffer pointed to by
the variant's bstrVal element.  Copy it into our local buffer and free
the string.
*/
    if (SUCCEEDED(hr))
    {
      wcscpy (pOut, var.bstrVal) ;
      SysFreeString (var.bstrVal) ;
    }.
    return hr ;
}
```

```c
typedef struct tagVARIANT VARIANTARG;
typedef struct tagVARIANT VARIANT;

typedef struct tagVARIANT
{
    VARTYPE vt;
    unsigned short wReserved1;
    unsigned short wReserved2;
    unsigned short wReserved3;

    union
    {
        short         iVal;            /* VT_I2                     */
        long          lVal;            /* VT_I4                     */
        float         fltVal;          /* VT_R4                     */
        double        dblVal;          /* VT_R8                     */
        VARIANT_BOOL  bool;            /* VT_BOOL                   */
        SCODE         scode;           /* VT_ERROR                  */
        CY            cyVal;           /* VT_CY                     */

        DATE          date;            /* VT_DATE                   */
        BSTR          bstrVal;         /* VT_BSTR                   */
        IUnknown      FAR* punkVal;    /* VT_UNKNOWN                */
        IDispatch     FAR* pdispVal;   /* VT_DISPATCH               */


        short         FAR* piVal;      /* VT_BYREF|VT_I2            */
        long          FAR* plVal;      /* VT_BYREF|VT_I4            */
        float         FAR* pfltVal;    /* VT_BYREF|VT_R4            */
        double        FAR* pdblVal;    /* VT_BYREF|VT_R8            */
        VARIANT_BOOL  FAR* pbool;      /* VT_BYREF|VT_BOOL          */
        SCODE         FAR* pscode;     /* VT_BYREF|VT_ERROR         */
        CY            FAR* pcyVal;     /* VT_BYREF|VT_CY            */
        DATE          FAR* pdate;      /* VT_BYREF|VT_DATE          */
        BSTR          FAR* pbstrVal;   /* VT_BYREF|VT_BSTR          */
        IUnknown FAR* FAR* ppunkVal;   /* VT_BYREF|VT_UNKNOWN       */
        IDispatch FAR* FAR* ppdispVal; /* VT_BYREF|VT_DISPATCH      */


        SAFEARRAY     FAR* parray;     /* VT_ARRAY|*                */
        VARIANT       FAR* pvarVal;    /* VT_BYREF|VT_VARIANT       */

        void          FAR* byref;      /* Generic ByRef             */
    };
} ;
```

7. Setting a property is slightly more complicated. We use the same IDispatch::Invoke( ) method, passing the dispatch ID of the property that we want to set. We also pass a flag saying that what we are doing is setting a property.

The trick in setting a property is packaging up the parameters in the DISPPARAMS structure. The DISPPARAMS structure, as previously shown, has an element called `rgvarg` which points to an array of VARIANTS containing the parameters that are passed to the method. It also has an element called `cArgs`, which contains the number of VARIANTS in the array, in this case one. We allocate a VARIANT and initialize it to default values via the function **VariantInit( )**. We use the function **SysAllocString( )** to allocate a BSTR containing the string we want to pass, place it in the VARIANT, and set the VARIANT's `vt` element to the flag **VT_BSTR**, indicating that this VARIANT contains a BSTR so that OLE will know how to marshal it. Finally, we set `rgvargs` to point to the VARIANT. Similar footwork is required when calling a method that requires parameters.

You would think this would be all we have to do, but it isn't. Parameters in OLE automation can be passed either by position, as in a compiled language, or by name. See Brockschmidt, pp. 752-753 for a discussion of named arguments. In a DISPPARAMS structure, the element `rgdispidNamedArgs` is a pointer to an array of dispatch IDs specifying the name of each argument in the `rgvargs` array, and the element `cNamedArgs` is the number of elements in the array. For historical reasons, when setting a property, it is necessary to provide an ID for the VARIANT containing the property's value, and the ID must have the reserved value **DISPID_PROPERTYPUT** (-3). The element `rgdispidNamedArgs` must point at an integer whose value is this, and the count of named arguments must be set to 1. Hey, I didn't design it. A working code example is shown on the facing page.

```
HRESULT CHelloDriver::SetString(LPOLESTR cp)
{
    HRESULT hr ;                DISPPARAMS dp ;
    VARIANTARG vString ;        EXCEPINFO ei ;
    UINT uiErr ;                DISPID dPutID ;
/*
Allocate a string from the system memory allocator.  Place it into the
element of a VARIANT structure, and set the flags.
*/

    BSTR bstr = SysAllocString (cp) ;
    VariantInit (&vString) ;
    vString.vt = VT_BSTR ;
    vString.bstrVal = bstr ;

/*
Set up the DISPPARAMS structure.  Point to the array of VARIANTs that
contains the parameters, and set the count in the array (here only 1).
*/

    dp.rgvarg = &vString ;          // variant array containing params
    dp.cArgs = 1 ;                  // # of elements in the array

/*
Now set the elements that identify the parameter passed to the method.
*/

    dPutID = DISPID_PROPERTYPUT ;   // use SET property function
    dp.rgdispidNamedArgs = &dPutID ; // needs it by reference
    dp.cNamedArgs = 1 ;             // number of elements

/*
Invoke the function.
*/
    hr = m_pDisp->Invoke (
      m_dHelloPropID,               // ID of property
      IID_NULL,                     // reserved
      LOCALE_SYSTEM_DEFAULT,        // system locale
      DISPATCH_PROPERTYPUT,         // set value of property
      &dp,                          // array of parameters to pass
      NULL,                         // no return value expected
      &ei,                          // exception info
      &uiErr ) ;                    // error info
/*
If function was successful, recipient should free string; otherwise we
have to.
*/
    if (!SUCCEEDED(hr))
    {
      SysFreeString (bstr) ;
    }
    return hr ;
}
```

C. BASIC SERVER FUNCTIONALITY

1. An automation object must provide the *IDispatch* interface, which is the means whereby the controller invokes the methods and accesses the properties of the object. To create and provide the server's objects to the world, the server must implement the *IClassFactory* factory interface, as was done in the previous chapter. The server may be either an in-proc (DLL) or local (.EXE) server. Thus:

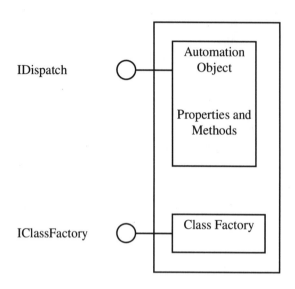

OLE Automation Interfaces

2. Exposing an automation object means writing your own dispinterface. Consider a very simple automation object used in the controller example. It exposes a single method called "SayHello( )", which draws a text string in a window on the screen. It also exposes a single property called "HelloMessage", which is the string drawn on the screen when the SayHello( ) method is invoked. We want to expose these features to other apps, which means wrapping them in an IDispatch interface. As we did when providing our own implementation of the IDataObject interface in Chapter 2, we would define our own C++ class derived from the predefined interface. The source code for this example is in the directory \chap03\helloau\hello32. We would call it CHelloDispatch, and its header file would look like this:

```c
#include <windows.h>

class CHelloDispatch : public IDispatch
{
 public:

/*
Data members
*/

    BSTR m_bstrHelloMsg;                // HelloMessage property
    ULONG m_RefCount;                   // Reference count

 /*
 Class constructor and destructor
 */

    CHelloDispatch();
    ~CHelloDispatch();

 /*
 IUnknown methods
 */

    STDMETHODIMP QueryInterface (REFIID riid, void FAR* FAR* ppv);
    STDMETHODIMP_(ULONG) AddRef (void);
    STDMETHODIMP_(ULONG) Release (void);

/*
IDispatch methods
*/

    STDMETHODIMP GetTypeInfoCount(UINT *pctinfo) ;
    STDMETHODIMP GetTypeInfo(UINT, LCID, ITypeInfo **pptinfo) ;
    STDMETHODIMP GetIDsOfNames(REFIID, LPOLESTR *, UINT, LCID,DISPID *);
    STDMETHODIMP Invoke(DISPID, REFIID, LCID lcid, WORD, DISPPARAMS *,
      VARIANT *, EXCEPINFO *, UINT *) ;

};
```

3. The class constructor, destructor, and QueryInterface( ) methods look like this:

```
#include "resource.h"
#include "hello.h"

extern HWND hMainWnd ;

/*
Class Constructor
*/

CHelloDispatch::CHelloDispatch()
{
    m_RefCount = 1;
    m_bstrHelloMsg = SysAllocString(TEXT("Hello, world"));
}

/*
Class Destructor
*/

CHelloDispatch::~CHelloDispatch()
{
    SysFreeString(m_bstrHelloMsg);
}


STDMETHODIMP CHelloDispatch::QueryInterface(REFIID riid, void ** ppv)
{

/*
Someone is asking us for our IDispatch or IUnknown.  Return a pointer to
our VTBL.
*/

    if (riid == IID_IUnknown  || riid == IID_IDispatch)
    {
      *ppv = this ;
      AddRef();
      return NOERROR;
    }

/*
Caller asked for an interface that we don't support.
*/
    else
    {
      *ppv = NULL;
      return E_NOINTERFACE;
    }
}
```

4. Now we have to implement the methods of the IDispatch interface. As before, some can be stubbed out completely, and some others are trivial. The methods **GetTypeInfoCount( )** and **GetTypeInfo( )** are optional, and can be stubbed out, thus:

```
STDMETHODIMP CHelloDispatch::GetTypeInfoCount(UINT *pNtypeInfo)
{
    *pNtypeInfo = 0;
    return E_NOTIMPL ;
}


STDMETHODIMP CHelloDispatch::GetTypeInfo(UINT itinfo, LCID lcid,
    ITypeInfo **pptinfo)
{
    *pptinfo = NULL ;
    return E_NOTIMPL ;
}
```

The method **GetIDsOfNames( )** is fairly simple. We are passed the name of a property or method, and simply return the dispatch ID to which it refers. If we do not support a member with that name, we return an error code. Note that the names are always passed in wide character strings. Thus:

```
STDMETHODIMP CHelloDispatch::GetIDsOfNames(REFIID riid,
    LPOLESTR *pNames, UINT cNames, LCID lcid, DISPID *pDispID)
{
    if ( _wcsicmp (*pNames, L"SayHello") == 0)
    {
      *pDispID = 2 ;
      return NOERROR ;
    }
    else if ( _wcsicmp (*pNames, L"HelloMessage") == 0)
    {
      *pDispID = 1 ;
      return NOERROR ;
    }

    return DISP_E_UNKNOWNNAME ;
}
```

5. As usual, there is one interface method that requires a significant amount of programming, and in this case it's the **Invoke( )** method. This method is passed the ID of the property or method being accessed, and the data that has been marshaled from the caller in an array of self-describing VARIANT structures. The method figures out what to do, and does it.

Unlike the normal implementation of a VTBL-based interface, you cannot assume that the compiler has checked for the correct number and type of parameters. The main drawback of OLE automation's late-bound architecture is that such checking must be done at run time. If an error is found, we return the appropriate error code and hope the controller has some mechanism to present the error to the user/programmer so it can be corrected. Thus:

```
STDMETHODIMP CHelloDispatch::Invoke(DISPID dispidMember, REFIID riid,
    LCID lcid, WORD wFlags, DISPPARAMS *pDispParams,
    VARIANT *pVarResult, EXCEPINFO *pexcepinfo, UINT *puArgErr)
{
/*
Caller wants to get or set the HelloMessage property.
*/
    if (dispidMember == 1)
    {
/*
Caller wants to get the HelloMessage property.
*/
      if (wFlags & DISPATCH_PROPERTYGET)
      {
/*
Check that the caller hasn't passed us any parameters.  That would be an
error.
*/
            if (pDispParams->cArgs != 0)
            {
                  return DISP_E_BADPARAMCOUNT ;
            }
/*
Allocate a string containing it, and place it in the VARIANT used for
the return value.
*/
            pVarResult->vt = VT_BSTR ;
            pVarResult->bstrVal = SysAllocString(m_bstrHelloMsg);
      }

      <continued on facing page>
```

```
/*
Caller wants to set the HelloMessage property.
*/
      else if (wFlags & DISPATCH_PROPERTYPUT)
      {
/*
Check parameter count and type.  If either is incorrect, return
appropriate error code.
*/
            if (pDispParams->cArgs != 1)
            {
                  return DISP_E_BADPARAMCOUNT ;
            }
            if (pDispParams->rgvarg[0].vt != VT_BSTR)
            {
                  return DISP_E_BADVARTYPE ;
            }
/*
Copy the new value from the array of VARIANTS holding the calling
parameters.
*/
            SysReAllocString(&m_bstrHelloMsg,
                  pDispParams-> rgvarg->bstrVal);
      }
      return NOERROR ;
    }
/*
Caller wants to call the SayHello( ) method.
*/

    else if (dispidMember == 2)
    {
/*
Check that there are no parameters.  If not, return an error code.
*/
      if (pDispParams->cArgs != 0)
      {
            return DISP_E_BADPARAMCOUNT ;
      }

/*
Put the current HelloMessage property into the edit control and beep to
signal the user.
*/
      MessageBeep (0) ;
      SetDlgItemText(hMainWnd, IDC_HELLOAREA, m_bstrHelloMsg);
      return NOERROR ;
    }

    return DISP_E_MEMBERNOTFOUND ;
}
```

D. OLE AUTOMATION IN THE MFC

1. The preceding implementation in the API may seem exceedingly bloody, and you may be wondering, "Isn't this stuff very similar from one app to another? Couldn't the plumbing somehow be pre-fabricated, requiring me to implement only the faucets on either end? Specifically, instead of hardwiring data such as member names and IDs directly into the code, couldn't data be abstracted into an array of self-contained structures and removed from the code? The code could then be written once and for all, and the differences from one app to another specified only in simple localized changes to data structures ? And wouldn't it be cool if there were some intelligent tools to manage these data structures? And wouldn't it be extra cool if it took care of all the nonsense about wide versus ANSI strings?" Yes it would be, and it has mostly been done for you in the MFC.

Suppose we want to make an MFC version of the simple automation server used in the preceding pages, exposing a string called "HelloMessage" and a method called "SayHello". The source code for this example is in the directory \chap03\helloau\mfchelloausv. To provide MFC support for OLE automation, choose the "Ole automation" check box while generating the project in App Wizard. The "OLE compound document support" on the tab refers to embedding and linking and has no bearing on automation; you can leave it unchecked. Thus:

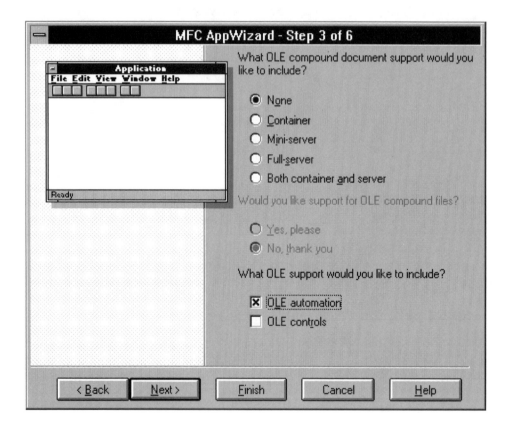

2. You may also provide an automation server in a DLL by checking the appropriate box when building an App Wizard DLL. Thus:

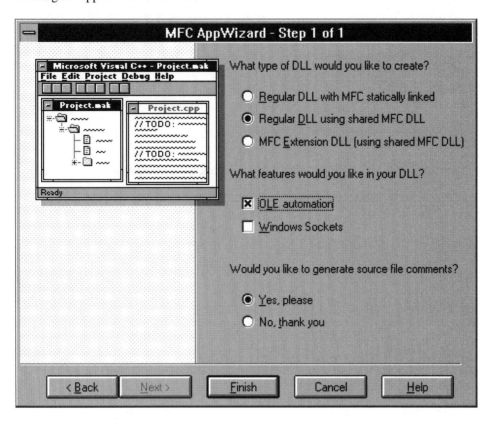

3. When you do this, the following changes are added to your app. The file **<afxdisp.h>** is added to your standard includes in the file stdafx.h, thus:

```
// stdafx.h : include file for standard system include files,
//   or project specific include files that are used frequently, but
//       are changed infrequently
//

#define VC_EXTRALEAN            // Exclude rarely used stuff from headers

#include <afxwin.h>             // MFC core and standard components
#include <afxext.h>             // MFC extensions
#include <afxdisp.h>            // MFC OLE automation classes
#ifndef _AFX_NO_AFXCMN_SUPPORT
#include <afxcmn.h>             // MFC support for Windows 95 Common Ctrls
#endif // _AFX_NO_AFXCMN_SUPPORT
```

4. Your CWinApp::InitInstance( ) method initializes the OLE libraries via the function **AfxOleInit( )**. App Wizard generates a CLSID for your automation object, which also appears in your CWinApp file. Thus:

```
<file mfchelloausv.cpp>


CMfchelloausvApp theApp;


// This identifier was generated to be statistically unique for yr app.
// You may change it if you prefer to choose a specific identifier.

// {79B3AC80-92C6-11CF-8A22-00AA00A58097}
static const CLSID clsid =
{ 0x79b3ac80, 0x92c6, 0x11cf, { 0x8a, 0x22, 0x0, 0xaa, 0x0, 0xa5, 0x80,
0x97 } };


/////////////////////////////////////////////////////////////////////
/////
// CMfchelloausvApp initialization

BOOL CMfchelloausvApp::InitInstance()
{
    // Initialize OLE libraries
    if (!AfxOleInit())
    {
      AfxMessageBox(IDP_OLE_INIT_FAILED);
      return FALSE;
    }
    <rest of InitInstance( )>
}
```

NOTE: App Wizard also generates the code that your automation server needs to provide a class factory. Since this is a general-purpose feature used for any MFC server, it is dealt with in Chapter 9, "Custom Interfaces."

5. The MFC support for OLE servers is implemented in the class CCmdTarget, from which your CDocument class is derived. App Wizard makes modifications to your CDocument class for supporting automation. The function **CCmdTarget::EnableAutomation( )**, called from the document's constructor, constructs internally an object of class *COleDispatchImpl*, which contains the actual code of MFC's IDispatch implementation. The functions **AfxOleLockApp( )** and **AfxOleUnlockApp( )** respectively increment and decrement an app's reference count, thereby keeping the app running as long as a document exists that is being used by OLE. Thus:

```
/*
Document constructor.
*/

CMfchelloausvDoc::CMfchelloausvDoc()
{

/*
My document's own initialization.
*/

    m_helloMessage = "Hello, World" ;

/*
OLE initialization added by App Wizard.
*/

    EnableAutomation();

    AfxOleLockApp();
}

/*
Document destructor.
*/

CMfchelloausvDoc::~CMfchelloausvDoc()
{
    AfxOleUnlockApp();
}
```

6. The MFC supports OLE automation by means of a *dispatch map*, an array of structures conceptually and operationally similar to the message map used for routing messages. The dispatch map contains an array of data structures, each of which contains all the elements needed to describe a single method or property. The dispatch ID for an entry is implied from the entry's position in the array. The entries between the //{AFX_DISPATCH_MAP comment blocks are maintained by Class Wizard. You may manually add entries outside this block if you wish. The following example is shown indented and commented for clarity; Class Wizard will place each entry on a single line. Thus:

```
BEGIN_MESSAGE_MAP(CMfchelloausvDoc, CDocument)
    //{{AFX_MSG_MAP(CMfchelloausvDoc)
      // NOTE - the ClassWizard will add and remove mapping macros here.
      //    DO NOT EDIT what you see in these blocks of generated code!
    //}}AFX_MSG_MAP
END_MESSAGE_MAP()


BEGIN_DISPATCH_MAP(CMfchelloausvDoc, CDocument)
    //{{AFX_DISPATCH_MAP(CMfchelloausvDoc)
    DISP_PROPERTY_NOTIFY(        // macro specifying automation property
      CMfchelloausvDoc,          // class containing property
      "HelloMessage",            // name of property
      m_helloMessage,            // member variable
      OnHelloMessageChanged,     // notification function called on change
      VT_BSTR)                   // type of property

    DISP_FUNCTION(               // macro specifying automation method
      CMfchelloausvDoc,          // class containing method
      "SayHello",                // name of method
      SayHello,                  // function to be called
      VT_EMPTY,                  // return type of function
      VTS_NONE)                  // parameter list of fn, here empty
    //}}AFX_DISPATCH_MAP
END_DISPATCH_MAP()
```

7. When the controller calls IDispatch::Invoke( ), the server code lives in the Invoke( ) method of the COleDispatchImpl object that the CDocument inherited from CCmdTarget. This code first checks for generic errors (1), such as the controller requesting a dispatch ID that doesn't exist or failing to set reserved fields to their required values. Next, it fetches the dispatch map entry describing the requested method or property (2). The code then checks for errors relating to the specific method or property being invoked, such as the wrong number or type of parameters. It will attempt to perform type conversion if necessary. Some conversions will succeed, such as ints to floats; some will fail, such as strings to IDispatch pointers (3). The code then sets or gets the specified property or calls the specified method (4). Finally, the results are reported to the controller. Thus:

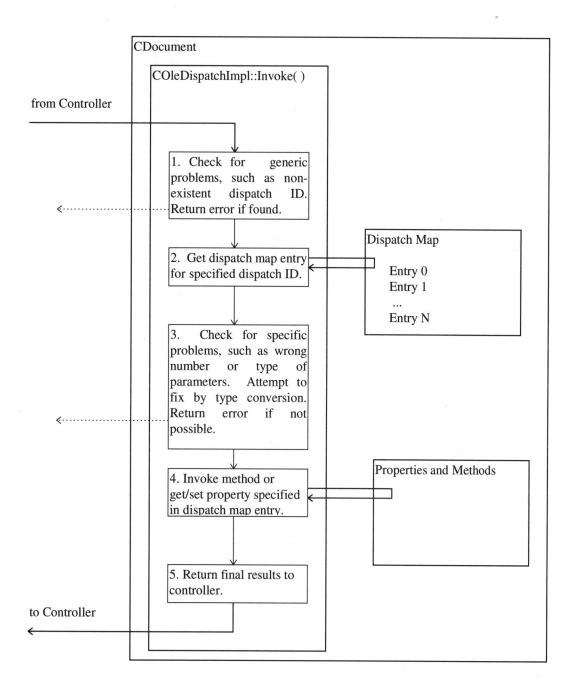

8. You add entries to your document's dispatch map with Class Wizard. The "Ole Automation" tab contains the necessary buttons. The process and its results are very similar to adding a message handler. Class Wizard makes entries in the dispatch map as shown on the preceding pages. It also makes entries in the document's header file. Thus:

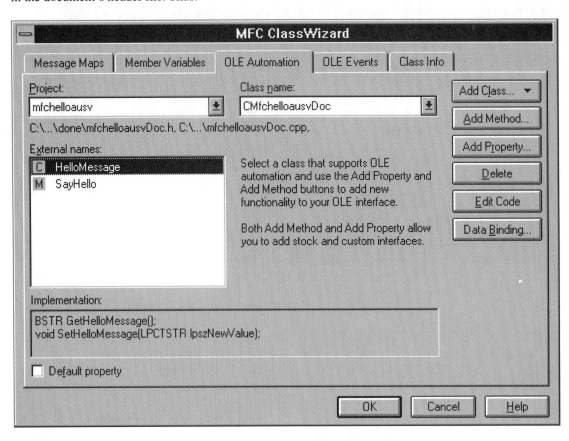

< header file showing entries made by Class Wizard >

```
class CMfchelloausvDoc : public CDocument
{
    < rest of header file omitted>

public:
    CString m_HelloMessage ;

protected:
    // Generated OLE dispatch map functions
    //{{AFX_DISPATCH(CMfchelloausvDoc)
    afx_msg BSTR GetHelloMessage();
    afx_msg void SetHelloMessage(LPCTSTR lpszNewValue);
    afx_msg void SayHello();
    //}}AFX_DISPATCH

    DECLARE_DISPATCH_MAP()
    DECLARE_INTERFACE_MAP()
};
```

9. When you add a method, you must specify its name, return type, and parameters if any. Class Wizard adds the method's declaration to your document's header file as shown on the previous page and generates a function skeleton for you as shown below, exactly as was done for a message handler. Thus:

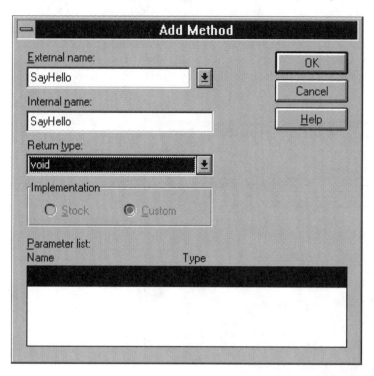

```
/*
Function shell added by Class Wizard.
*/


void CMfchelloausvDoc::SayHello()
{

/*
My own code added.
*/

    UpdateAllViews (NULL) ;
}
```

10. When you add a property, you specify its name and type. You have the choice of two ways to handle the controller's access to the property. You can use the traditional Get and Set( ) method pair as shown below, which is useful if you want to validate the new property value before allowing it to be used. Or you can have Class Wizard add a member variable and automatically handle requests to set and get its value. Class Wizard will generate a notification function which will be called when a controller changes the property's value. In either case, Class Wizard makes the necessary additions to the dispatch map and the header files, and generates skeletons of the required functions. Note in the sample code how the MFC handles all of the conversion between wide and narrow character strings. Thus:

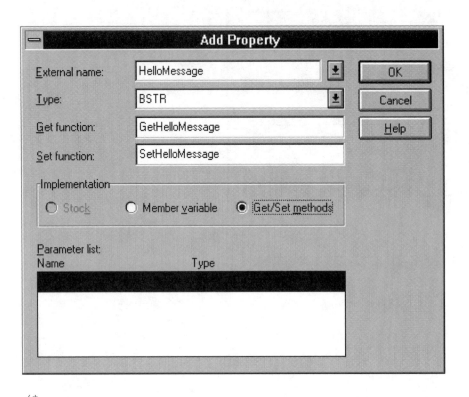

```
/*
Function skeletons generated by Class Wizard.
*/

BSTR CMfchelloausvDoc::GetHelloMessage()
{
    CString strResult;
/*
Next line only added by me:
*/
    strResult = m_HelloMessage ;
    return strResult.AllocSysString();
}


void CMfchelloausvDoc::SetHelloMessage(LPCTSTR lpszNewValue)
{
/*
Next line only added by me.
*/
    m_HelloMessage = lpszNewValue ;
}
```

11. You may generate as many automation-supporting classes as you wish by using Class Wizard to derive a class from CCmdTarget. Since an MFC DLL does not provide a document class, this is the only way to specify the automation object in an in-proc server.

When you generate your new class, you must choose one of the radio buttons to specify how the class is to be exposed to the world. If you pick "Createable by type ID" as shown below, Class Wizard will generate the code to add a class factory for your new class, thereby making it accessible to controllers via CoCreateInstance( ). However, if you simply pick "Automation," Class Wizard will not generate the class factory code and your new class will not be accessible via CoCreateInstance( ). This is customarily done to implement an object hierarchy. Only the top-level object, such as the application, is createable. Objects lower in the hierarchy are provided by calling the methods of higher objects, such as providing a file object by calling a method on the application object. Thus:

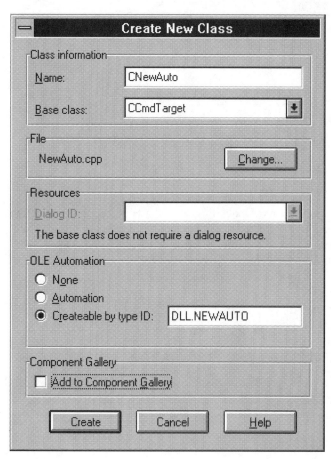

12. Our SDK server apps to this point have required separate .REG files to make the entries in the system registry that clients need to locate them. An MFC server contains code to make it register itself via the method **COleObjectFactory::UpdateRegistryAll( )**. In an app, this is provided in the CWinApp::InitInstance( ) method. The function is called every time the app is run as a standalone program, but not when it is run as an automation server. Thus:

```
BOOL CMfchelloausvApp::InitInstance()
{
    // Initialize OLE libraries
    if (!AfxOleInit())
    {
      AfxMessageBox(IDP_OLE_INIT_FAILED);
      return FALSE;
    }

    COleObjectFactory::UpdateRegistryAll();

    // Dispatch commands specified on the command line
    if (!ProcessShellCommand(cmdInfo))
      return FALSE;

    return TRUE;
}
```

In an in-proc server, the call to COleObjectFactory::UpdateRegistryAll() is placed in the function DllRegisterServer( ), which the server DLL exports by name. A development tool or setup program will load the library, call GetProcAddress( ) to obtain a pointer to DllRegisterServer( ), and call it. Thus:

```
STDAPI DllRegisterServer(void)
{
    AFX_MANAGE_STATE(AfxGetStaticModuleState());
    COleObjectFactory::UpdateRegistryAll();
    return S_OK;
}
```

E. Exception Info

1. The **EXCEPINFO** structure passed as part of the method IDispatch::Invoke( ) is a holder for extensive error information that a friendly OLE automation server can return to a controller for the purpose of informing the user exactly what is wrong with a failed Invoke( ) call. The server can specify an error code and a human-readable string. Most powerfully, the server can specify the help file in which further information can be found and even the context ID of the specific topic within the help file. It's like saying to the caller, "RTFM, and here's the page, you #$%@ idiot !" The structure looks like this:

```
typedef struct FARSTRUCT tagEXCEPINFO
{
    unsigned short wCode;        // app-specific error code
    unsigned short wReserved;    // reserved, must be 0
    BSTR bstrSource;             // server app in which error occurred
    BSTR bstrDescription;        // text description of error
    BSTR bstrHelpFile;           // server's help file path
    unsigned long dwHelpContext; // server's help context ID for error
    void FAR* pvReserved;        // reserved, must be NULL
    HRESULT (STDAPICALLTYPE FAR* pfnDeferredFillIn)(EXCEPINFO *);
                                 // ptr to function for delayed fill-in
    SCODE scode;                 // SCODE describing error
} EXCEPINFO
```

2. An EXCEPINFO structure is passed to the server by the controller as one of the parameters in the IDispatch::Invoke( ) method. If the server at any time finds an error in the invocation of the desired action, it fills in the fields of the EXCEPINFO structures and returns the code DISP_E_EXCEPTION. In the example on the next page, when the controller tries to set the HelloMessage property, the server uses the API function **VariantChangeType( )** to attempt to convert whatever data the caller actually passed us into a BSTR. If an error is found, the method fills in the EXCEPINFO structure with data describing the error. It is up to the controller to present that data to the user in a meaningful manner. Thus:

```
STDMETHODIMP CHelloDispatch::Invoke(DISPID dispidMember, REFIID riid,
    LCID lcid, WORD wFlags, DISPPARAMS *pDispParams,
    VARIANT *pVarResult, EXCEPINFO *pExcepInfo, UINT *puArgErr)
{

/*
Caller wants to set the HelloMessage property.
*/
    if (dispidMember == 1)
    {
      else if (wFlags & DISPATCH_PROPERTYPUT)
        {

/*
Perform type checking on the passed VARIANT.  If it can't be converted
into  a BSTR, then fill out the EXCEPINFO structure and return the
failure code that says the EXCEPINFO contains valid information.
*/

            VARIANT vResult ; HRESULT hr ;

            hr = VariantChangeType (&vResult,      // output variant
                pDispParams->rgvarg,               // input variant
                0,                                 // flags
                VT_BSTR) ;                         // desired output type

            if (hr != S_OK)
            {
                pExcepInfo->wCode = 0 ;
                pExcepInfo->wReserved = 0 ;
                pExcepInfo->pvReserved = NULL ;
                pExcepInfo->pfnDeferredFillIn = NULL ;

                pExcepInfo->bstrSource = SysAllocString(
                    "Hello32.exe");
                pExcepInfo->bstrDescription = SysAllocString(
                    "Expecting string parameter") ;
                pExcepInfo->scode = DISP_E_TYPEMISMATCH ;
                pExcepInfo->bstrHelpFile = SysAllocString (
                    "c:\\hello32.hlp") ;
                pExcepInfo->dwHelpContext = 1 ;

                return DISP_E_EXCEPTION ;
            }

/*
Successful set of the property.
*/
            SysReAllocString(&m_bstrHelloMsg, vResult.bstrVal);
        }
    return NOERROR ;
    }
```

3. The controller needs to check the return value for the Invoke( ) method. If it returns the code that says there is information in the EXCEPINFO, it is up to the controller to package the information and present it to the user. One such way is in a dialog box. Thus:

```
if (!SUCCEEDED(hr))
{

/*
No EXCEPINFO provided by server.
*/
    if (hr != DISP_E_EXCEPTION)
    {
      MessageBox (hMainDlg, TEXT("Unsuccessful, and no EXCEPINFO."),
          TEXT("Error"), MB_ICONSTOP) ;
    }
/*
Server provided EXCEPINFO extended error information. Assemble the app's
name and error into a string, and pop it up in a dialog box.
*/

    else
    {
      TCHAR out [256] ;
      wsprintf (out,
          TEXT("The app %s reported the following error:%c%c%s"),
          ei.bstrSource, 0x0d, 0x0a, ei.bstrDescription) ;
      int ret = DialogBoxParam (hInstance, MAKEINTRESOURCE(IDD_DIALOG2),
          hMainDlg, (DLGPROC) ErrorDlgProc, (long) out) ;

/*
If user clicked the HELP button, invoke WinHelp on the help file and
help context supplied in the EXCEPINFO.
*/
      if (ret == IDC_HELP)
      {
          WinHelp (hMainDlg, ei.bstrHelpFile, HELP_CONTEXT,
              ei.dwHelpContext) ;
      }

/*
Controller is responsible for freeing the BSTR elements.
*/
      if (ei.bstrHelpFile) SysFreeString(ei.bstrHelpFile) ;
      if (ei.bstrSource) SysFreeString(ei.bstrSource) ;
      if (ei.bstrDescription) SysFreeString (ei.bstrDescription) ;
    }

}
```

4. In the MFC, you can throw an EXCEPINFO in any function called from an automation handler via the function **AfxThrowOleDispatchException( )**. This fills out an EXCEPINFO structure with the app-specific error code, a human-readable string, and the help context ID. The name of the help file is retrieved from the CWinApp base class. Thus:

```
void CMfchelloausvDoc::SetHelloMessage(LPCTSTR lpszNewValue)
{

/*
Check the new value of the property passed by the controller before
allowing it to be used. This controller will not accept any string that
contains the word "bad".  If it does, fire back an EXCEPINFO and don't
set the value.
*/
    if (strstr (lpszNewValue, "bad"))
    {
      AfxThrowOleDispatchException (
            1,                          // app error code
            "I can't take bad news",// human-readable string
            99) ;                       // help context

      return ;
    }

/*
String was acceptable.  Set the value of our property.
*/
    m_HelloMessage = lpszNewValue ;
}
```

When called from a Visual Basic controller, the EXCEPINFO is presented to the user as shown below. The MFC sample app does not contain a help file; this is left as an exercise for the student. Thus:

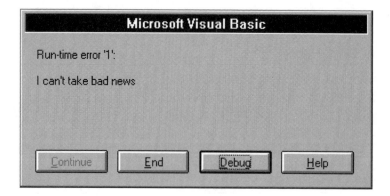

94

F. Accessing Automation Objects from Visual Basic

1. The reason OLE automation got started, and one of the main reasons it caught on, is that it allows programmers to write relatively simple programs in Visual Basic which connect together sophisticated components purchased from other vendors. <u>Real</u> programmers of the type who purchase this book tend to look down their noses at anything having the word "basic" in it, but let's face it:

A) There's lots of money to be made in quickly gluing together components purchased from other vendors, and

B) We like making lots of money.

2. Consider the following very simple VB project. It contains a single form with two edit controls ("text boxes" in VB parlance) and three pushbuttons. It took all of 30 seconds to put together from the VB control palette. You can find the VB source code in the directory \chap03\helloau\vbhelloclient.

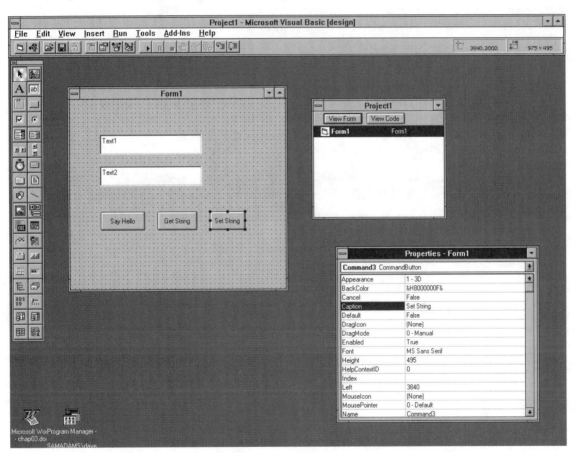

3. To create an object, you must first use the `Dim` keyword in the form's general declarations section to declare a variable as an object. Thus:

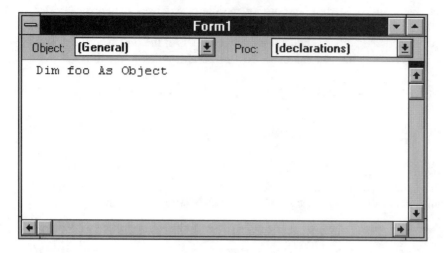

4. Once you have declared the object, you create it via the VB function **CreateObject( )**. This takes the human-readable name of the object and hey, presto, wakes up the server and creates the object. Since you have studied the guts of OLE to this point, you know that internally, this function is reading the registry to find the class ID value under the human-readable name, then calling CoCreateInstance( ) to make OLE find the server identified with the class ID, deal with the class factories, and return a pointer to the object's IDispatch interface. Thus:

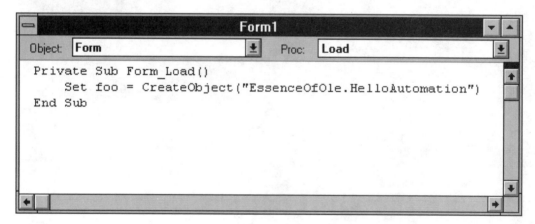

5. To call the object's SayHello( ) method in response to a button click, you simply access the method using the dot notation, as if it were a member of the local object. VB will use the IDispatch interface to query for the dispatch ID, then invoke it. All the heavy lifting is done for you by VB.

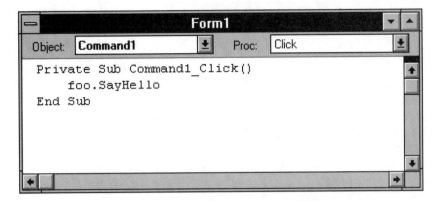

6. To get the object's HelloMessage property, you simply access it using the dot notation as if it was a local property. VB does all of the negotiation with the IDispatch interface. Thus:

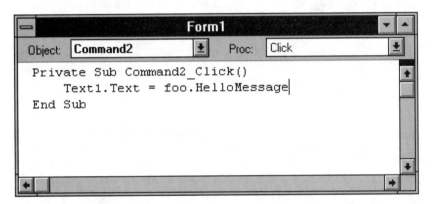

7. To set the object's HelloMessage property, you simply assign into it on the left-hand side of the equals sign. Again, VB does all the negotiation with the IDispatch interface. Thus:

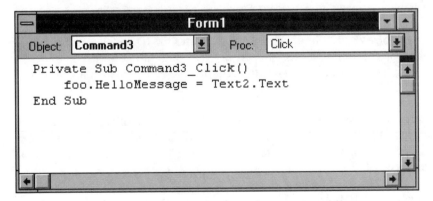

Lab Exercises
Chapter 3
OLE Automation Controller

Directory: \EssenceofOLE\chap03\helloau\hlodrv32\templ

In this lab, we'll create the automation controller discussed in the first part of this chapter. All of the interesting code will take place in the file HELLODRV.CPP.

1. To develop and test the controller, it is necessary to have a server to interact with. Go to the root directory of this example and run the registry file HELLO32.REG. This will make the necessary entries in the system registry to connect the server HELLO32.EXE in the \helloau\hello32\done directory as the automation server for the object whose human-readable name is "EssenceofOLE.HelloAutomation". If the root directory you are using for your samples is anything other than C:\, you will need to edit the .REG file to make the LocalServer32 entry point to the exact path location of the server file.

2. The method CHelloDriver::Create( ) is the place where the connection is first made between the automation controller and the object provided by the server. The first thing the controller needs to do is create the automation object by calling the API function CoCreateInstance( ). The class ID of the object has already been read from the registry for you and may be found in the variable "clsid". The interface that you need returned is IID_IDispatch. Store the returned object pointer in the member variable "m_pDisp". You should build and run your app at this point. The server should appear, but none of the automation methods should work because you have not yet gotten the dispatch IDs needed to identify them. If the server does not come up, you probably have the registry path wrong.

3. Having gotten the IDispatch interface, we need to get the IDs within it that correspond to the named dispatch elements via the method IDispatch::GetIDsOfNames( ). You will have to do this twice, once for the property "HelloMessage" and once for the method "SayHello". Store the IDs in the member variables "m_dHelloPropID" and "m_dSayHelloId" respectively. Remember that the strings you pass to GetIDsOfNames( ) must always be a wide character string, even if your app is not a wide character app.

4. The first actual invocation of the automation object's method takes place in the method CHelloDriver::SayHowdy( ). Use the method IDispatch::Invoke( ) to call the automation object's SayHello( ) method. Pass an empty parameter array to the function and expect no return value.

5. Next implement the CHelloDriver::GetString( ) method. This uses the IDispatch interface to get the value of the automation object's HelloMessage property. You must allocate and initialize a VARIANT structure to receive the return value. The code to put it into the dialog box's edit control has already been written for you.

6. Finally, implement the CHelloDriver::SetString( ) method. You must now allocate a VARIANT to hold the input parameters, and a DISPPARAMS structure to hold the variant and other flags. Initialize them and set their values as shown in the text. Use the IDispatch::Invoke( ) method to set the value of the automation object's HelloMessage property.

EXTRA CREDIT: Examine the CHelloDriver::BadSetString( ) method until you feel comfortable with the processing of the EXCEPINFO structure. The first time you select the "Help" button in the dialog box, WinHelp will probably not be able to find the specified file. You will have to locate it yourself, in the directory \helloau\hello32\help. The operating system will then remember where it lives, so subsequent calls to WinHelp will find it.

Directory: \EssenceofOLE\chap03\helloau\hello32\templ

1. Now that your controller is working, you have something to test the server with. Before starting to work on the server, you must change the entries in the registry so that the controller will use the new server that you are developing rather than the finished one supplied in the \done directory. You can do this either by editing the .REG file to point to the new server's path (in the directory \templ\windebug) and reregistering the whole thing, or by using the registry editor and changing only the path itself.

2. The server app is a small one. All the interesting code takes place in the file HELLO.CPP. As you are already conversant with the concepts, the class factory registration has been done for you, as have the two trivial methods of the IDispatch interface. First, you must implement the method IDispatch::GetIDsOfNames( ). Compare the name supplied by the caller with the names "HelloMessage" and "SayHello". The ID for the former is 1, and that of the latter is 2. Note that the caller always supplies these names in a wide character string, even though it might not be a wide character app and you might not be either.

3. Now you must implement the IDispatch::Invoke( ) method. Since it's complex, we'll do it a piece at a time. First, let's handle the property get case. Check the wFlags element for DISPATCH_PROPERTYGET. If found, the caller is trying to get the HelloMessage property. Set the vt element of the pVarResult parameter to the proper value to indicate a string. Use the function SysAllocString( ) to allocate a new BSTR containing the string in the member variable m_bstrHelloMsg. Place this BSTR in the return variant and return the success code. Test with your controller; you should now be able to get the value of this property.

4. Next, let's implement the set operation. Check the wFlags element for DISPATCH_PROPERTYPUT. If found, the caller is trying to set the HelloMessage property. Check the vt element of the supplied variant to make sure it contains a BSTR. If so, use the function SysReAllocString( ) to reset the value of the member variable m_bstrHelloMsg to the new value supplied in the VARIANT. Return success or failure code. The SayHello( ) method has been implemented for you so you will be able to see the results.

5. Finally, let's implement the EXCEPINFO structure. Use the function VariantChangeType( ) to attempt to coerce the passed parameter into a BSTR. If this function doesn't succeed, then fill out the fields of the EXCEPINFO structure passed in the parameter list. Your app comes with a help file called "hello32.hlp". The context for the topic inside it that explains this error is 1. Return the error code DISP_E_EXCEPTION to indicate to the controller that extended error information can be found in the EXCEPINFO structure.

Lab Exercises
Chapter 3
OLE Automation Server

Directory: \EssenceofOLE\chap03\helloau\mfchelloausv

The MFC is a powerful development environment that lets us construct OLE automation servers in a fraction of the time it would take to hardwire one in the API. No \templ directory is provided for this exercise, as the MFC will generate all the code you need. The \done directory contains a finished example.

1. Start VC++ and generate a new project using App Wizard. On the appropriate App Wizard pane (number 3 at the time of this writing), check the "OLE automation" box. You can choose the "Finish" button after this selection. Build your app and run it; it will register itself.

2. Now we need a controller for the MFC server app. We can use the controller built in the first part of this lab. If you haven't done that part, use the controller from the \done directory. The controller is hardwired to use the server whose class ID is in the registry under the key HKEY_CLASSES_ROOT\ EssenceofOLE.HelloAutomation\CLSID. Open your MFC app's .CPP file that contains the CWinApp-derived class. You will find a variable named "clsid". Just above that variable, in a comment line, you will find the same class ID as a string inside curly braces. Take this string, curlies and all, and place it in the CLSID key listed above, replacing the previous contents. This will cause your controller to launch the MFC server when it starts up. Run your controller and test it. The controller's call to CoCreateInstance( ) will succeed, but its call to GetIDsOfNames( ) will fail because the server currently contains no methods or properties with the names the controller is querying for. The server should not become visible, as this is the user interface convention for servers.

3. In your MFC server's project, go to Class Wizard and select the "Ole Automation" tab. Select your document class in the list box if it isn't already. Use Class Wizard to add a method called "SayHello" and a CString property called "HelloMessage" to your app. Build it and test it with the controller, which should at this point find everything it needs.

4. In the previous step, Class Wizard generated function skeletons for you. Add whatever code you want to implement these features, perhaps by drawing the string on your server's main window. If you want the server window to be visible, go to the CWinApp::InitInstance( ) method and just after the call to COleTemplateServer::RegisterAll( ), comment out the line that says "return TRUE;".

Chapter 4

Type Libraries

A. CONCEPTS AND DEFINITIONS

1. An OLE automation server can greatly enhance its usability by providing self-description information for the use of intelligent tools that program it, such as VB or VC++. You will never be able to sell an OLE object server that doesn't provide one. Such a description usually contains:

- The types of objects the server supports

- Each object's methods with their parameters and types

- Each object's properties with their types

- References to specific items of on-line documentation

2. An automation object provides a description of itself by means of a *type library*, a collection of static data structures provided by the object vendor and accessed via the *ITypeLib* interface. A type library is a container for one or more *type infos*. A type info is a static data structure provided by the object vendor that contains information about a single automation object in a binary machine-readable format, accessed via the *ITypeLib* interface. Thus:

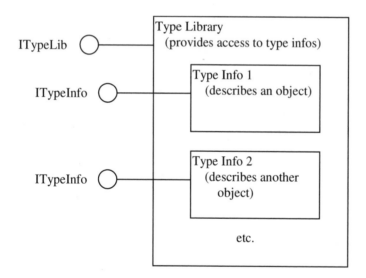

WARNING: A type library and its contents are nothing but a fancy software manual. They are not generated by runtime examination of an object's binary code; they contain whatever descriptive information the author decided to put in them and are only as good as their contents. What's the first law of computer science? Garbage in, garbage out. If the library contains misinformation, you are, as we say here in Boston, "scrod."

3. An example of the utility of type libraries is shown below. In Visual Basic, the Object Browser dialog box will read the type libraries provided by the objects it uses and display their contents. In the example below, the Object Browser displays the properties and methods described by the type library of the simple Hello32 automation server created in the previous chapter. The HelloMessage property is selected, causing its type ("String") to be shown in the lower left corner of the box. The button containing the question mark provides access to the on-line help file provided by the object vendor. The name of the file and the context ID for the topic explaining the selected property are provided in the type library. Thus:

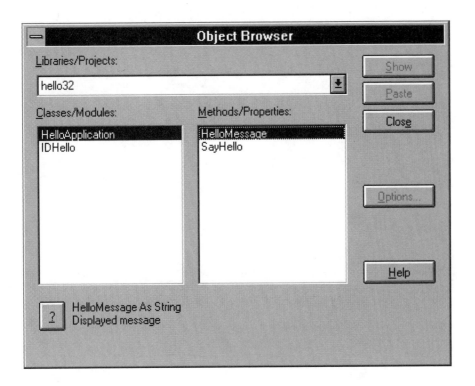

This page intentionally contains no text other than this sentence.

B. BUILDING TYPE LIBRARIES

1. A type library is created by writing a file in *Object Descriptor Language* containing statements which describe your objects. The file will have the extension .ODL and is added to the VC++ project. When the project is built, the .ODL file is compiled into a type library file with extension .TLB. Thus:

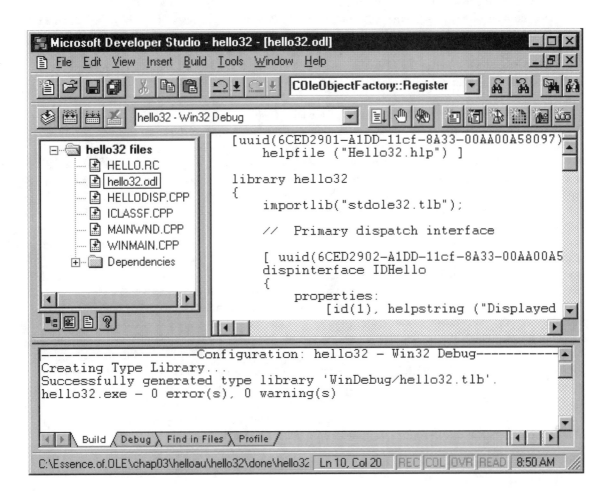

2. The example shown on the facing page is "hello32.odl", the .ODL file that compiles into the type library describing the simple Hello32 automation server created in the previous chapter. Each of the sections of the .ODL file contains a set of *attributes* enclosed in square brackets, followed by the *definitions* of the objects to which the attributes apply. Attributes used in the sample file include **uuid**, the globally unique ID of the object being defined.

The file starts off with the attributes block of the library itself, which contains the library's uuid and its version number. Next appears the definition of the library, which consists of the keyword **library** followed by the name of this library ("hello32") and a set of curly braces. Everything appearing between the opening and closing curly braces will be compiled into the library.

The first statement inside the library is **importlib**. This is the .ODL equivalent of #include, used to incorporate other type libraries by reference. The file "stdole32.tlb" is the .ODL equivalent of "windows.h".

Next appear a number of .ODL code blocks, each of which describes a type info that we want the library to contain. The first one we encounter is that of the dispinterface IDHello. Remembering from the previous chapter, a dispinterface is the set of properties and methods accessed through a specific IDispatch interface. First we see the attributes of dispinterface, which at present contain only its uuid. Next comes the keyword **dispinterface**, followed by its name and a set of curly braces. Everything appearing within the curly braces will be exposed as an element of the IDHello type info.

A dispinterface contains properties and methods, which are respectively denoted in .ODL via the keywords **properties** and **methods**. Each property and method has its own attributes section, in this case containing only its dispatch ID, denoted via the keyword **id**. Then follows the name of the property or method, its type, and its parameters if any. The dispinterface IDHello contains a single property, of type BSTR, called "HelloMessage", whose dispatch ID is 1. It also exposes a single method called "SayHello( )", whose parameter list and return type are both void and whose dispatch ID is 2.

The final type info that we see in this library is **coclass**, which denotes an object that is creatable via the API function CoCreateInstance( ). Our coclass attributes contain the uuid of the creatable object, which if you check back to the sample code for the previous chapter, you will find matches the class ID passed to CoCreateInstance( ) in the controller program. Inside the coclass is a reference to the dispinterface IDHello, which is telling the programmer that he ought to be able to create an object of the coclass and successfully query it for the dispinterface IDHello. The attribute **default** signifies that IDHello is what the caller will get if he queries for the default IDispatch interface.

A more in-depth description of the .ODL language can be found in Brockschmidt, pp. 150-154 and 160-168. The complete reference for it is in the Win32 SDK documentation.

```
// attributes of the type library itself, here uuid and version.

[uuid(6CED2901-A1DD-11cf-8A33-00AA00A58097), version(1.0)]

// Definition of library.

library hello32
{

// Standard types incorporated by reference.

    importlib("stdole32.tlb");

//  A dispinterface is a custom set of methods and properties accessed
// via the IDispatch interface mechanism.

    [ uuid(6CED2902-A1DD-11cf-8A33-00AA00A58097)]
    dispinterface IDHello
    {

// properties and methods contained in the dispinterface with their
// dispatch ids and types.

        properties:
                [id(1)] BSTR HelloMessage;

        methods:
                [id(2)] void SayHello();
    };


// A coclass is an object that can be created by calling
// CoCreateInstance( ).

    [ uuid(6CED2900-A1DD-11cf-8A33-00AA00A58097)]
    coclass HelloApplication
    {

// If you create an object of this coclass, you ought to be able to
// successfully query it for IDHello. And if you query it simply for
// IDispatch, IDHello is what you will get.

        [default] dispinterface IDHello ;

    };
};
```

3. The type libraries we have seen so far have listed only the types and names of an object's properties, methods, and parameters. This isn't anywhere near enough to be able to program it intelligently. A type info may provide a *help string*, a small string provided within the type info itself. In the VB Object Browser example on page 104, the string "Displayed Message" is a help string. To place a help string in a type info, add the ODL attribute **helpstring( )** within the square brackets enclosing a type description as shown below. The string that you want to display is placed inside the parentheses in quotes. A development environment that wants to display the string can retrieve it via the ITypeLib and ITypeInfo interfaces as shown in the latter part of this chapter.

4. A help string is generally displayed in a cramped location inside a development environment, so there is a fairly low limit on the amount of explanation it can usefully provide, perhaps a dozen words or so. To provide more detailed explanation of a property or method, you can place references in the type library to specific topics within your object's on-line help file (which you must provide anyway if you expect anyone to buy it). A smart development environment will provide the programmer with a button that launches WinHelp (via the API function WinHelp( )) and jumps directly to the specified topic. You specify the help file that contains the help topics via the ODL attribute **helpfile( )**, containing the name of the help file in parentheses. This attribute must appear only once in the library's attributes section. Any attributes section within the library may contain the ODL attribute **helpcontext( )**, which specifies the context integer of the topic within the specified help file that (you hope) explains the item. The development environment retrieves these elements via the ITypeLib and ITypeInfo interfaces as shown in the latter part of this chapter. Thus:

```
// Help file for library specified here.

[ uuid(6CED2901-A1DD-11cf-8A33-00AA00A58097), version(1.0),
    helpfile ("Hello32.hlp") ]

library hello32
{
    importlib("stdole32.tlb");

// Help string explaining this type info specified here.

    [ uuid(6CED2902-A1DD-11cf-8A33-00AA00A58097),
      helpstring ("IDispatch for Hello32 Object") ]

    dispinterface IDHello
    {

// Help string explaining this property and help context of further
// explanation specified here.

    properties:
            [id(1), helpstring ("Displayed message"), helpcontext(1)]
                BSTR HelloMessage;

<rest of .ODL file>
```

C. Providing and Registering Type Libraries

1. An object may provide its type libraries in several ways. You can ship a separate .TLB file along with your application. This is especially good if your type library is large. Microsoft Excel, for example, comes with a type library file named "xl5en32.olb", which is 223 Kbytes long.

2. If you do not want to provide the type library in an external file, you can bind it into your .EXE or .DLL as a resource, thereby making your app self-contained. This is the method used by OCX controls. To bind the type library as a resource, add a **TYPELIB** directive to your .RC file, specifying the name of the typelib you want included. **The resource id of the type library within your .EXE or .DLL must be 1, as shown here, or the system's type library access functions will have difficulty finding it.** This probably means that you will have to add it to your .RC file by hand.

```
<.RC file>

//////////////////////////////////////////////////////////////////////////////
/////
//
// TYPELIB
//

1              TYPELIB DISCARDABLE      "hello32.tlb"
```

3. However you decide to distribute your type library files, you must make entries in the system registry so that client applications and development tools can find the correct type library for your object. The registry does not contain the type library itself; rather, it contains references to the file in which the type library can be found. First, under the automation object's CLSID key, you must place the subkey "TYPELIB" with a value of the uuid which identifies the type library in which the type info describing the specific automation object can be found. Thus:

```
HKEY_CLASSES_ROOT
   CLSID
     <your app's clsid>
       TYPELIB=<uuid of your object's type library>
```

In the hello32 example, these entries are:

```
HKEY_CLASSES_ROOT
   CLSID
     {6CED2900-A1DD-11cf-8A33-00AA00A58097}
       TYPELIB={6CED2901-A1DD-11cf-8A33-00AA00A58097}
```

4. The TYPELIB section of the registry contains an entry for every type library registered on the system. The entry structure provides the capability of specifying different type libraries for different version numbers, language IDs, and 16- or 32-bit servers. Since the type library frequently contains references to an object's on-line help files, the registry entry structure also contains an entry specifying the directory in which these may be found. Its keys will look like this:

```
HKEY_CLASSES_ROOT
   TYPELIB
     <type library uuid> >
       <version> = <human-readable name of your type library>
         <language id, 0 == any language>
           Win32 = <your type library file name>
         HelpDir = <directory containing help files>
```

In the hello32 example, these entries are:

```
HKEY_CLASSES_ROOT
   TYPELIB
     {6CED2901-A1DD-11cf-8A33-00AA00A58097}
       1.0 = OLE Automation Hello 1.0 Type Library
         0
           Win32 = c:\EssenceofOLE\chap03\helloau\hello32\done\h ello32.tlb
         HelpDir = c:\EssenceofOLE\chap03\helloau\hello32\help
```

Note: Brockschmidt, p. 170 gives a slightly different layout for the registry entries; however, the ones shown above are the ones that you will see if you actually go and look at the registry.

D. TYPE LIBRARIES IN THE MFC

1. When you add methods or properties to an OLE Automation object in the MFC by using Class Wizard, entries are also made in the .ODL file. Thus:

```
// mfchelloausv.odl : type library source for mfchelloausv.exe
// This file will be processed by the Make Type Library (mktyplib) tool
// to produce the type library (mfchelloausv.tlb).

[ uuid(79B3AC81-92C6-11CF-8A22-00AA00A58097), version(1.0) ]
library Mfchelloausv
{
    importlib("stdole32.tlb");

    //  Primary dispatch interface for CMfchelloausvDoc

    [ uuid(79B3AC82-92C6-11CF-8A22-00AA00A58097) ]
    dispinterface IMfchel
    {
      properties:
            // NOTE - ClassWizard will maintain property information
            //     Use extreme caution when editing this section.
            //{{AFX_ODL_PROP(CMfchelloausvDoc)
            [id(1)] BSTR HelloMessage;
            //}}AFX_ODL_PROP

      methods:
            // NOTE - ClassWizard will maintain method information here.
            //     Use extreme caution when editing this section.
            //{{AFX_ODL_METHOD(CMfchelloausvDoc)
            [id(2)] void SayHello();
            //}}AFX_ODL_METHOD

    };

    //  Class information for CMfchelloausvDoc
    [ uuid(79B3AC80-92C6-11CF-8A22-00AA00A58097) ]
    coclass Document
    {
      [default] dispinterface IMfchel;
    };
    //{{AFX_APPEND_ODL}}
};
```

NOTE: The .ODL file generated by the MFC does not contain any of the help-related attributes shown on the preceding page, even if you check the "Context-sensitive Help" box in App Wizard while generating the project. You must add them manually.

WARNING: Class Wizard assigns dispatch IDs in alphabetical order, first to properties and then to methods. When you add a new property or method, it will be inserted into the dispatch map at its alphabetical location and the dispatch IDs of all elements which follow it will change. Class Wizard will properly maintain the .ODL file, but any external code that depends on a hardwired class ID will have to be rewritten or regenerated.

2. In the Hello32 example in the previous chapter, we had to write our own proxy (wrapper) class on the controller side to encapsulate the IDispatch interface and provide easy access to the automation server's object. This was a repetitive pain in the ass, making it a prime candidate for automation by intelligent software tools. Class Wizard provides the capability of generating the wrapper class for you from a type library. Pick the "Add Class" button from any Class Wizard tab, then select "From an OLE TypeLib..." A dialog box will ask you to name the type library file. Thus:

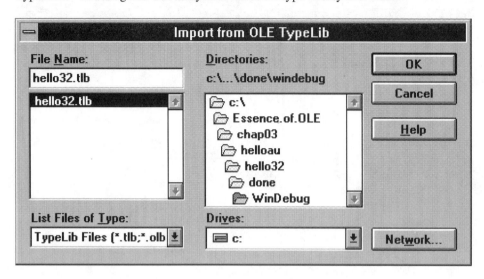

When you select a type library, Class Wizard will read it and provide you with a list of all the type infos it contains. You select the ones for which you want a wrapper class generated. Thus:

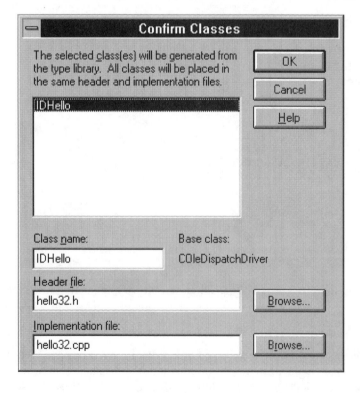

3. Class Wizard will read the specified type info(s) and generate a wrapper class based on their contents. The MFC base class for the wrapper is *COleDispatchDriver*, which contains helper functions used for accessing the IDispatch interface. Class Wizard generates an access function for each method, and a get/set function pair for each property. Thus:

```
// Machine generated IDispatch wrapper class created with ClassWizard
////////////////////////////////////////////////////////////////////////
/////
// IDHello wrapper class

class IDHello : public COleDispatchDriver
{
public:
    IDHello() {}         // Calls COleDispatchDriver default constructor
    IDHello(LPDISPATCH pDispatch) : COleDispatchDriver(pDispatch) {}
    IDHello(const IDHello& dispatchSrc) :
        COleDispatchDriver(dispatchSrc) {}

// Attributes
public:
    CString GetHelloMessage();
    void SetHelloMessage(LPCTSTR);

// Operations
public:
    void SayHello();
};
```

4. The implementation of the wrapper class uses the base class methods **GetProperty( )** and **SetProperty( )** to provide type-safe mediation between the caller and the underlying IDispatch interface. The base class method **InvokeHelper( )** performs the same function for a method. Thus:

```
//////////////////////////////////////////////////////////////////////
/////
// IDHello properties

CString IDHello::GetHelloMessage()
{
    CString result;
    GetProperty(0x1, VT_BSTR, (void*)&result);
    return result;
}

void IDHello::SetHelloMessage(LPCTSTR propVal)
{
    SetProperty(0x1, VT_BSTR, propVal);
}


//////////////////////////////////////////////////////////////////////
/////
// IDHello operations

void IDHello::SayHello()
{
    InvokeHelper(0x2, DISPATCH_METHOD, VT_EMPTY, NULL, NULL);
}
```

WARNING: As you can see in the above example, the dispatch IDs used in the wrapper class generated by Class Wizard are hardwired. If they change on the server, which is quite common during development, your wrapper class will no longer work correctly and will need to be regenerated.

5. To use the wrapper class, you must instantiate one of its objects. In the sample program, this is done by including it as a member variable of our view, thus:

```
#include "hello32.h"      // wrapper class header file generated by CW

class CMfchelloauclView : public CView
{
protected: // create from serialization only
    CMfchelloauclView();
    DECLARE_DYNCREATE(CMfchelloauclView)

    IDHello m_dispHello ;


}
```

6. Once you have the wrapper object, you must create the IDispatch object which it wraps. This is done via the method **COleDispatchDriver::CreateDispatch( )**. This you know by now simply queries the registry for the class ID of the specified name, then calls CoCreateInstance( ), passing the class ID and requesting the IDispatch interface. If you acquire an IDispatch interface pointer by other means, for example, as a property of another object, you can attach it to your wrapper via the method **COleDispatchDriver::Attach( )** (not shown). Thus:

```
int CMfchelloauclView::OnCreate(LPCREATESTRUCT lpCreateStruct)
{
    if (CView::OnCreate(lpCreateStruct) == -1)
      return -1;

    if (!m_dispHello.CreateDispatch ("Hello.Application"))
    {
      return -1 ;
    }

    return 0;
}
```

7. Now that the dispatch is hooked up, all we have to do is call the wrapper class's methods, thus:

```
void CMfchelloauclView::OnLButtonDown(UINT nFlags, CPoint point)
{
    m_dispHello.SayHello ( ) ;
}
```

E. Writing Type Library Browsers

1. Writers of programming tools or other apps that use type libraries need to be able to open the type libraries and read their contents. This section discusses the objects and interfaces provided by the operating system for this purpose. You will find the source code for this sample app in the directory \chap04\typlib32. Because of the frequency of dealing with text strings, this is a Unicode app and will run only under Windows NT.

2. If the user specifies a file name containing the type library, you can load the type library via the function **LoadTypeLib( )**. This returns a pointer to an interface of type *ITypeLib*, which provides access to the newly opened type library. Thus:

```
/*
User clicked "By File Name..." button.
*/


case IDC_BYFILENAME:
{
    OPENFILENAME of ;   TCHAR File [128] ;        HRESULT hr ;
    LPTYPELIB pTypeLib ;
    < fill OPENFILENAME struct with needed values>
/*
Pop up common dialog box, get user's selection of the name.
*/
    if (GetOpenFileName (&of))
    {
/*
Load the type library from the file specified by the user. Get back a
pointer to the ITypeLib interface controlling the new type library.
*/
        hr = LoadTypeLib (File,       // name of file containing type lib
            &pTypeLib) ;              // ptd to output variable
/*
If file name is successfully loaded, create dialog box to display its
contents, passing a pointer to the ITypeLib interface as its lParam.
*/
        if (SUCCEEDED(hr))
        {
            CreateDialogParam (hInst, MAKEINTRESOURCE(IDD_BROWSE), NULL,
                (FARPROC)TypeBrowseProc, (LPARAM)          ) ;
            pTypeLib->Release( ) ;
        }
/*
Otherwise, display error box.
*/
        else
        {
            MessageBox (hDlg, TEXT("Couldn't open type lib file"),
                TEXT("Error"), MB_ICONSTOP) ;
        }
    }
    return TRUE ;
}
```

3. The user may specify a type library by means of its registered ID, generally acquired by reading the registry. If you have a type library ID, you can load it via the function **LoadRegTypeLib( )**, which returns a pointer to the ITypeLib interface. Thus:

```
/*
User clicked on the "Open Selected" button.
*/

extern TYPEINFOBLOCK tib[ ] ;

case IDC_OPENSELECTED:
{
    LPTYPELIB pTypeLib ;

/*
Get the current selection in the list box.
*/
    LRESULT lr = SendDlgItemMessage (hDlg, IDC_LIST1, LB_GETCURSEL,
            0, 0L) ;

/*
Current selection is an index in an array of TYPEINFOBLOCK structures.
Use the class ID from the current selection to load a type library from
the registry.
*/

        HRESULT hr = LoadRegTypeLib (
                tib[lr].clsid,        // class ID of type library
                tib[lr].wVerMajor,    // version number, major
                tib[lr].wVerMinor,    // version number, minor
                0,                    // locale ID, 0 == any
                &pTypeLib) ;          // output variable
/*
If file name successfully loaded, create dialog box to display its
contents, passing a pointer to the ITypeLib interface.
*/
    if (SUCCEEDED(hr))
    {
      CreateDialogParam (hInst, MAKEINTRESOURCE(IDD_BROWSE), hDlg ,
            (DLGPROC)TypeBrowseProc , (LPARAM)pTypeLib) ;
      pTypeLib->Release( ) ;
    }
/*
Otherwise, display error box.
*/

    else
    {
      MessageBox (NULL,TEXT("Couldn't load type lib"),TEXT("Error"), 0);
    }
    return TRUE ;
}
```

117

4. A type library is manipulated by means of the *ITypeLib* interface. Its methods are:

ITypeLib::FindName   // *Finds name of a type description in a type library.*
ITypeLib::GetDocumentation   // *Get library's documentation strings.*
ITypeLib::GetLibAttr   // *Get attributes of library.*
ITypeLib::GetTypeComp   // *Get pointer to the ITypeComp for a compiling a type library.*
ITypeLib::GetTypeInfo   // *Get a type description from the library.*
ITypeLib::GetTypeInfoCount   // *Get the number of type descriptions in the library.*
ITypeLib::GetTypeInfoType   // *Get the type (function or variable) of a type description in the lib.*
ITypeLib::GetTypeInfoOfGuid   // *Get type description corresponding to the specified GUID.*
ITypeLib::IsName   // *Does lib contain member of this name?*
ITypeLib::ReleaseTLibAttr   // *Release TLIBATTR structure obtained from ITypeLib::GetLibAttr.*

5. Once you have a type library, you can look inside it to see what sorts of type info objects it contains. The method **ITypeLib::GetTypeInfoCount( )** returns the number of type info objects contained within the type library. The method **ITypeLib::GetDocumentation( )** retrieves descriptive information about an item. This function will give you the name of the object, a short descriptive help string, the name of the on-line help file in which more detailed information may be found, and the help context (an index value) within that file. It returns its information in the form of BSTRs, which we must release via the function **SysFreeString( )**. Thus:

```
BOOL InitTypeLib (ITypeLib *pTypeLib, HWND hParent)
{
    unsigned int utypeinfoCount, i;
    BSTR bstrDoc, bstrHelpFile ;    DWORD dwHelpContext ;
    TCHAR out [256], *psz;

/*
Get help string, help file, and help context for type library itself and
place into text controls. The strings come in the form of a BSTRING
which we must free.
*/

    pTypeLib->GetDocumentation(
      (unsigned int)-1,        // index of type in lib
      NULL,                    // output ptr to item name
      &bstrDoc,                // output ptr to item help string
      &dwHelpContext,          // output ptr to item help context
      &bstrHelpFile);          // output ptr to item help file

    wsprintf(out, TEXT("%ld"), dwHelpContext);
    SetDlgItemText (hParent, IDC_HELPCONTEXT, out);

    psz = (bstrDoc != NULL) ? bstrDoc : TEXT("<none>");
    SetDlgItemText (hParent, IDC_HELPSTRING, psz);
    if (bstrDoc) SysFreeString (bstrDoc) ;

    psz = (bstrHelpFile != NULL) ? bstrHelpFile : TEXT("<none>") ;
    SetDlgItemText (hParent, IDC_HELPFILE, psz) ;
    if (bstrHelpFile) SysFreeString (bstrHelpFile) ;
    <continued on next page>
```

```c
/*
Get the number of type infos this type lib contains.
*/
    utypeinfoCount = pTypeLib->GetTypeInfoCount();


/*
For each type info in the library, get its name and add it to the type
list control in the dialog box.
*/

    BSTR bstrName;

    for(i = 0; i < utypeinfoCount; i++)
    {
      pTypeLib->GetDocumentation(i, &bstrName, NULL, NULL, NULL);

      SendDlgItemMessage (hParent, IDC_TYPELIST,  LB_ADDSTRING, 0,
        (LPARAM)bstrName);
      SysFreeString(bstrName);
    }

    return TRUE;
}
```

6. When you have selected a type info within the type library, you can find the type of typeinfo it describes via the method **ITypeLib::GetTypeInfoType( )**. The method **ITypeLib::GetDocumentation( )** now gets information describing the selected type, thus:

```
char * TypeKind[] = {
    "Enum",             /* TKIND_ENUM */
    "Struct",           /* TKIND_RECORD */
    "Module",           /* TKIND_MODULE */
    "Interface",        /* TKIND_INTERFACE */
    "Dispinterface",    /* TKIND_DISPATCH */
    "Coclass",          /* TKIND_COCLASS */
    "Typedef",          /* TKIND_ALIAS */
    "Union",            /* TKIND_UNION */
};


void SetSelectedType(LPTYPELIB pTypeLib, DWORD dwIndex, HWND hParent)
{
    BSTR bstrDoc, bstrHelpFile ;
    TCHAR FAR* psz;
    TCHAR szBuf[40];
    unsigned long dwHelpContext;
    TYPEKIND tkind;


/*
Find the type of typeinfo this one is -- interface, class, etc.  Set
into dialog item text control.
*/

    pTypeLib->GetTypeInfoType(
       (unsigned int)dwIndex,           // index within type lib
       &tkind);                         // output ptr

    SetDlgItemText(hParent, IDC_TYPEKIND, TypeKind[tkind]);

/*
Get the documentation string and help context from the type lib.
Place into their dialog items.
*/

    pTypeLib->GetDocumentation((unsigned int)dwIndex,
       NULL, &bstrDoc, &dwHelpContext, &bstrHelpFile);

    wsprintf(szBuf, TEXT("%ld"), dwHelpContext);
    SetDlgItemText (hParent, IDC_HELPCONTEXT, szBuf);

    psz = (bstrDoc != NULL) ? bstrDoc : TEXT("<none>");
    SetDlgItemText (hParent, IDC_HELPSTRING, psz);
    psz = (bstrHelpFile != NULL) ? bstrHelpFile : TEXT("<none>") ;
    SetDlgItemText (hParent, IDC_HELPFILE, psz) ;
    SysFreeString(bstrDoc);
    SysFreeString(bstrHelpFile) ;
}
```

This page intentionally contains no text other than this sentence.

7. A type library is a container for type info objects. Each type info describes a single type of object. A type info is created via the method **ITypeLib::GetTypeInfo**( ). Thus:

```
/*
User clicked the "Open Type Info" button.
*/

case IDC_OPENTYPEINFO:
{
    LPTYPEINFO pTypeInfo ;

/*
Ask the list box for its current selection.
*/

    LRESULT lr = SendDlgItemMessage (hDlg, IDC_TYPELIST, LB_GETCURSEL,
        0, 0L) ;

/*
Open the selected type info.  They are conveniently arranged so that the
index in the list box is the number of the type info within the type
lib.
*/

    HRESULT hr = pTypeLib->GetTypeInfo(
            lr,                        // index within type lib
            &pTypeInfo)  ;             // output ptr

/*
If we successfully got the type info, then launch a new dialog box to
show its contents, passing a pointer to the new ITypeInfo in its lParam.
*/
    if (!SUCCEEDED(hr))
    {

      CreateDialogParam (hInst, MAKEINTRESOURCE(IDD_DIALOG2),
            hDlg , (DLGPROC)TypeInfoDlgProc , (LPARAM)pTypeInfo) ;
      pTypeInfo->Release( ) ;
    }
/*
Otherwise, show an error box.
*/
    else
    {
      MessageBox (NULL,TEXT("Couldn't open type info"),TEXT("Error"),0);
    }
    break ;
}
```

8. A type info is manipulated by means of the ITypeInfo interface, which has the following methods:

ITypeInfo::AddressOfMember	*// Get address of static functions or variables*
ITypeInfo::CreateInstance	*// Create a new instance of a component object class (coclass)*
ITypeInfo::GetContainingTypeLib	*// Get type library containing the type info*
ITypeInfo::GetDllEntry	*// Get entry point for a function in a DLL*
ITypeInfo::GetDocumentation	*// Get documentation string describing type info*
ITypeInfo::GetFuncDesc	*// Get description of a function, in a FUNCDESC structure*
ITypeInfo::GetIDsOfNames	*// Map between names and IDs*
ITypeInfo::GetMops	*// Get marshaling information*
ITypeInfo::GetNames	*// Map between IDs and names*
ITypeInfo::GetRefTypeInfo	*// Get type descriptions referenced by other type descriptions*
ITypeInfo::GetTypeAttr	*// Get attributes of a type, in a TYPEATTR structure*
ITypeInfo::GetTypeComp	*// Get ITypeComp interface for a type, used for compilers*
ITypeInfo::GetRefTypeOfImplType	*// Get description of the specified interface types*
ITypeInfo::GetVarDesc	*// Get description of a variable, in a VARDESC structure*
ITypeInfo::Invoke	*// Invokes a method or accesses a property of an described object*
ITypeInfo::ReleaseFuncDesc	*// Releases a FUNCDESC previously returned by GetFuncDesc*
ITypeInfo::ReleaseTypeAttr	*// Releases a TYPEATTR previously returned by GetTypeAttr*
ITypeInfo::ReleaseVarDesc	*// Releases a VARDESC previously returned by GetVarDesc*

9. A type info contains global information, such as GUID, locale, and version, in a structure called a **TYPEATTR**, which you get via the method **ITypeInfo::GetTypeAttr( )**. This allocates and returns a structure, which you must later release via the method **ITypeInfo::ReleaseTypeAttr( )**. Thus:

```
void InitTypeInfo (LPTYPEINFO pTypeInfo, HWND hParent)
{
    MEMBERID memid;
    BSTR bstrName;
    unsigned int i;
    FUNCDESC FAR *pfuncdesc;
    VARDESC  FAR *pvardesc;
    TCHAR out [256], *pStr ;
    HRESULT hr ;

/*
Get the TYPEATTR structure from the type info.
*/
    TYPEATTR *pTypeAttr ;

    pTypeInfo->GetTypeAttr(&pTypeAttr);

/*
Get the GUID from the attributes and set it into its edit control.
*/

    hr = StringFromCLSID(pTypeAttr->guid, &pStr);
    SetDlgItemText(hParent, IDC_GUID, pStr) ;
    SysFreeString (pStr);

/*
Same for the locale.
*/

    wsprintf (out, TEXT("0x%x"), pTypeAttr->lcid) ;
    SetDlgItemText (hParent, IDC_LOCALE, out) ;
/*
Do the same for the version.
*/
    wsprintf(out, TEXT("%u.%02u"),pTypeAttr->wMajorVerNum,
        pTypeAttr->wMinorVerNum);
    SetDlgItemText (hParent, IDC_VERSION, out);

/*
Get the function and variable names, shown later.
*/
    < code omitted, shown on page 127>

/*
Release the type attr.
*/

    pTypeInfo->ReleaseTypeAttr (pTypeAttr) ;
}
```

10. A **TYPEATTR** structure looks like this:

```
typedef struct FARSTRUCT tagTYPEATTR
{
    GUID guid;                          // GUID of the TypeInfo
    LCID lcid;                          // locale of names and doc strings
    unsigned long dwReserved;           // reserved
    MEMBERID memidConstructor;          // ID of constructor
    MEMBERID memidDestructor;           // ID of destructor
    char FAR* lpstrSchema;              // reserved
    unsigned long cbSizeInstance;       // size of an instance of this type
    TYPEKIND typekind;                  // kind of this type
    unsigned short cFuncs;              // number of functions
    unsigned short cVars;               // number of variables/data members
    unsigned short cImplTypes;          // number of implemented interfaces
    unsigned short cbSizeVft;           // size of this type's VTBL
    unsigned short cbAlignment;         // byte-alignment for this type
    unsigned short wTypeFlags;          // flags
    unsigned short wMajorVerNum;        // major version number
    unsigned short wMinorVerNum;        // minor version number
    TYPEDESC tdescAlias;                // type this type is an alias for
    IDLDESC idldescType;                // IDL attributes of the type

} TYPEATTR, FAR* LPTYPEATTR;
```

11. The most interesting thing to see in a type is its list of member functions and variables. These are presented by the **FUNCDESC** and **VARDESC** structures, respectively. We fetch them via the methods **ITypeInfo::GetFuncDesc( )** and **ITypeInfo::GetVarDesc( )**. The structures are allocated dynamically and need to be released via the methods **ITypeInfo::ReleaseFuncDesc( )** and **ITypeInfo::ReleaseVarDesc( )**. The member ID item that each contains is necessary for getting the documentation names for the item via the method **ITypeInfo::GetDocumentation( )**. It also represents the item's Dispatch ID for OLE Automation. Thus:

```
< code excerpted from page 125>

/*
For each function in the TYPEATTR, get its description in a FUNCDESC.
Use the member id from the funcdesc to get the function's name from the
TypeInfo. Place the name into the list box, then release the string and
the funcdesc.
*/
    for(i = 0; i < pTypeAttr->cFuncs; i++)
    {
      pTypeInfo->GetFuncDesc(i, &pfuncdesc) ;
      memid = pfuncdesc->memid;
      pTypeInfo->GetDocumentation(memid, &bstrName, NULL, NULL, NULL);

      SendDlgItemMessage (hParent, IDC_LIST1, LB_ADDSTRING,
            0, (LPARAM)bstrName);
      SysFreeString(bstrName);
      pTypeInfo->ReleaseFuncDesc(pfuncdesc);
    }


/*
For each variable in the TYPEATTR, get its description in a VARDESC.
Use the member ID from the vardesc to get the variable's name from the
TypeInfo. Place the name into the list box, then release the string and
the vardesc.
*/

    for(i = 0; i < pTypeAttr->cVars; i++)
    {
      pTypeInfo->GetVarDesc(i, &pvardesc) ;
      memid = pvardesc->memid;
      pTypeInfo->GetDocumentation(memid, &bstrName, NULL, NULL, NULL);

      SendDlgItemMessage (hParent, IDC_LIST1, LB_ADDSTRING,
            0, (LPARAM)bstrName);
      SysFreeString(bstrName);
      pTypeInfo->ReleaseVarDesc(pvardesc);
    }
```

12. The FUNCDESC and VARDESC contain many interesting entries, thus:

```
typedef struct tagFUNCDESC
{
    MEMBERID memid;                 // function member ID
    SCODE FAR* lprgscode;           // legal SCODES for the function
    ELEMDESC FAR* lprgelemdescParam;        // array of param types
    FUNCKIND funckind;              // is fn virtual, static, or dispatch-only
    INVOKEKIND invkind;             // is fn method, prop-get or prop-set
    CALLCONV callconv;              // function's calling convention
    short cParams;                  // total number of parameters
    short cParamsOpt;               // number of optional parameters
    short oVft;                     // offset in virtual function table
    short cScodes;                  // count of permitted Scodes
    ELEMDESC elemdescFunc;          // return type of the function
    unsigned short wFuncFlags;// flags
}
FUNCDESC;

typedef struct FARSTRUCT tagVARDESC
{
    MEMBERID memid;                 // member ID
    char FAR* lpstrSchema;          // reserved
    union
    {
      unsigned long oInst;          // offset of variable within the instance
      VARIANT FAR* lpvarValue;  // value of the constant

    }UNION_NAME(u);
    ELEMDESC elemdescVar;           // Variable data, in a VARIANT
    unsigned short wVarFlags;  // Flags
    VARKIND varkind;                // kind of variable
} VARDESC, FAR* LPVARDESC;
```

13. A function isn't a function without its parameters and return type, which you can get by examining the FUNCDESC structure in detail. Thus:

```
extern LPTYPEATTR pTypeAttribs ;

void SetSelectedMember(LPTYPEINFO pTypeInfo, DWORD index, HWND hParent)
{
    MEMBERID memid;
    TCHAR out [256], *psz ;
    BSTR bstrDoc, bstrHelpFile ;
    DWORD dwHelpContext ;

/*
Get the TYPEATTR structure from the type info.
*/
    TYPEATTR *pTypeAttr ;
    pTypeInfo->GetTypeAttr(&pTypeAttr);

/*
If this is a function, fill the param list.
*/

    if(index < pTypeAttr->cFuncs)
    {
      int i;
      unsigned int cNames;
      FUNCDESC *pfuncdesc;
      const unsigned int MAX_NAMES = 40;
      BSTR rgNames[MAX_NAMES];
/*
Get the funcdesc of the function.
*/
      pTypeInfo->GetFuncDesc((unsigned int) index, &pfuncdesc) ;
      memid = pfuncdesc->memid;
/*
Get the type of the function from our own utility function mapping name
strings to invocation types; set name into text control.
*/

      GetFuncTypeName (pfuncdesc->invkind, out, sizeof(out));
      SetDlgItemText (hMainWnd, IDC_FUNCTYPE, out) ;
/*
Do the same for the return type.
*/
      GetVarTypeName (pfuncdesc->elemdescFunc.tdesc, out) ;
      SetDlgItemText (hParent, IDC_RETURNTYPE, out) ;
```

```
/*
Check for number of params; if none, put VOID in listbox.
*/
      if (pfuncdesc->cParams == 0)
      {
            SendDlgItemMessage(hMainWnd, IDC_PARAMLIST, LB_ADDSTRING, 0,
                  (LPARAM)(LPSTR)"[void]") ;
      }


/*
Use the memid of the funcdesc to get the list of names from the
TypeInfo. Loop through them all to put them in the list box.  Free each
when done, and release the funcdesc.
*/
      else
      {
            pTypeInfoCur->GetNames(memid, rgNames, MAX_NAMES, &cNames) ;
/*
First returned name is the func itself.  If there is more than 1, then
functions parameters are named.  Loop through and put each name in list.
*/
            if (cNames > 1)
            {
                  for(i = 1; i < cNames; i++)
                  {
                        SendDlgItemMessage(hMainWnd, IDC_PARAMLIST,
                              LB_ADDSTRING, 0, (LPARAM)rgNames[i]);
                        SysFreeString(rgNames[i]);
                  }
            }
/*
Otherwise, parameters aren't named.  Examine each type, get the name of
the type from our own utility function, and put in list.
*/
            else
            {
                  char type [128] ;
                  for (i = 0 ; i < pfuncdesc->cParams; i++)
                  {
                        VARTYPE vtype ;
                        vtype = ((pfuncdesc->lprgelemdescParam) + i)->
                              tdesc.vt ;
                        GetVarTypeName (vtype, out, sizeof(out)) ;
                        wsprintf (type, "[%s]", out) ;
                        SendDlgItemMessage(hMainWnd, IDC_PARAMLIST,
                              LB_ADDSTRING, 0, (LPARAM)type);
                  }
            }
            SysFreeString(rgNames[0]);
      }
      pTypeInfoCur->ReleaseFuncDesc(pfuncdesc);
}
```

<continued on following page>

14. The type of a variable may be found by examining its VARDESC, thus:

```
/*
Otherwise it's a variable.
*/
    else
    {
            VARDESC FAR *pvardesc;
            char type [128] ;

/*
Get variable descriptor and use memid.
*/


            pTypeInfoCur->GetVarDesc(
                    (unsigned int)(dwIndex - pTypeAttribs->cFuncs),
                    &pvardesc);
            memid = pvardesc->memid;
            UpdateMemberInfo(memid);


/*
Get type of variable; get its name from our utility function.  Set
strings into edit controls.
*/

            VARTYPE vtype = (pvardesc->elemdescVar).tdesc.vt ;
            GetVarTypeName (vtype, out, sizeof(out)) ;
            wsprintf (type, "[%s]", out) ;
            SendDlgItemMessage(hMainWnd, IDC_PARAMLIST, LB_ADDSTRING,
                    0, (LPARAM)type);
            SetDlgItemText (hMainWnd, IDC_FUNCTYPE, (LPSTR)"Variable") ;
            pTypeInfoCur->ReleaseVarDesc(pvardesc);
    }
}
```

130

15. To jump to a given context number in a help file, use the function **WinHelp( )** , thus:

```
case ID_DOHELP:
{
  OLECHAR HelpFileName [128], HelpContextName [128] ;
  long HelpContext ;

/*
Get help file name and context number from edit controls.  Convert the
latter into a long integer.
*/
    GetDlgItemText (hDlg, IDC_HELPFILE, HelpFileName,
        sizeof(HelpFileName)) ;
    GetDlgItemText (hDlg, IDC_HELPCONTEXT, HelpContextName,
        sizeof(HelpContextName)) ;
    HelpContext = _wtol (HelpContextName) ;

/*
Invoke the help system for the specified file and context number.
*/

    WinHelp (
            hDlg,                   // owner window
            HelpFileName,           // help file name (.HLP)
            HELP_CONTEXT,           // flags
            HelpContext) ;          // context number

    break ;
}
```

Lab Exercise
Chapter 4
Creating and Using Type Libraries

Directory: \EssenceofOLE\chap03\helloau\hello32\templ
(note: this exercise uses the last chapter's files)

1. Our automation server from the previous chapter has a type library, but the library does not contain any properties or methods. In the file HELLO32.ODL, go to the appropriate section and add .ODL language entries for the HelloMessage property and the SayHello( ) method. Add references to the help file found in the \HELP directory, which has been constructed such that the help contexts for the properties and methods are the same as their dispatch IDs. (Clever, no?) Build the type library. Examine the .REG file in the \HELLOAU directory and make sure the entries point to the location of the type library on your system. Use the type browser app from the \DONE directory of the next example to examine it.

2. Now that we have a type library, we want to use it to generate an MFC controller app. To emphasize the fact that we are starting from scratch with the MFC, there is no \templ directory, although a finished example may be found in \EssenceofOLE\chap04\mfchelloaucl\done. Use App Wizard to generate a new project, checking the "OLE Automation" box in App Wizard's step 3. Build it and run it to make sure everything worked right.

3. Now we want to use Class Wizard to generate a wrapper class from our server's type library. Bring up Class Wizard, select the "Add Class" button, and the "From an OLE TypeLib" option. When the "Import" dialog box appears, navigate to the location of the type library you generated in step 1 and select this file. When the "Confirm Classes" dialog box appears, there should only be one option. Change the class and file names if desired, or take the one given. Click OK.

4. Class Wizard now has generated a new wrapper class from the type library. You will find it in your Project Workspace's class view and file views. In your CView-derived class, add a member variable of the wrapper class. Add a handler for the WM_CREATE message to your CView class. In this handler, call the CreateDispatch( ) method of your wrapper class, passing the name "EssenceofOLE.HelloAutomation", which should still be registered from the previous chapter's exercises, or whatever other name you might have used when registering the server. If this operation is successful, return 0, thereby continuing the startup; otherwise return -1, which will cause the view to refuse to be created and the MFC client app to shut down. Signal the shutdown with a message box if you like.

5. Now you need to add a human interface to the controller. Use any MFC features you like to get the input from the user, perhaps a mouse click to call SayHello( ) and a dialog box to specify the HelloMessage string. If you are good with the MFC, these should take you under 5 minutes for both. In response to the user input, call the wrapper class's SayHello( ), SetHelloMessage( ), and GetHelloMessage( ) methods. It's pretty easy.

EXTRA CREDIT: Add a help button to your MFC app. When the user clicks it, use the features shown in the type browser lab to open the type library, read the name of the help file from it, and show it to the user. This is a nontrivial exercise.

Directory: \EssenceofOLE\chap04\typbro32\templ

1. This lab is the type browser shown in the latter section of this chapter. First, the app queries the registry to see all the type libraries installed on the system, in file MAINDLG.CPP, case WM_INITDIALOG. Examine this code until you feel comfortable with it.

2. When the user clicks the "By File Name" button, the file-open dialog box pops up. This code is in the file MAINDLG.CPP, case WM_COMMAND, subcase IDC_BUTTON1. If the user selects a name from it, attempt to get a type library from the specified file via the function LoadTypeLib( ). Place the pointer to the new type lib in the output variable pTypeLib.

3. If the user clicks "Open Selected" or double-clicks the list box, he has selected a type library from the registry. This code is in the file MAINDLG.CPP, case WM_COMMAND, subcase IDC_BUTTON2. Load the type library via the function LoadRegTypeLib( ). The class ID of the selected type lib is in the array tib[lr].clsid. Store the output pointer in the variable pTypeLib.

4. The type library has now been loaded, so the type library dialog box is on the screen. We need to fill its controls with information describing the type library. In the file TYPELIB.CPP, go to the function InitTypeLib( ). You are passed a pointer to the type library that has just been opened. Use the GetDocumentation( ) method to get the type library's (offset == -1) help file, help string, and help context. The placement of these into the dialog box's controls has been done for you.

5. Now we want to know the names of all the type infos that this type library contains. Use the method ITypeLib::GetTypeInfoCount( ) to get the number of type info objects in the type lib. Then for each type info, use the method ITypeLib::GetDocumentation( ) to get its name. The code that puts it in the list box has been done for you.

6. When the user clicks on a type info in the list box, the function SetSelectedType( ) will be called. This means that the dialog box should now show information relating the selected type info. Use the method ITypeLib::GetTypeInfoType( ) to get the type of the type info. The code to find its name and put it into its edit control has already been written for you. Also, use the method ITypeLib:: GetDocumentation( ) to get the type infos document string, its help context, and its help file. Code is supplied for you to place all of these members into their edit controls.

7. When the user clicks the "Open Type Info" button, or double-clicks a type info name in the list box, it means that he wants to examine the selected type info in more detail. To do this, we must open the type info. In the file TYPEDLG.CPP, case WM_COMMAND, subcase IDC_BUTTON2, use the method ITypeLib::GetTypeInfo( ) to do this. The index of the type info is the same as the index of the list box, which you will find the variable "lr". Store the pointer in the variable "pTypeInfo".

8. Now that the type info is open, we want to start examining it. In the file TYPEINFO.CPP, go to the function InitTypeInfo( ). You are passed a pointer to a type info. Get a TYPEATTR structure describing this type via the method ITypeInfo::GetTypeAttr( ). Store a pointer to the TYPEATTR structure in the variable pTypeAttr. Code is supplied for you that takes the TYPEATTR structure and displays its elements in the dialog box. At the end of the function, release the TYPEATTR via the method ITypeInfo::ReleaseTypeAttr( ).

9. Now that we have selected a type info, we need to show the member functions and variables within it. For each function in the TYPEATTR, get its description in a FUNCDESC. Use the member id from the funcdesc to get the function's name from the TypeInfo via the method GetDocumentation( ). The placement of the name into the text control has been done for you. Finally, release the string and the funcdesc. Do the same for the variables.

10. The filling of the parameter list for a function was deemed too painful to make you do in the time allotted. In the file TYPEINFO.CPP, go to the function SetSelectedMember( ). Examine the completed code until you feel comfortable with it.

11. Finally, we want to hook up the on-line help to connect to the help files provided by the vendors of the type library. In the file TYPEDLG.CPP, case WM_COMMAND, subcase IDC_DOHELP, use the function WinHelp( ) to bring up the on-line help engine, open to the specified help file and context gotten from the type library. The file name and help context have already been fetched for you.

EXTRA CREDIT: Find more useful things in the typelib, the TYPEATTR, the funcdesc or the vardesc. Place them in their own text controls on the box.

EXTRA EXTRA CREDIT: Add a button to the type info dialog box. When the user clicks it, use the method ITypeInfo::CreateInstance( ) to create one of them. Then start writing code to provide access to its member functions and variables. When you finish this one, you will have written VB4.

Chapter 5
ActiveX Controls

A. CONTROL THEORY AND HISTORY: BUY COMPONENTS, DON'T MAKE THEM

When Windows was first designed, the visual user interface demanded some common set of gizmos to allow the user to provide input or commands to the program. For example, every app needed some form of pushbutton. Rather than force every developer of Windows software to write his own pushbutton from scratch, the providers of Windows wrote a pushbutton global window class that all app designers were able to use. The control was a simple child window so communication between the control and its container was handled by Windows messages. The container would send the control a message such as WM_SETTEXT to set the button's text, and the control would send its parent window a WM_COMMAND message to indicate that the user had clicked on it. This was enormous bang for the buck at the time.

The child window control architecture was a fine first cut, but as the concept took hold and controls' intelligence increased, the bandwidth of the message-based communication channel between child and parent became too narrow. The messages from container to control proliferated and were hard to use, having only two parameters. For example, look at the edit control which has no fewer than 78 custom messages as of this writing. The communication channel from control to container was even tighter since it relied on the WM_COMMAND message, which allows only a single 16-bit int for the control's customized status information, not even enough for a pointer to a structure. The child window control architecture had reached its limit.

The VBX control model, released with Visual Basic, solved the bandwidth problem. Controls could export *methods*, functions that a container could call directly and pass an arbitrary number of parameters. The control could also expose *properties*, data values that the container could directly set or get. Better yet, the control could signal the container of asynchronous *events*, again passing any number and type of parameters. A virtuous cycle began as more and better VBX controls attracted more and richer buyers and more buyers stimulated development of more and better controls. You didn't have to write a calendar control to allow the user to input a date; you could buy a VBX control off the shelf. One of my favorites was an electrocardiogram monitor control (although I wouldn't want to be a patient in a coronary care unit run by a 16-bit VB app on Windows 3.1).

Trouble arose with the switch to 32-bit Windows. The techniques used to make VBX controls efficient in 16-bit Windows were heavily tied not only to the Intel chip, with lots of assembler code, but also into the 16-bit segmented architecture, particularly the stack frame. Porting it to 32 bits and processor independence would have required a complete rewrite and led to other troubles. Microsoft decided to take the top-level concepts of the VBX architecture and implement it using the new OLE 2.0 specification, and they dubbed their new control mechanism ActiveX. In the spring of 1996, the name was changed to ActiveX.

B. WHAT THE HELL IS ACTIVEX ANYWAY ?

The term "ActiveX" has gotten an enormous amount of airplay since its release in the spring of 1996. As usual, once Microsoft finds an adjective they like, they tack it onto everything in sight until it loses all meaning, as they did with the word "Visual", leading to a great deal of confusion. At the time of this writing, the term is defined thus:

ActiveX is an extension of existing OLE technologies, originally code-named "Sweeper", that allows OLE-aware apps to do useful things with and over the Internet. Confusingly, *ActiveX Controls* is the new name for all OLE controls, whether or not they have anything to do with the Internet. The basics of ActiveX controls are discussed in this chapter, and the basics of their containers in the following chapter. The features of ActiveX controls used on the Internet are discussed in Chapter 11. *ActiveX Scripting* is the ability of apps to execute run-time interpreted scripts in languages such as Java or Visual basic, generally involving ActiveX controls. This allows HTML pages to contain active content. ActiveX Scripting is discussed in Chapter 12. *ActiveX Documents* deal with the embedding and linking of objects which reside on the Internet. As this book does not cover embedding and linking, neither does it cover ActiveX Documents.

The Internet portion of ActiveX was originally developed for use in an HTML environment, and the examples in Chapters 11 and 12 concentrate on this use. However, there is no reason to confine their use to this environment. You really can use them anywhere you want, in any app.

C. ActiveX Control Architecture

1. An ActiveX control must be an in-process COM server whose objects expose at least the IUnknown interface. As a COM server, it must provide a class factory and export the named functions DllGetClassObject( ) and DllCanUnloadNow( ). A control must also provide the capability of self-registering, exposing the named functions DllRegisterServer( ) and DllUnregisterServer( ). This allows any container app that obtains the control's file to register it programmatically and begin using it. See Appendix A for a detailed description of self-registration functionality. The required pieces of a control are shown graphically below:

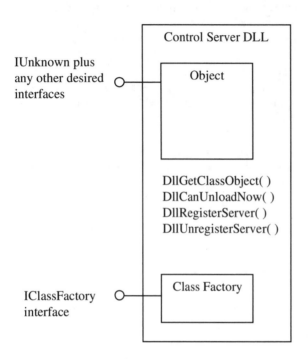

2. If a control wants to have a visible window and receive Windows messages, it must support all the interfaces necessary for being an embedded object server with in-place activation. Fortunately, this support is built into the MFC base class for an ActiveX control, the discussion of which begins on page 142. The container in which the control resides must provide all the functionality of an embedded object container with in-place activation. A discussion of embedding and in-place activation is beyond the scope of this book. See Brockschmidt, Chapters 17, 18, 22, and 23.

Note: Some Microsoft documentation refers to in-place activation as "Visual Editing," no doubt to distinguish it from tactile editing or olfactory editing. This term manages to be ambiguous, misleading, and inaccurate, quite an accomplishment for a two-word phrase. See Brockschmidt, pp. 1011-1012 for a discussion of its origins.

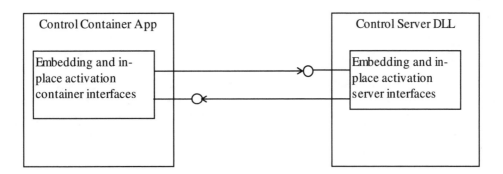

3. A control will generally want to exposes methods and properties to its container. It does this by being an automation server supporting the IDispatch interface as discussed in Chapter 3. The container accesses the methods and properties by means of the method IDispatch::Invoke( ). The discussion of control properties and methods begins on page 150.

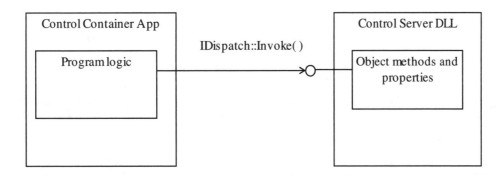

4. A control may also signal events to its container. It does this by being an automation controller and calling the Invoke( ) method of an IDispatch interface provided by its container. The discussion of control events begins on page 161.

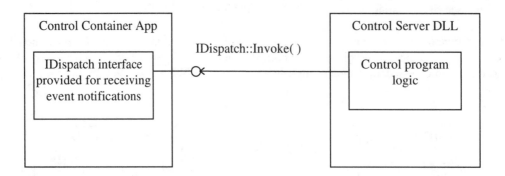

5. A control may also get, but not set, ambient properties provided by its container. An ambient property tells the control about the container environment in which it lives, for example, the color of the form on which it has been placed. A control exposes its ambient properties by providing a second IDispatch interface from which the control reads the desired property. The use of ambient properties by a control is discussed on page 169.

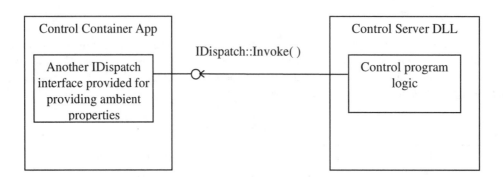

6. A control usually needs to provide a way of remembering its persistent properties from one session to another. This is done by supporting the IPersistStream interface as discussed in Chapter 7. The control's container will query for this interface and use it to store the control's properties in a configuration file or other persistent medium. The use of persistent properties is discussed beginning on page 157.

7. A control may provide programming support, such as type libraries and property pages, for the design time use of its programming environment. The type libraries in an ActiveX control are described on pages 153 and 163; the discussion of property pages begins on page 166. This programming support is the first feature I would expect to see removed when slimming down controls for the Internet. Real-world controls will probably come in two flavors: full-featured design flavor, which will include the programming support, and run-time flavor, which won't.

D. MFC CONTROL BASICS

1. You've probably noticed that many apps including VC++ like to display a clock in the lower right-hand corner of their status bar. In this example, we are going to create an ActiveX control that performs this function for us. Instead of having to write a clock, app designers will be able to buy ours and just drop it in, saving lots of development time. While relatively simple in its own function, this example will demonstrate all of the features of an ActiveX control. You will find the sample code in the directory \chap05\timer.

You create a new control via VC++'s Control Wizard, which you will find on the "New Project Workspace" dialog box as shown below. When you select "Create...", Control Wizard will take you through two wizard sheets allowing you to specify choices for your new control's configuration. In this sample app, we select only the default options. Thus:

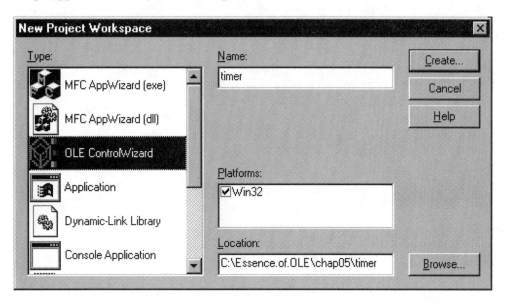

2. When you create a new control project, Control Wizard will derive a new class for you from the base class **COleControl**, which in turn derives from CWnd. An ActiveX control requires a complex support framework. The in-place activation code alone makes strong men weep, but the framework is essentially identical from one control to the next. This lends itself beautifully to the inheritance mechanism of C++ and the MFC. The COleControl class provides most of the nuts-and-bolts functionality common to all ActiveX controls. The derived class declaration looks like this:

```
class CTimerCtrl : public COleControl
{
    DECLARE_DYNCREATE(CTimerCtrl)

// Constructor
public:

// Overrides

    // Drawing function
    virtual void OnDraw(CDC* pdc, const CRect& rcBounds,
      const CRect& rcInvalid);

    // Persistence
    virtual void DoPropExchange(CPropExchange* pPX);

    // Reset control state
    virtual void OnResetState();

// Implementation
protected:
    ~CTimerCtrl();

    DECLARE_OLECREATE_EX(CTimerCtrl)      // Class factory and guid
    DECLARE_OLETYPELIB(CTimerCtrl)        // GetTypeInfo
    DECLARE_PROPPAGEIDS(CTimerCtrl)       // Property page IDs
    DECLARE_OLECTLTYPE(CTimerCtrl)        // Type name and misc status

    <declaration of message, dispatch, and event maps omitted>
};
```

3. Control Wizard will also create two more classes for you. You will find a class derived from **COleControlModule**, which is the control's version of CWinApp. In the timer example, this is called CTimerApp, shown below. App Wizard will override the InitInstance( ) and ExitInstance( ) of this class for you and place their shells in this class's implementation file, here "timer.cpp". You can do app-level initialization and cleanup by placing your own code here, but that is relatively rare and this simple example provides none.

Control Wizard will also create a property page for you, derived from the MFC base class **COlePropertyPage**. This is discussed in more detail on page 166.

<file timer.h>

```
class CTimerApp : public COleControlModule
{
public:
    BOOL InitInstance();
    int ExitInstance();
};
```

<file timer.cpp>

```
///////////////////////////////////////////////////////////////////////
///
// CTimerApp::InitInstance - DLL initialization

BOOL CTimerApp::InitInstance()
{
    BOOL bInit = COleControlModule::InitInstance();

    if (bInit)
    {
      // TODO: Add your own module initialization code here.
    }

    return bInit;
}
```

4. All controls must export the named function DllRegisterServer( ), which is the function used by external agencies to order the control to make all the necessary entries in the registry. Control Wizard will generate this function for you; you will find it in your control's App class. If you want to make additional registry entries, you can add the code here to do so. When you build your control, VC++ will automatically find this function and call it, producing registry entries similar to the following:

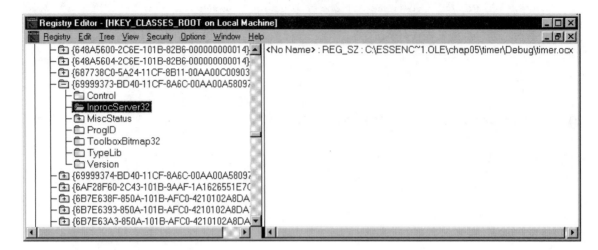

The key "InProcServer32", with which you are already familiar, identifies the full path to the server which produces objects of the specified class. In this case, you can see that it points to the control DLL "timer.ocx". The presence of the key "Control" identifies this registry entry as belonging to a full-featured ActiveX control. Programming environment apps that want to provide a list of registered ActiveX controls, such as Visual Basic or the test container on page 149, will look for the presence of this key to determine whether or not the registered server is a control.

In the forthcoming ActiveX control architecture, where not every control will support every feature, there will be more registry keys here denoting *component categories*. These entries will specify which interfaces the control supports, so the container will be able to determine the control's capabilities without actually having to create and query the control itself. This can be an expensive operation when the control lives out on the Internet.

5. Similar to the CView class, our control contains an **OnDraw( )** method which is called when the control needs to render its appearance. As with the method CView::OnDraw( ), you are provided with a pointer to a CDC object which represents the output device context. When your control is active, this CDC will be mapped to the control's window. When your control is inactive, the CDC will represent a metafile which the container uses to present a picture of your control that looks right even when it isn't active. This is the *presentation format* required in an embedding operation. The beauty of the MFC is that you don't have to do anything different in either case. You simply write code to draw on the CDC to make your control look the way you want it to look, and the MFC magically routes the pixels to the right place.

There are two important differences between drawing in COleControl::OnDraw( ) and drawing in a view. First, in a control you CANNOT assume that the control's drawing area starts at coordinates (0,0) and extends for your window's width and height. If the control is inactive, the provided DC might not be a window, it might actually be a metafile DC with a different bounding rectangle. You must use the bounding rectangle **rcBounds** provided as the second parameter as shown in the source code sample below. The invalid rectangle in the DC is likewise unreliable; if you care about the invalid rectangle, you must use the last parameter, **rcInvalid**. Second, the COleControl base class does not automatically fill the control's background with a default brush as does a view. If you want the background filled with a certain color or pattern, you must do that yourself. This is not shown in the example below, but is demonstrated on page 156 where the background color property is explained.

In the timer example, we get the current time from the operating system, format it into a string, and draw it centered in the control. Thus:

```
void CTimerCtrl::OnDraw(CDC* pdc, const CRect& rcBounds,
    const CRect& rcInvalid)
{

/*
Get current time.
*/
    SYSTEMTIME st ;
    GetLocalTime (&st) ;

/*
Convert time into colon-separated string.
*/
    char out [128] ;
    wsprintf (out, "%2.2d:%2.2d:%2.2d", st.wHour, st.wMinute,
      st.wSecond) ;

/*
Draw within bounding rectangle presented by framework.
*/
    pdc->DrawText (out, -1, (LPRECT)&rcBounds,
      DT_CENTER | DT_VCENTER | DT_SINGLELINE) ;

}
```

6. The COleControl class can process messages exactly like any other class derived from CCmdTarget. Simply use Class Wizard to add message handlers to your message map. In this example, we add handlers for the WM_CREATE to start a one-second timer, the WM_DESTROY message to kill the timer, and the WM_TIMER message to repaint our control's window to display the current time. The added code is on the facing page. Thus:

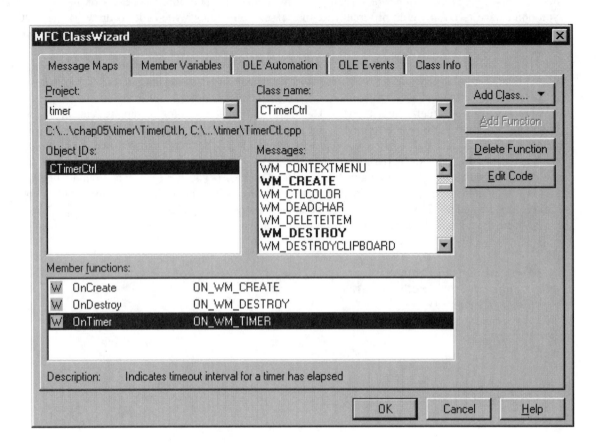

```
/*
When window is created, start a one-second timer which will be used to
refresh the display.
*/

int CTimerCtrl::OnCreate(LPCREATESTRUCT lpCreateStruct)
{
    if (COleControl::OnCreate(lpCreateStruct) == -1)
      return -1;

    m_TimerID = SetTimer (0, 1000, NULL) ;

    return 0;
}

/*
When the timer signals, invalidate the window to force a repaint.
*/

void CTimerCtrl::OnTimer(UINT nIDEvent)
{
    Invalidate ( ) ;
}

/*
When the window is destroyed, kill the timer too.
*/

void CTimerCtrl::OnDestroy()
{
    COleControl::OnDestroy();

    KillTimer (m_TimerID) ;
}
```

7. To test your control, you will need to use the test container app TSTCON32.EXE. This will probably appear as "OLE Control Test Container" on the "Tools" menu of VC++. If not, you can add it via the "Tools – Customize" menu item. This app provides easy GUI access to all the standard features of any control. It will allow you to create and destroy controls, activate and deactivate them, set their properties, call their methods, and respond to their events. You place a control into the test container via the "Edit – Insert OLE Control…" menu item, which will bring up a list of all registered controls on your system. Thus:

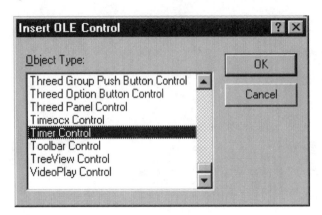

When you choose a control, the test container will create it and activate it. The sizing border and hatching are drawn by the container itself, not by your control. Try inserting several instances of the control and moving them around. You should also experiment with the "Edit – Embedded Object Functions" menu, which provides access to the activation and deactivation of the control. These menu items are actually calling methods on the *IOleObject* interface exposed by the control. You don't have to write code to make it happen, you have inherited all of this functionality from the COleControl base class. Thus:

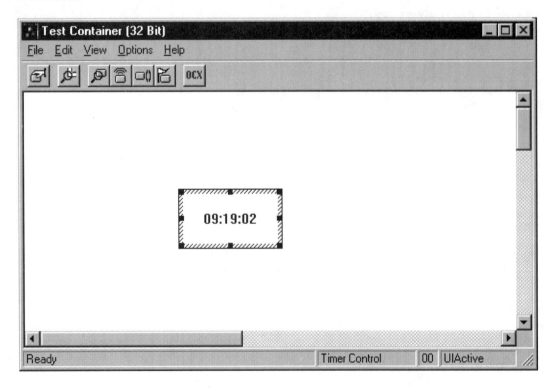

148

E. CONTROL PROPERTIES AND METHODS

1. A control exposes properties and methods to its container by being an OLE automation server, supporting the IDispatch interface as discussed in Chapters 3 and 4. A property in a control is exactly the same as an automation property introduced in Chapter 3, a variable that makes sense to the control and which the control's container may want to set or get.

2. The buyer of any control is a programmer writing an app. We want to make our control as useful as possible so the programmer will buy our control and not someone else's. In order to be versatile, we will give our control the capability of displaying the time either showing the seconds (01:23:45) or not (01:23). We accomplish this by creating a property, called "ShowSeconds", which the programmer will set to TRUE or FALSE. Some programmers will hardwire the property at development time, and some will provide their own UI to allow the user to choose. We expose this property to the world do this exactly as we did in Chapter 3 by using the "OLE Automation" tab of Class Wizard and selecting the "Add Property..." button. The MFC framework adds exactly the same support. Thus:

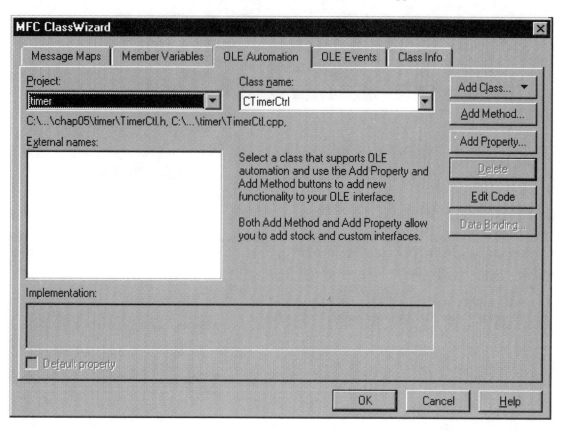

3. When we add a property, we enter its name and type as shown below. Class Wizard will add a member variable added to the control class and automatically connect it to the control's IDispatch::Invoke( ) method. When the property is changed by the container, the specified notification function will be called. Thus:

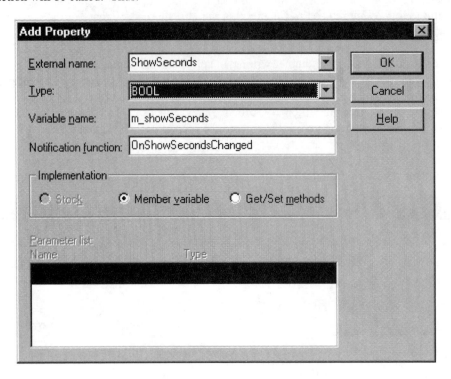

```
/*
This notification function will be called when the ShowSeconds property
is changed by the control's container.  Simply invalidate to force a
repaint.
*/

void CTimerCtrl::OnShowSecondsChanged()
{
    Invalidate( ) ;
    SetModifiedFlag();
}
```

4. Our ShowSeconds property is exposed automatically for us by Class Wizard. It is up to us to write code that uses the property intelligently. In the timer example, we modify the OnDraw( ) method to examine the value of the ShowSeconds property and display the current time with or without the seconds accordingly. Thus:

```
void CTimerCtrl::OnDraw(CDC* pdc, const CRect& rcBounds,
    const CRect& rcInvalid)
{

/*
Get current time.
*/
    SYSTEMTIME st ;
    GetLocalTime (&st) ;

/*
Convert time into colon-separated string. If ShowSeconds property is
set, then compose string showing time in seconds.  Otherwise, compose
string showing time to nearest minute.
*/
    char out [128] ;

    if (m_showSeconds)
    {
      wsprintf (out, "%2.2d:%2.2d:%2.2d", st.wHour, st.wMinute,
          st.wSecond) ;
    }
    else
    {
      wsprintf (out, "%2.2d:%2.2d", st.wHour, st.wMinute) ;
    }

    <rest of OnDraw( ) method>
}
```

5. Just as in Chapter 4, our control contains an .ODL file for creating a type library. When we add a property, Class Wizard adds an entry to the .ODL file describing the property. In the case of an ActiveX control, the type library is bound into the control DLL itself as a resource. Thus:

```
#include <olectl.h>

[ uuid(69999370-BD40-11CF-8A6C-00AA00A58097), version(1.0),
  helpstring("timer OLE Control module"), control ]
library TIMERLib
{
    importlib(STDOLE_TLB);
    importlib(STDTYPE_TLB);

    //  Primary dispatch interface for CTimerCtrl

    [ uuid(69999371-BD40-11CF-8A6C-00AA00A58097),
      helpstring("Dispatch interface for Timer Control"), hidden ]
    dispinterface _DTimer
    {
    properties:
            // NOTE - ClassWizard will maintain prop information here.
            //     Use extreme caution when editing this section.
            //{{AFX_ODL_PROP(CTimerCtrl)
            [id(1)] boolean ShowSeconds;
            //}}AFX_ODL_PROP

    methods:
            // NOTE - ClassWizard will maintain method information here.
            //     Use extreme caution when editing this section.
            //{{AFX_ODL_METHOD(CTimerCtrl)
            //}}AFX_ODL_METHOD

            [id(DISPID_ABOUTBOX)] void AboutBox();
    };
```

NOTE: The type library information is useful only at programming time, not at run time. To make controls smaller for better Internet support, I would expect that the type library will be removed from a runtime control in the future.

6. To access a property from the test container, create or select a control and select "View – Properties…" from the menu. This will bring up a dialog box that reads the control's type library and lists all of the exposed properties contained therein. When you select a property in the list box, the test container will call IDispatch::Invoke( ) to fetch its value. You can set the property by typing in a value and clicking "Apply", in which case the test container will call IDispatch::Invoke( ) to set its value. Thus:

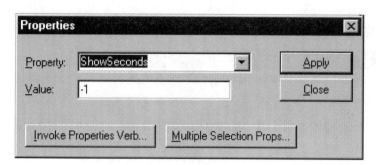

WARNING: The test container and all other programming environments get their information from reading the type library supplied by the control, not by examining the code. If they get out of sync, you're scrod. This would seem unusual because of the automatic .ODL file management provided by the MFC, but you would not believe the amount of money I've made cleaning up after clients who did exactly that. It is especially deadly when you are developing container and control simultaneously.

7. Some properties are so common among controls that they have been designated by Microsoft as *stock properties*. A stock property is a property whose name, type, and dispatch ID are reserved for a specific purpose.

Although the name "stock property" might lead you to think that these were always exposed and functional, this is not the case. A control specifies each stock property that it wants to support via the OLE Automation tab of Class Wizard. When you pick "Add Property", the drop-down combo box contains the names of all the stock properties. When you select one, entries will be made in your control's dispatch map and .ODL file, similar to those used for custom properties. Thus:

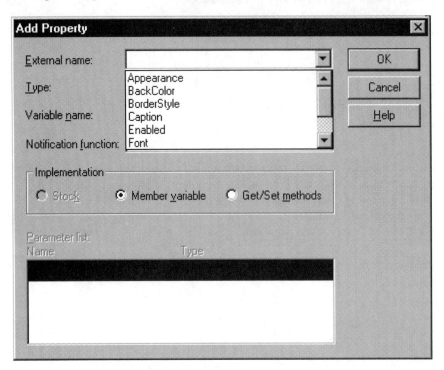

Using a stock property means that when you expose one via Class Wizard, you do not have to add the member variable or notification function; the base class already contains it. The property is available to you via a member function or variable in the COleControl base class. The stock properties and their access mechanisms are:

Property	COleControl member function/variable
Appearance	m_sAppearance
BackColor	GetBackColor( )
BorderStyle	m_sBorderStyle.
Caption	InternalGetText( )
Enabled	m_bEnabled
Font	InternalGetFont( )
ForeColor	GetForeColor( )
hWnd	m_hWnd
Text	InternalGetText( ) [same as Caption]

8. Having added a stock property, it is up to the control to use it intelligently. Here we add support for the "BackColor" property to our timer control. Every time we draw our control, we get the current background color via the method **COleControl::GetBackColor( )**, which returns a variable of type **OLE_COLOR**.

The programmer using our control in his container might want to set the background color to a permanently fixed value such as blue. Alternatively, he might want to set it to a system color specified by the user in the Control Panel, such as the button face color, which obviously can vary from one user to another. Look at the color property page shown on page 168 for an example of how a programmer could specify this arrangement. The method **COleControl::TranslateColor( )** looks at the OLE_COLOR and returns the actual COLORREF to use, either the color hardwired by the container programmer or the system color set by the user.

In the example below, we get the background color and translate it. We then create a brush, fill the control's rectangle with it, and set the text background color to use it. Thus:

```
void CTimerCtrl::OnDraw(CDC* pdc, const CRect& rcBounds,
    const CRect& rcInvalid)
{

    <set up string as shown previously>
/*
Having exposed it via Class Wizard, use the stock property
"BackColor" to draw the background of the control.
*/
    OLE_COLOR oc = GetBackColor ( ) ;
    COLORREF cr = TranslateColor (oc) ;

    CBrush BackBrush (cr) ;
    pdc->FillRect(rcBounds, &BackBrush);

    pdc->SetBkColor (cr) ;

/*
Draw within bounding rectangle presented by framework.
*/
    pdc->DrawText (out, -1, (LPRECT)&rcBounds,
      DT_CENTER | DT_VCENTER | DT_SINGLELINE) ;

}
```

9. A control must deal with the issue of persistence. The programmer who buys our control sets its properties when he places it into the app he is writing. He then ships to his customer, the end user, an app containing our control. When the end user starts the programmer's app and the control is first created, the control's properties will be those specified in the class constructor that you wrote, not the state to which the programmer set them when he designed the app. The control needs some mechanism to change its properties from these default values to the state specified by the programmer when he used our control to build his app. The control accomplishes this by supporting the IPersistStream interface discussed in Chapter 7.

The control does not know where it will live or what storage resources are available to it. It is up to the container to provide a stream in which the control will store its properties at design time and read them out again at run time. This stream can be in a configuration file, or in the final app's .EXE file. See Chapter 6 for an example of the latter. At design time, the development environment creates the stream, queries the control for IPersistStream, and uses the methods of that interface to make the control write its properties into the stream. At run time, the app will find the stream and use the IPersistStream interface to make the control read its properties from it.

In the COleControl class, the interfaces are written for you and connected to the **COleControl::DoPropExchange( )** method. This method is conceptually similar to the CWnd::DoDataExchange( ) method used for initializing and saving the initial state of a dialog box's member variables. All you have to do is to add code to handle your own properties to the method COleControl::DoPropExchange( ), which does the actual reading or writing when the control is loaded or stored. There are functions beginning with the letters PX_ for storing each type of variable. In this example, the function **PX_Bool( )** is used to fetch or store a BOOL variable to the control's persistent stream. If the stream does not contain the specified element, such as when the control is initially created, then the PX_Bool( ) function will fail and the variable will be unmodified. Thus:

```
void CTimerCtrl::DoPropExchange(CPropExchange* pPX)
{

/*
These two lines were added by Control Wizard.  They store the control's
version number and the stock properties of the base class.
*/

    ExchangeVersion(pPX, MAKELONG(_wVerMinor, _wVerMajor));
    COleControl::DoPropExchange(pPX);

/*
We added this line ourselves to save our custom ShowSeconds property
into the stream provided by the container.
*/

    PX_Bool (pPX, "ShowSeconds", m_showSeconds) ;
}
```

10. To test the persistence of your control, run the test container, insert a control, and change its properties from their default values. Then choose "File – Save to Stream" from the main menu. The container will create a stream internally and serialize your control's properties into it. You can then delete the original control. Selecting the somewhat misnamed "File – Load" item from the menu will cause the test container to create a control of the specified class and call its DoPropExchange( ) method, passing the stream in which the properties were saved. The control that appears in the container should have the previously set property values, not the control's default values. You can examine the contents of the saved stream by selecting the "View – Saved Control Stream" from the test container's menu. Thus:

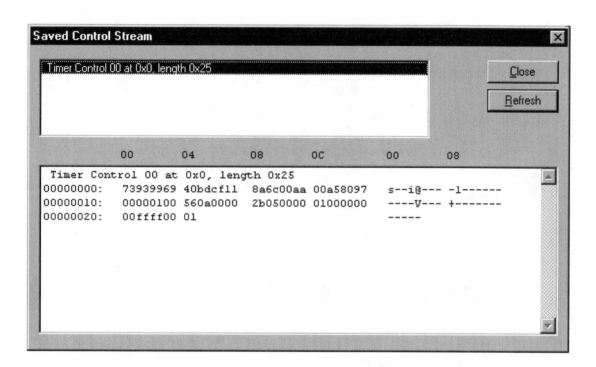

Note: You are not restricted to storing only exported automation properties in your control's stream; you can put anything you want in it. However, there is no guarantee that the container will use this persistence mechanism. It might just save all the property values itself and restore them one by one – kludgey, but legal. Make sure that your control works reasonably if the DoPropExchange( ) method is not used, or is used and fails.

11.   In addition to properties, a control may also expose *methods* to its container. These are functions, exposed via the same IDispatch interface that exposes properties. Methods are added via Class Wizard, exactly as they were in Chapter 3. There are two stock methods, Refresh( ) and DoClick( ). The former forces a repaint of the control, the latter simulates a mouse click. Their implementation is similar to stock properties.

In the following example, we add a method called "SetAlarm" to our timer control. It accepts a single parameter, the delay in seconds until an alarm event is fired. Class Wizard handles the plumbing; all we have to do is add the code that we want executed. In this case, we simply calculate the tick count at which the specified delay will have expired and store it in a member variable. Thus:

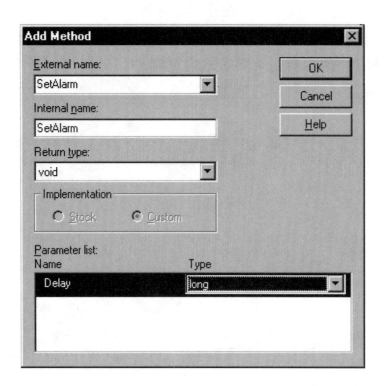

```
/*
This method is exposed to OLE Automation. Calculate and save expiration
time.
*/

void CTimerCtrl::SetAlarm(long Delay)
{
    m_Expiration = GetTickCount( ) + Delay * 1000 ;
}
```

12. To call a method from the test container, use the "Edit – Invoke Methods..." menu item. This will pop up a dialog box that reads the control's type library. It will show you all the methods the control contains along with their parameters. To invoke the method, enter values for the parameters and click the "Invoke" button. Thus:

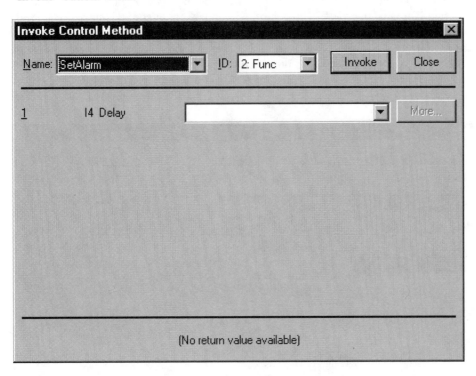

F. EVENTS

1. A control may use *events* to notify its container asynchronously of anything that takes place in the control that it thinks the container might care about. To receive notification of events, a container must create and expose an IDispatch interface. The control will obtain a pointer to this interface from the container and call its Invoke( ) method to signal the event, passing it the ID of the event and whatever parameters the event requires to describe it. You can think of an event as an OLE automation method call in the opposite direction. A container is free to process or ignore events it receives from its controls. A control adds events by using the "OLE Events" tab of Class Wizard. Thus:

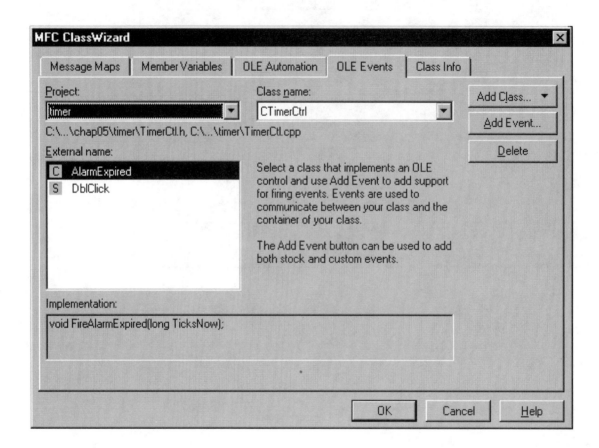

2. When you click "Add Event", Class Wizard will pop up a dialog box for you to enter the name of the event and its parameters. In this example, we define an event named "AlarmExpired", which passes a single LONG parameter named "TicksNow". Class Wizard will add a member function to our control class with the word "Fire" prepended to the name of the event, "FireAlarmExpired( )" in the example below. This code is added inline in the header file. When our control determines that the criteria for the event have been met, we call the appropriate Fire function. Thus:

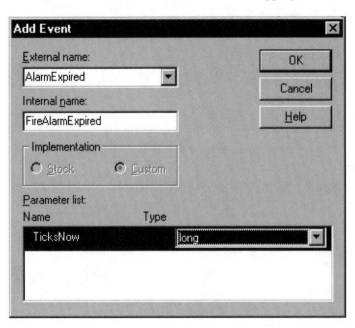

```
<file TimerCtrl.h>

/*
This function added inline to class definition header file.
*/
void FireAlarmExpired(long TicksNow)
{
    FireEvent(eventidAlarmExpired, EVENT_PARAM(VTS_I4), TicksNow);
}

<file TimerCtrl.cpp>

void CTimerCtrl::OnTimer(UINT nIDEvent)
{
    Invalidate ( ) ;
/*
If system time has passed alarm time, fire the event signaling the
container that the alarm has expired.
*/
    if (m_Expiration != 0 && m_Expiration <= GetTickCount( ))
    {
      FireAlarmExpired (m_Expiration) ;
      m_Expiration = 0 ;
    }
}
```

3. The control's .ODL file contains a second typeinfo to describe the events to be fired by the control. In the incoming dispinterface descriptions that we have seen so far in this book, the control has been saying, "When you invoke ID #1 to me, here's what I take it to mean." In the outgoing events dispinterface shown on this page, the control is saying, "When I invoke ID #1 to you, here's what I mean has happened." Class Wizard makes entries in this file to describe the events that you place in the control. Thus:

```
#include <olectl.h>

[ uuid(69999370-BD40-11CF-8A6C-00AA00A58097), version(1.0),
  helpstring("timer OLE Control module"), control ]
library TIMERLib
{
    importlib(STDOLE_TLB);
    importlib(STDTYPE_TLB);

    <primary timer IDispatch definition omitted>

    // Event dispatch interface for CTimerCtrl

    [ uuid(69999372-BD40-11CF-8A6C-00AA00A58097),
      helpstring("Event interface for Timer Control") ]
    dispinterface _DTimerEvents
    {
      properties:
            // Event interface has no properties

      methods:
            // NOTE - ClassWizard will maintain event information here.
            //     Use extreme caution when editing this section.
            //{{AFX_ODL_EVENT(CTimerCtrl)
            [id(DISPID_DBLCLICK)] void DblClick();
            [id(1)] void AlarmExpired(long TicksNow);
            //}}AFX_ODL_EVENT
    };

    // Class information for CTimerCtrl

    [ uuid(69999373-BD40-11CF-8A6C-00AA00A58097),
      helpstring("Timer Control"), control ]
    coclass Timer
    {
      [default] dispinterface _DTimer;
      [default, source] dispinterface _DTimerEvents;
    };


    //{{AFX_APPEND_ODL}}
};
```

4. The base class COleControl contains a number of stock events. These are events which are so commonly used that Microsoft has reserved their names, dispatch IDs, and parameters, similar to stock methods and stock properties. The stock events are:

Click	*// Button-up received with capture on and mouse over control.*
DblClick	*// Double-click received with capture on and mouse over control .*
Error	*// Error occurred OLE control.*
KeyDown	*// WM_SYSKEYDOWN or WM_KEYDOWN message received.*
KeyPress	*// WM_CHAR message received.*
KeyUp	*// WM_SYSKEYUP or WM_KEYUP message received.*
MouseDown	*// Any BUTTONDOWN received. Mouse captured just before event fired.*
MouseMove	*// WM_MOUSEMOVE message is received.*
MouseUp	*// Any BUTTONUP is received. Mouse capture is released before event is fired.*

To make your control signal a stock event, simply select the event in Class Wizard's "OLE Events" dialog box tab. Firing the event is handled by the base class in response to the Windows messages that it receives. For example, if you add a handler for the stock event "DblClick" as shown below, the base class will automatically fire it when it receives the WM_LBUTTONDBLCLK message. Thus:

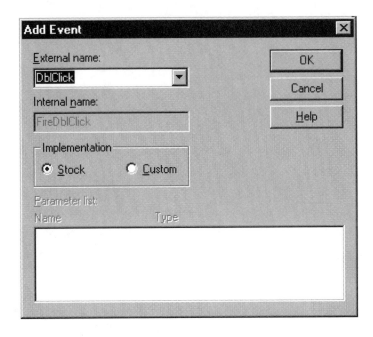

5. To view events from the test container, choose "Options – Event Log" from the main menu. This will show you a modeless dialog box in which events are reported as they occur. The event's parameters, if any, appear in the box as well. Thus:

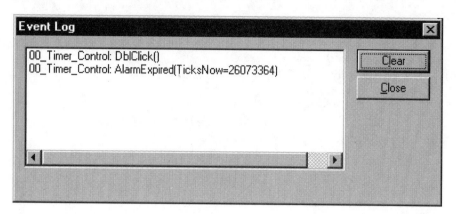

G. PROPERTY PAGES

1. The programmer who buys a control usually sets the control's properties in some kind of programming environment such as the dialog box editor or Visual Basic. While the programming environment can read the names and types of the control's properties and present them to the user in a contiguous list, a more friendly mechanism for presenting and receiving choices would be a big selling point. Imagine programming the edit control if you had to look up all the style flags and type in a single hex value combining them, instead of having a tabbed dialog box containing nice check boxes for each style flag.

A control can provide its own user interface for accessing its properties by supporting one or more *property pages*, which are the individual panes used in property sheets (tabbed dialog boxes). OLE provides a mechanism for a server such as our control to specify the property pages it supports, and for a client app such as a development environment to create a property sheet containing those property pages. The underlying mechanism is quite involved, see Brockschmidt, pp. 761-774.

By providing property pages, you can make your control much easier to program and therefore much more attractive to buyers. Even in this very simple example, providing a check box for the ShowSeconds property graphically illustrates its boolean nature. Controls with many different properties could group them logically.

The MFC provides support for OLE's property page mechanism via the class *COlePropertyPage*. If you look in the file "TimerPpg.h", you will find the ID of a dialog resource. This is the dialog template that is used for the specified property page. You may add controls to it in the dialog editor for the purpose of manipulating your control's properties. To pop up the property page in the test container, choose "Edit – Properties" from the main menu. After you add a single check box to the supplied dialog template, the test container will show you a property page that looks like this:

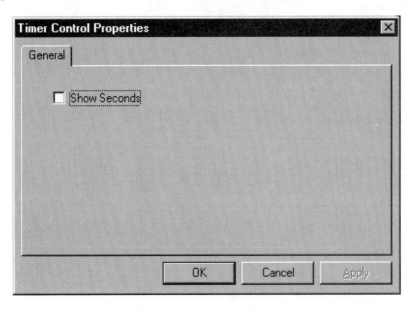

NOTE: By convention, property pages are only supposed to have one of two standard sizes, either 250 x 62 dialog box units or 250 x 100 dialog box units. If you make yours any other size, you run the risk that not all of your controls will be visible.

NOTE: Like the type library, the property page mechanism is useful only at programming time, not at runtime. To make controls smaller for better Internet support, I would expect that it will be removed from a runtime control in the future.

2. The property page is created by an external app via the IOleObject::DoVerb( ) method, which is automatically handled for you by the COleControl base class. As with a dialog box, the only thing you really care about on a property page is setting the initial state of its controls when it first comes up, and reading the final state of its controls if the user clicks OK. And as with a dialog box, this operation is so highly standardized that it has been automated with MFC support.

To connect an ActiveX property to a dialog control on a property page, use Class Wizard to add a member variable to the property page class in the same manner as you would for a dialog box. Enter the name of the OLE property in the "Optional OLE property name" control at the bottom of the box. When you do this, Class Wizard will add code to the property page's DoDataExchange( ) method that accesses the value of the specified property through the ActiveX control's OLE automation mechanism and either sets the dialog control to the property's value or vice versa. The data movement is accomplished with a function in the DDP_ family, as in the **DDP_Check( )** function in the example below. Thus:

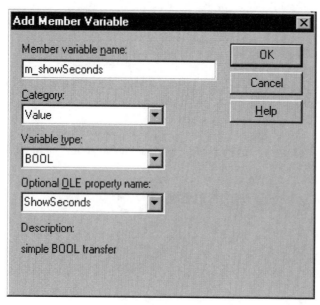

```
/*
Code added by Class Wizard.  Function DDP_Check( ) maps the value of the
property "ShowSeconds" to the member variable m_showSeconds and the
checkbox IDC_CHECK1.
*/

void CTimerPropPage::DoDataExchange(CDataExchange* pDX)
{
    //{{AFX_DATA_MAP(CTimerPropPage)
    DDP_Check(pDX, IDC_CHECK1, m_showSeconds, _T("ShowSeconds") );
    DDX_Check(pDX, IDC_CHECK1, m_showSeconds);
    //}}AFX_DATA_MAP
    DDP_PostProcessing(pDX);
}
```

3. Control Wizard generated a single property page for your control. If you want more, you may create them by using Class Wizard to derive a new class from the base class COlePropertyPage (not CPropertyPage, that is a bare dialog box class that has no connection to OLE). The MFC supplies stock property pages for specifying colors, fonts, and pictures, which you may also use.

Each property page is a separate OLE object with its own class ID, class factory, and registry entries. Your COleControl file will contain a section of property page IDs beginning with the macro **BEGIN_PROPPAGEIDS( )**. This macro specifies the control class and the number of property pages it contains. After this macro, you place one **PROPPAGEID( )** macro for each property page you want your control to support. Inside this macro, you place the class ID of the property page. In the example below, we add the MFC stock property page for colors, whose class ID is the constant **CLSID_CColorPropPage**. This causes the property sheet displayed by the test container to have two pages in it, as shown at the bottom of this page. Thus:

```
<file timerctl.cpp>

//////////////////////////////////////////////////////////////////////
/////
// Property pages

// TODO: Add property pages as needed.  Remember to increase the count!

BEGIN_PROPPAGEIDS(CTimerCtrl, 2)
    PROPPAGEID(CTimerPropPage::guid)
    PROPPAGEID(CLSID_CColorPropPage)
END_PROPPAGEIDS(CTimerCtrl)
```

They work thus:

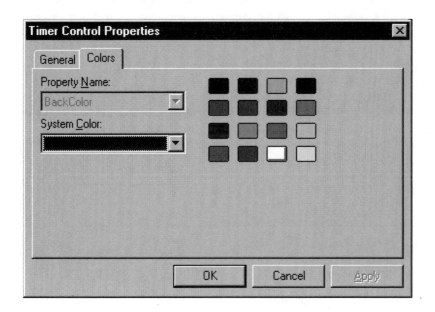

167

H. Ambient Properties

1. A container may choose to expose *ambient properties* to the control. These are standard properties that describe the environment in which a control resides. For example, the ambient background color is the background color of the form containing the control. The container exposes ambient properties via a second IDispatch interface. Connecting to and accessing the ambient IDispatch fortunately is handled by the COleControl base class. A control may get an ambient property's value but may not set it.

An ambient property is sort of like the button face color specified in the control panel – most apps use it for their buttons, but they don't have to if they don't want to, and there's no way to make them use it or even find out if they do or not. The supported ambient properties are:

    BackColor
    DisplayName
    Font
    ForeColor
    LocaleID
    ScaleUnits
    TextAlign
    UserMode
    UIDead
    DisplayHatching
    DisplayGrabHandles

All ambient properties have helper functions to make them available to the programmer, such as **COleControl::AmbientForeColor( )**, which gets the ambient foreground color. There is no conflict between ambient properties and stock or custom properties with the same name. They represent different properties of different objects and are accessed via different mechanisms.

Exactly what a control is supposed to do with an ambient property is still somewhat murky. For example, should a control set its background color to the container's ambient, or should it choose a contrasting color ? It depends on what the control is for. A text control probably wants to use this information to help it blend in. An alarm control probably wants to use this information to help it stand out. The one important rule is that if the programmer explicitly sets a control property that conflicts with the ambient, then the explicitly set property should govern.

The base class is notified of changes to ambient properties (which ought to be rare) via the method COleControl::OnAmbientChanged( ). The default implementation simply invalidates the control, which is fine for most purposes.

In the following example on the facing page, we use the ambient foreground color to draw the text of our control.

```
void CTimerCtrl::OnDraw(CDC* pdc, const CRect& rcBounds,
    const CRect& rcInvalid)
{

    <set up string as shown previously>
/*
Having subscribed to be notified of it, use the stock property
"BackColor" to draw the background of the control.
*/
    OLE_COLOR oc = GetBackColor ( ) ;
    COLORREF cr = TranslateColor (oc) ;

    CBrush BackBrush (cr) ;
    pdc->FillRect(rcBounds, &BackBrush);

    pdc->SetBkColor (cr) ;

/*
Use ambient foreground color for text.
*/

    oc = AmbientForeColor ( ) ;
    cr = TranslateColor (oc) ;

    pdc->SetTextColor (cr) ;

/*
Draw within bounding rectangle presented by framework.
*/
    pdc->DrawText (out, -1, (LPRECT)&rcBounds,
      DT_CENTER | DT_VCENTER | DT_SINGLELINE) ;
}
```

2. To set ambient properties in the test container, choose "Edit – Set Ambient Properties ..." from the menu. The container will pop up the following dialog box, which provides access to all ambient properties.

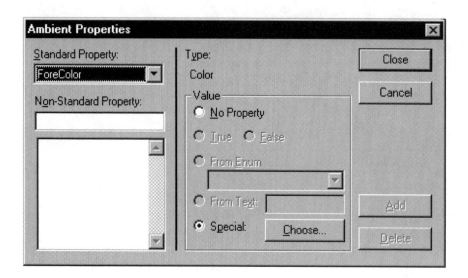

Lab Exercises
Chapter 5
ActiveX Controls

Directory: \chap05\timer

1. This lab starts from an empty directory. Pick "File — New" from the main menu, then pick "Project Workspace" from the dialog box. In the next dialog box, select "OLE Control Wizard". Pick all the default options from the resulting Control Wizard dialog boxes. Build the resulting control. Run the test container by picking "Tools — OLE Control Test Container" from the main menu. In the test container, pick "Edit — Insert OLE Control" from the main menu. Pick your newly built control from the resulting dialog box. You should see a fairly boring ellipse that doesn't do much. You now know that all of your control development tools are installed and working properly.

2. Next, we want to process timer messages. Bring up Class Wizard. In your COleControl-derived base class, add methods to handle the WM_CREATE, WM_DESTROY, and WM_TIMER methods. In the OnCreate( ) handler, start a timer with an interval of 1 second. In the OnDestroy( ) handler, destroy the timer. In the OnTimer( ) handler, simply invalidate your control's window to force a repaint. Modify your OnDraw( ) method to get the current time via the API function GetLocalTime( ) and draw it centered in your controls window via the method CDC::DrawText( ). Build your control and run it in the test container. You should see it ticking, but the background is transparent, which looks crummy.

3. Now add a stock property to your control. In Class Wizard, pick the "OLE Automation" tab, then click the "Add Property" button. If you click the drop-down list box in the "External Name" field, you will see the property "BackColor". Select it, note the values filled in for the other fields, and click OK. Click OK again to close Class Wizard. Examine your control's header file and .ODL to see the new entries made by Class Wizard. Modify your OnDraw( ) handler to call the function GetBackColor( ), the base class's access function for the stock property. Call TranslateColor( ) to translate it into an RGB value. Instantiate a CBrush of the same color and use it to fill paint the control's background area. Use the method CDC::SetBkColor( ) to set the background color of your timer's text to the specified value before drawing it. Build your control and run it in the test container. Pick "View — Properties" from the test container's main menu. Pick BackColor from the resulting dialog box and choose a value. Your timer's text background should change to the selected color. How did the test container know the property was there and what type it should be ?

4. Now add a custom property to your control. In Class Wizard, pick "Add Property" again. This time, type in your own name "ShowSeconds" for the name of the property. Set its type to BOOL. Modify your OnDraw( ) handler to use the value of this property to show or not show the seconds in the ticking timer. Set this property from the test container and watch your timer show and remove its seconds display.

5. Now we want to show a property page to allow access to our custom property. In your control's .RC file, you will find a dialog box entry whose ID contains the word "PROPPAGE". Open this and add a checkbox to it. Label the check box "Show Seconds". Then bring up Class Wizard and go to the "Member Variables" tab. Add a BOOL variable that binds to the checkbox. Place the "ShowSeconds" property name in the "Optional OLE property name" field. Build your control and run it in the test container. Pick "Edit — Embedded Object Functions — Properties" from the test container's main menu to show the property page.

6. Your control now has most of its features. What it does not have is a way to remember its properties from one session to another. In the method DoPropExchange( ), use the function PX_Bool to save and restore the ShowSeconds property. Build your control and place it in the container. Save its properties into a stream, delete the control, then create another control with using the stored set of properties, as explained on page 158.

171

7. Your control contains a bitmap which is used for display in the tool palettes of development environments such as VB. You will find that bitmap in your control's .RC file; it will be the only one. Edit the bitmap to something at least halfway recognizable. Build your control and run it in the test container. When you insert the control, you will see its bitmap appear on the test container's toolbar.

EXTRA CREDIT: Add a second property page to your control. Use the standard property page CLSID_CColorPropPage to manipulate the background color property of your control.

Chapter 6
ActiveX Control Containers

A. SUPPORTING CONTROLS IN YOUR CONTAINER

1. The MFC provided support in version 4.0 for containers of ActiveX controls. To add ActiveX control container support to your app, you must choose the "Ole Controls" box in step 3 of App Wizard. Thus:

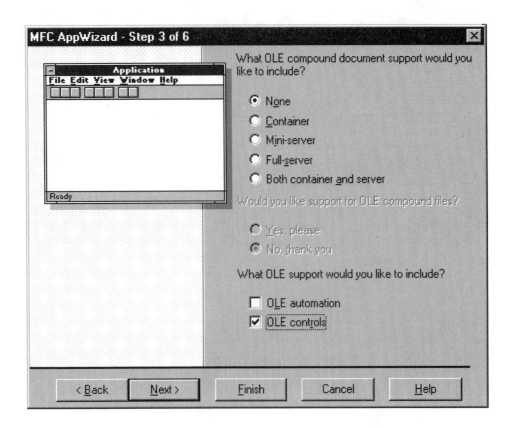

The sample code for this chapter can be found in the directory \chap06\timeruser. It is a container app that uses the timer control we created in Chapter 5. It is meant as a demonstration of what you can do to use controls that you know about at design time. It does not attempt to demonstrate what you have to do to access any arbitrary control, reading the type library and generating support on the fly, which is a problem at least an order of magnitude greater.

2. If you do not check the box when you are generating the project and want to add ActiveX control support after the fact, you must add the include file "**afxdisp.h**" to your stdafx.h file, and call the function **AfxEnableControlContainer( )** from your app's CWinApp::InitInstance( ). Thus:

```
< stdafx.h file>

// stdafx.h : include file for standard system include files,
//   or project specific include files that are used frequently, but
//       are changed infrequently
//

#define VC_EXTRALEAN            // Exclude rarely used stuff

#include <afxwin.h>          // MFC core and standard components
#include <afxext.h>          // MFC extensions
#include <afxdisp.h>         // MFC OLE automation classes
#ifndef _AFX_NO_AFXCMN_SUPPORT
#include <afxcmn.h>          // MFC support for Windows 95 Common Controls
#endif // _AFX_NO_AFXCMN_SUPPORT


< file containing CWinApp-derived class>

BOOL CTimerUserApp::InitInstance()
{
    AfxEnableControlContainer();

    <rest of InitInstance>

    return TRUE ;
}
```

B. Control Container Architecture

1. ActiveX control containment is built into the CWnd class in a rather cool transparent way. Each control that your container app uses is wrapped by a proxy class derived from CWnd. The creation of this class can be done in several different ways, as discussed on pages 185 and 191. You manipulate the window aspects of the control by calling the CWnd base class methods as for any other CWnd. For example, to move the control, you would call the proxy class's CWnd::MoveWindow( ).

The actual connection of the CWnd methods to the control is provided by the barely documented class *COleControlSite*. Each control proxy CWnd contains a member variable called **m_pCtrlSite**, which is a pointer to an object of this class. For a standard CWnd which is not a control proxy, this value will be NULL. Thus:

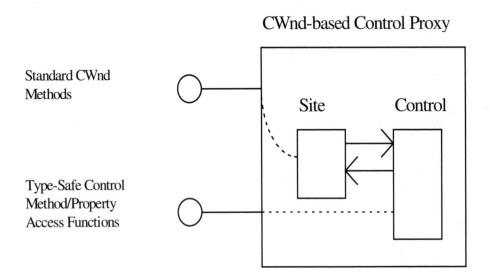

2. When you call a method such as CWnd::MoveWindow( ), the framework checks this member variable. If it is NULL, then the CWnd is a standard non-ActiveX CWnd, in which case the framework simply calls the API function MoveWindow( ) as before. If this member is not NULL, then the CWnd is a wrapper for an ActiveX control. In this case, the framework calls the COleControlSite::MoveWindow( ), which negotiates with the ActiveX control to move and resize its window. A pseudo-code listing would look somewhat like this:

```
void CWnd::MoveWindow(int x, int y, int nWidth, int nHeight,
    BOOL bRepaint)
{

/*
If this member variable is NULL, then this CWnd is a regular old common-
garden-variety CWnd, not a proxy wrapper for a control.  Execute the
standard call to MoveWindow( ).
*/

    if (m_pCtrlSite == NULL)
    {
       ::MoveWindow(m_hWnd, x, y, nWidth, nHeight, bRepaint);
    }

/*
Otherwise, this CWnd is a wrapper for a control.  Delegate the call to
the COleControlSite's MoveWindow( ) method.
*/

    else
    {
      m_pCtrlSite->MoveWindow(x, y, nWidth, nHeight, bRepaint);
    }
}
```

3. The COleControlSite class is not well documented. Perhaps the developers of VC++ thought that you should never have to touch it directly, as all negotiation with it should have been handled at the CWnd level. Its code is found in the file "OCCSITE.CPP". The method COleControlSite::MoveWindow( ) uses the IOleObject and IOleInPlaceObject interfaces to negotiate the placement of the control's window on the container's window. A pseudo-code listing would look somewhat like this:

```
void COleControlSite::MoveWindow(int x, int y, int nWidth, int nHeight,
    BOOL)
{

/*
Set the proxy's location and size to that specified by the caller.
*/

    CRect rectOld(m_rect);
    m_rect.SetRect(x, y, x + nWidth, y + nHeight);

/*
Call the control's IOleObject::SetExtent( ) method, telling the embedded
control object how big its container wants it to be.
*/

    if (SetExtent())
    {

/*
If      that      was      successful,      call      the      control's
IOleInPlaceObject::SetObjectRects( ) method, telling the control object
how much space it is allowed to have in the in-place container's window.
*/

        m_rect.SetRect(x, y, x + m_rect.Width(), y + m_rect.Height());
        m_pInPlaceObject->SetObjectRects(m_rect, NULL);
    }
    else
    {
      m_rect = rectOld;
    }
}
```

This page intentionally contains no text other than this sentence.

C. ActiveX Controls in Dialog Boxes

1. One of the primary uses of any type of control is to communicate with the user in a dialog box. The VC++ dialog editor contains extensive support for ActiveX controls, making it quite easy for you to employ them in this manner.

To add an ActiveX control to a dialog box, open the desired dialog box template in the dialog editor. Then click the right mouse button on the dialog box and select "Insert OLE Control ..." from the context menu. You will see a dialog box containing all the ActiveX controls currently registered on your system. Select the one that you want, in this case the timer control that we built in the previous chapter. Thus:

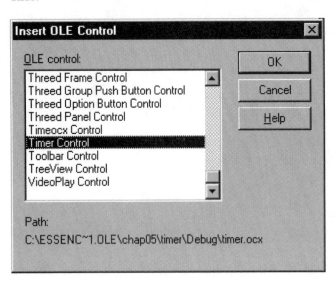

2. When you select a control, the dialog editor will create an instance of it and place it on your template. The control will not be active at this point, so you will not see the timer ticking. The appearance of the control that you see on the screen is the presentation format discussed in the previous chapter, a metafile supplied by your control. Thus:

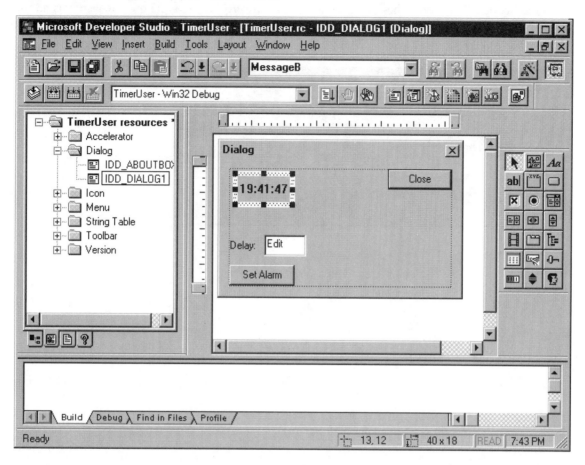

NOTE: If you want to see your control activated, select "Layout — Test" from the main menu. A test dialog box will appear containing another instance of your control which will be ticking.

3. You will probably want to set most, if not all, of the control's properties in the dialog editor. The editor is smart enough to access the control's property pages that we built in the previous chapter. You bring up the "Properties" dialog box in the same manner as for any other control — either double click on the timer control, or right click on the timer control and select "Properties" from the context menu.

The dialog editor creates the "General" and "All" property pages on its own. It then gets all the property pages from the control and places them in the middle. In this example, the "Control" and "Colors" tabs were supplied by the control itself as shown in the previous chapter. Thus:

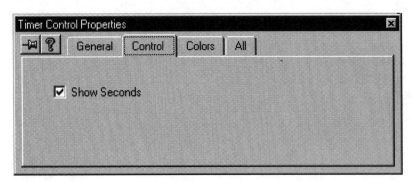

4. The template of a dialog box containing ActiveX controls is similar to any other dialog template. If you examine your app's .RC file, you will see that the template uses the **CONTROL** statement to generate an ActiveX control, with the control's class ID in place of the registered window class. Thus:

```
IDD_DIALOG1 DIALOG DISCARDABLE  0, 0, 186, 95
STYLE DS_MODALFRAME | WS_POPUP | WS_CAPTION | WS_SYSMENU
CAPTION "Dialog"
FONT 8, "MS Sans Serif"
BEGIN
    DEFPUSHBUTTON     "Close",IDOK,129,7,50,14
    EDITTEXT          IDC_EDIT1,33,52,33,16,ES_AUTOHSCROLL
    PUSHBUTTON        "Set Alarm",IDC_SETALARM,7,74,50,14
    LTEXT             "Delay:",IDC_STATIC,7,56,21,8
    CONTROL           "",IDC_TIMERCTRL1,
                      "{69999373-BD40-11CF-8A6C-00AA00A58097}",
                      WS_TABSTOP,13,12,40,18
END
```

5. The dialog editor also stores the control's properties in the .RC file in a resource type called **DLGINIT**. When the editor saves the template, it creates a stream and goes through the OLE functions that eventually connect to your control's DoPropExchange( ) method, causing your control to write its properties into the stream. The dialog editor then takes the contents of the stream and writes them into the .RC file as shown below. At runtime, when the dialog pops up and the control is created, the dialog box generator will read the DLGINIT resource into a stream and present it to the control in the DoPropExchange( ) method, thereby causing your control to read the property values set by the programmer. Thus:

```
IDD_DIALOG1 DLGINIT
BEGIN
    IDC_TIMERCTRL1, 0x376, 25, 0
0x0000, 0x0000, 0x0000, 0x0001, 0x0634, 0x0000, 0x02ff, 0x0000, 0x0001,
0x0000, 0xc0c0, 0x00c0, "\315"
    0
END
```

6. If all the dialog box ever needs to do with the control is to show it to the user with the properties set at design time, you don't have to do anything else. However, for most controls, you will probably want to access their properties and methods at runtime or respond to their events. To make this happen, you have to generate the proxy wrapper class for that control referred to on page 177. Bring up Class Wizard and select the "Member Variables" tab. In the "Control IDs" list, select your ActiveX control, then click "Add Variable...". Thus:

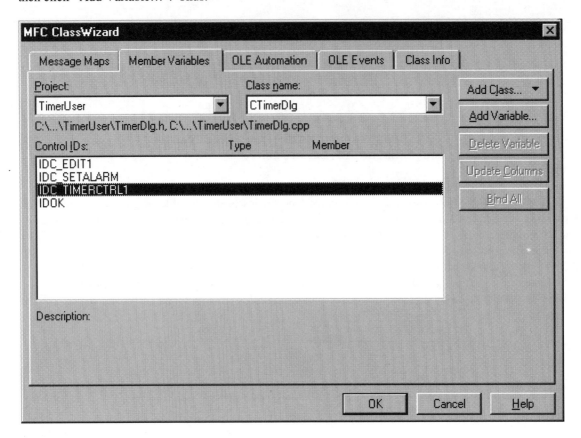

7. When you attempt to add the member variable for the ActiveX control, Class Wizard will automatically detect that this control does not have a wrapper class available, and so will generate one for you. You will see the following dialog box. Select OK and Class Wizard will read your app's type library and generate the proxy class shown on the next page. Thus:

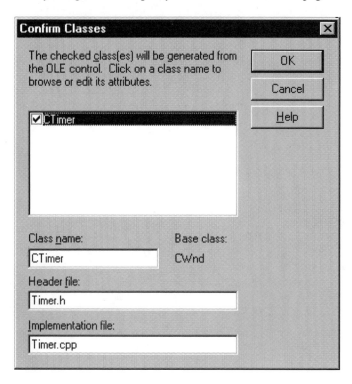

8. When you generate the proxy wrapper class, Class Wizard reads the control's type library and generates type-safe access functions for the properties and methods in the control, in a manner similar to generating an OLE automation controller class as shown in Chapter 4. The wrapper class's header file looks like this:

```
class CTimer : public CWnd
{
protected:
    DECLARE_DYNCREATE(CTimer)
/*
Type-safe access functions for control's properties.
*/

public:
    BOOL GetShowSeconds();
    void SetShowSeconds(BOOL);
    OLE_COLOR GetBackColor();
    void SetBackColor(OLE_COLOR);

/*
Type-safe access functions for control's methods.
*/

public:
    void SetAlarm(long Delay);
    void AboutBox();

/*
Creation methods for this control. Not used in a dialog box, but used in
the nondialog case dealt with on page 191.
*/

public:
    CLSID const& GetClsid()
    {
      static CLSID const clsid = { 0x69999373, 0xbd40, 0x11cf,
            { 0x8a, 0x6c, 0x0, 0xaa, 0x0, 0xa5, 0x80, 0x97 } };
            return clsid;
    }
    virtual BOOL Create(LPCTSTR lpszClassName,
      LPCTSTR lpszWindowName, DWORD dwStyle, const RECT& rect,
      CWnd* pParentWnd, UINT nID, CCreateContext* pContext = NULL)
    { return CreateControl(GetClsid(), lpszWindowName, dwStyle, rect,
            pParentWnd, nID); }

    BOOL Create(LPCTSTR lpszWindowName, DWORD dwStyle, const RECT& rect,
      CWnd* pParentWnd, UINT nID, CFile* pPersist = NULL,
      BOOL bStorage = FALSE, BSTR bstrLicKey = NULL)
    { return CreateControl(GetClsid(), lpszWindowName, dwStyle, rect,
      pParentWnd, nID, pPersist, bStorage, bstrLicKey); }
};
```

9. The wrapper class's member functions that provide access to the control's methods and properties will look similar to those you saw in Chapter 4. The member function which provides the SetAlarm( ) method looks like this:

```
void CTimer::SetAlarm(long Delay)
{
    static BYTE parms[] =
      VTS_I4;
    InvokeHelper(0x2, DISPATCH_METHOD, VT_EMPTY, NULL, parms,
      Delay);
}
```

You use the wrapper class member variables and functions just like you did in Chapter 4. When the user clicks the "Set Alarm" button, we read the requested delay from the edit control and access the wrapper class's "SetAlarm" method. Thus:

```
/*
User clicked the "Set Alarm" button. Use type-safe member function of
wrapper class to access that method on the control.
*/

void CTimerDlg::OnSetalarm()
{
    UINT DelaySeconds = GetDlgItemInt(IDC_EDIT1) ;
    m_Timer.SetAlarm (DelaySeconds) ;
}
```

10. Responding to events is even easier. Simply select the "Message Map" tab of Class Wizard and select the ID corresponding to the ActiveX control. When you generated the wrapper class and added the member variable, Class Wizard read the control's type library, specifically the event typeinfo discussed in the previous chapter, and found the names and parameters of all the events that it supports. The events' names will appear in the "Messages" list box. Simply select the desired event and add a handler function as for any other message. Thus:

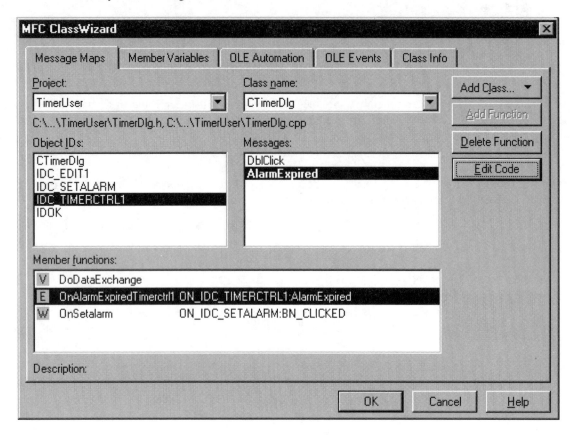

188

11. As you recall from Chapter 5, the container handles events by exposing an IDispatch interface which the control calls. All the heavy lifting is done for you by the MFC. When you add an event response to your dialog class, Class Wizard will add an event sink map to the dialog class that contains the control. This will look exactly like a dispatch map because it is exactly like a dispatch map. It connects your handler function to the generic IDispatch implementation provided by the container and called by the control. Thus:

```
BEGIN_EVENTSINK_MAP(CTimerDlg, CDialog)
    //{{AFX_EVENTSINK_MAP(CTimerDlg)
    ON_EVENT(CTimerDlg, IDC_TIMERCTRL1, 1, OnAlarmExpiredTimerctrl1,
        VTS_I4)
    //}}AFX_EVENTSINK_MAP
END_EVENTSINK_MAP()

/*
SetAlarm event has been signaled.  Beep to alert user and dismiss the
dialog box.
*/

void CTimerDlg::OnAlarmExpiredTimerctrl1(long TicksNow)
{
    MessageBeep(0) ;
    OnCancel ( ) ;
}
```

D. ACTIVEX CONTROLS ON STANDARD WINDOWS

1. The dialog editor has very nice support for ActiveX controls, but suppose you want to use them outside of a dialog box, for example on a view. The easiest way is to use a CFormView, because then you get the dialog editor back again. But suppose you want to create and destroy the controls dynamically. What do you do?

2. The first thing you need to do is to generate the control's proxy wrapper class if this hasn't been done already. You do this via VC++'s Component Gallery, accessed via the "Insert — Component" menu item. If you select the "OLE Controls" tab, you will see a list of all the registered controls on your system along with their toolbar icons, as shown below. Click "Insert" to generate the wrapper class and add it to your project. The wrapper class for the timer control, called CTimer, was generated earlier in this chapter and may be found on page 187.

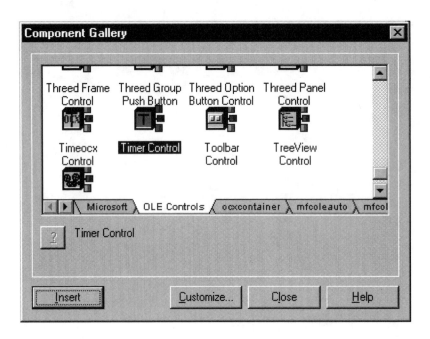

3. In the TimerUser example program, we add to our view a member variable which points to an object of class CTimer. Thus:

```
class CTimerUserView : public CView
{
protected: // create from serialization only
    CTimerUserView();
    DECLARE_DYNCREATE(CTimerUserView)

    CTimer *m_pTimer ;

    <rest of view class declaration>
} ;
```

4. When the user picks "Control Test — Add to View" from our app's menu, we need to instantiate a CTimer and call its Create( ) method. This is identical to the process used for creating a new child window. Thus:

```
void CTimerUserView::OnControltestAddtoview()
{

/*
Instantiate new CTimer proxy object.
*/
    m_pTimer = new CTimer ( ) ;

/*
Call CTimer::Create( ), which does the actual creation of the proxy
window and its control.
*/
    RECT r = {10, 10, 100, 50} ;

    m_pTimer->Create ("",                        // text
      WS_CHILD | WS_VISIBLE | WS_BORDER,         // style
      r,                                         // window rectangle
      this,                                      // parent CWnd
      1) ;                                       // child window ID
}
```

5. When the user picks "Control Test — Remove from View" from our sample app's menu, we destroy the control by calling its DestroyWindow( ) method. We then destroy the proxy object that wraps it and NULL out the pointer to it. Thus:

```
void CTimerUserView::OnControltestRemovefromview()
{
    m_pTimer->DestroyWindow ( ) ;
    delete m_pTimer ;
    m_pTimer = NULL ;
}
```

6. You access the control's properties and methods simply by calling the type-safe access functions provided in the wrapper class. In the following example, the "Control Test — Show Seconds" menu item is connected to the "ShowSeconds" property. The "Control Test — Wait 5 Seconds" menu item is connected to the SetAlarm( ) method. Thus:

```
/*
User picked "Show Seconds" menu item. Use proxy's access function to
find current setting of this property.  Then if it's on, turn it off and
vice versa.
*/

void CTimerUserView::OnControltestShowsecondsproperty()
{
    if (m_pTimer->GetShowSeconds( ) == TRUE)
    {
      m_pTimer->SetShowSeconds (FALSE) ;
    }
    else
    {
      m_pTimer->SetShowSeconds (TRUE) ;
    }
}


/*
User picked "Wait 5 Seconds" menu item.  Use proxy's access function to
call the SetAlarm( ) method. This function returns immediately.  The
control signals expiration of the alarm by means of an event as shown on
the facing page.
*/

void CTimerUserView::OnControltestWait5seconds()
{
    m_pTimer->SetAlarm (5) ;
}
```

7. Connecting to the events of a control is a little trickier. Remembering back to the dialog box, Class Wizard added an event sink map to the CDialog class when we added a handler function for the first event. You can't make Class Wizard do this for a view, but you can do it in a dummy dialog box and transfer everything by hand. This isn't as hard as it sounds, really about a two-minute job. You add the declaration of your event handler function and the macro **DECLARE_EVENTSINK_MAP( )** to your view's header file. Thus:

```
<file TimerUserView.h>

class CTimerUserView : public CView
{
    < rest of view declaration >

    afx_msg void OnAlarmExpiredTimerctrl1(long TicksNow) ;
    DECLARE_EVENTSINK_MAP()

};
```

You then add the macros **BEGIN_EVENTSINK_MAP( )** and **END_EVENTSINK_MAP( ) to** your view's implementation file. Between them, you place an **ON_EVENT( )** macro for each event that you want to handle. Finally, you add the actual handler function to the header file and implementation as shown here. While this sounds hard, it isn't really. Just create a dummy dialog box, add the control to it and use Class Wizard to add handlers for the events. Then just cut from the dialog box class and paste into the view class. Sounds kludgey and it is, but it's very quick and that makes you money.

```
<file TimerUserView.cpp>

BEGIN_EVENTSINK_MAP(CTimerUserView, CView)
    //{{AFX_EVENTSINK_MAP(CTimerDlg)
    ON_EVENT(CTimerUserView, 1, 1, OnAlarmExpiredTimerctrl1, VTS_I4)
    //}}AFX_EVENTSINK_MAP
END_EVENTSINK_MAP()

void CTimerUserView::OnAlarmExpiredTimerctrl1(long TicksNow)
{
    MessageBeep (0) ;
}
```

E. AMBIENT PROPERTIES

1. The container exposes ambient properties by means of an IDispatch interface. The undocumented MFC base class *COleControlContainer*, contained inside CWnd, takes care of creating the IDispatch and connecting a default set of ambient properties to it. The ambient properties exposed by an MFC container are:

Appearance	1 if 3d controls enabled, 0 otherwise
AutoClip	TRUE
BackColor:	background color returned in DC by WM_CTLCOLORSTATIC
DisplayAsDefault	TRUE if button is default, FALSE otherwise
ForeColor	foreground color returned in DC by WM_CTLCOLORSTATIC
Font	result of CWnd::GetFont( )
LocaleID	result of API function GetThreadLocale( )
Message Reflect	TRUE
Scale Units:	pixels
ShowGrabHandle	FALSE
ShowHatching	FALSE
Supports Mnemonics	TRUE
UI Dead	FALSE
User Mode	TRUE

If for some reason you need to change the ambient properties, you can override the method COleControlContainer::GetAmbientProp( ), which you can find in the file OCCCONT.CPP. It's deeply buried and modifications to it are likely to be bloody, but if you can't live without it, that's where to start.

This page intentionally contains no text other than this sentence.

F. Licensing of Controls

1. Controls represent the main product of control developers, who naturally want to be protected against unauthorized use to the extent technically feasible. Remember the three-tier structure in the control business. You build a control and sell it to a programmer. The programmer takes your control, builds it into his apps, and sells them to end users. The programmer has to ship your control DLL with his app in order for the latter to run on the end users' machines. What you don't want is for the end users to take your control and start building it into their own apps without paying for it. You want some way of allowing the control to run in an end user app while blocking it from being used by a development environment.

The ActiveX control spec provides support for a low level of this capability through the *licensing* of controls. In practice, the security provided isn't very tight, and I find the hype over it to be vastly inflated. I discuss it in this book only for the purpose of completeness. It's potentially useful as a reminder for users who download trial versions of your control from the Internet to pay their licensing fees. It isn't protection against a determined assault and can't easily be turned into such. In practice, most controls sell for a few hundred bucks or less. All you need from a licensing scheme is to make it cost more than that for someone to pirate your control. The way licensing works is as follows:

A. You build your ActiveX control with licensing support as shown on the next page. This means that whenever a control of this type is created, the control checks for a *key*, some combination of characters that you specify when you develop the control. If the control does not find the required key, its class factory will refuse to hand over a pointer to it.

B. The key can be supplied to the control in one of two ways. When your customer the programmer buys the control, he gets the control and also a *license file* containing the key. When he inserts the control into the app he is building, the control finds the license file, checks that the key contained therein matches its own internal setting, knows that it is legal to run, and so comes up fully functional.

C. When the programmer compiles his app, his development environment asks the control for the key, which it binds into the app's .EXE file. The programmer ships his app to the end user, including your control DLL but not the license file. When the end user starts the app, the app creates the control using the key that the programmer bound into the app. The control comes up and runs fine. If the end user tries to use your control in VB or VC++, his new app will have neither the key nor the license file, so the control will refuse to allow itself to be created.

2. What protects you against the end user reverse engineering the app and finding the key? Only that the time it takes costs more than buying it legally, and the customer wouldn't get any upgrades (hah!) or support (hah! hah!). What protects you against your customer shipping the license file to the end user or posting it anonymously on the Internet? Nothing at all. I told you this scheme wasn't very secure. It doesn't buy you any more, and possibly less, than creating two versions of the control, one with development support such as property pages and type libraries and one without. The runtime version of the control could be freely distributed. The developer version could contain a serial number so that if one got loose, you'd know who let it go.

3. This section refers to a sample licensed control which you will find in the directory \chap06\lic. It doesn't do anything except draw an ellipse on the screen so you know it's there. If the control finds a satisfactory license on creation, it simply allows itself to be created. If it does not, it allows creation anyway but shows the user a nagging dialog box to encourage him to pay the license fee. This way, if an end user likes your control enough to want to program with it, he can go ahead and try it right away, which might generate more sales. Also, if for some reason a bug appears in the licensing code or the key embedded in the container app gets damaged, the end user isn't completely out of action and you are less likely to be threatened with dismemberment.

4. You create a control with licensing support by clicking the appropriate box in Control Wizard. Thus:

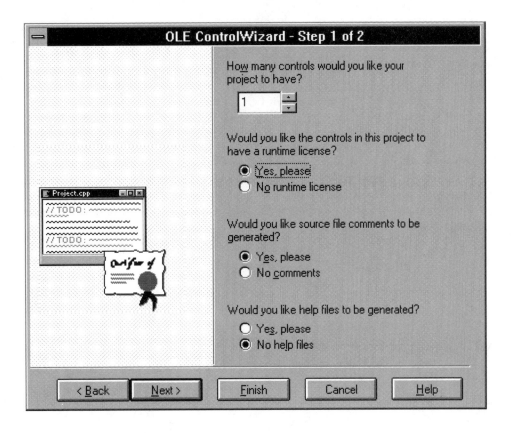

5. At the lowest level, licensing support is provided by the interface *IClassFactory2*, which is similar to IClassFactory except that it adds three additional methods to support licensing. This interface is supplied in the MFC by the class COleObjectFactory. Its additional methods are:

IClassFactory2::RequestLicKey( )   *// get lic key from control to embed in compiled app*
IClassFactory2::GetLicInfo( )   *// get lots of licensing information*
IClassFactory2::CreateInstanceLic( )   *// create object, checking license key*

When you build the control, App Wizard internally generates a *license key*, a combination of characters that the container provides to the control so that the latter can verify that it is being created by an authorized licensee. At design time, this key is provided in a *license file* supplied by the control vendor. When you are writing a container app and create an instance of a control, your development tool does so by calling the **IClassFactory2::CreateInstanceLic( )** method, passing a license key of NULL. The control will then check for the existence of the licensing file that contains the specified key. If the control fails to find this license file or fails to find the required contents within it, the control will refuse to be created. Thus:

Design Time: Creating Control

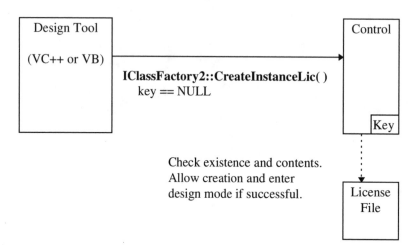

198

6. The base class COleObjectFactory implements IClassFactory2 in the MFC. The default COleObjectFactory ignores any licensing issues and simply creates the control. When you check the box in App Wizard to request licensing support in your control, this class's methods VerifyUserLicense( ) and GetLicenseKey( ) are overridden and default implementations of them to your control source file. The name of the licensing file and the text of the licensing string are generated and hardwired into your code as shown below.

When a caller attempts to create an instance of your control without passing the proper key, the method **COleObjectFactory::VerifyUserLicense( )** is called from within the internal IClassFactory2::CreateInstanceLic( ). You place here whatever verification code you want, returning TRUE if your conditions are satisfied, thereby allowing the creation to proceed, or FALSE if they aren't, thereby causing the creation to fail. In the example shown below, creation is always allowed, but unlicensed users are shown a nagging dialog box to encourage them to pay their license fees. The MFC function **AfxVerifyLicFile( )** checks that the license file with the hardwired name exists and contains the hardwired string. Thus:

```
/*
Name of license file.
*/

static const TCHAR BASED_CODE _szLicFileName[] = _T("lic.lic");

/*
Required license string, either from license file or from container app.
*/

static const WCHAR BASED_CODE _szLicString[] =
    L"Copyright (c) 1996 Rolling Thunder Computing";

/*
This function is called by the class factory if the container attempts
to create the control without passing the specified license string.
*/

BOOL CLicCtrl::CLicCtrlFactory::VerifyUserLicense()
{
/*
Use MFC function to verify that license file exists and contains the
required string.  If not, then show a nagging dialog box but allow
creation anyway.
*/
    if (!AfxVerifyLicFile(AfxGetInstanceHandle(), _szLicFileName,
      _szLicString))
    {
      CNagDlg dlg ;
      dlg.DoModal ( ) ;
    }
    return TRUE ;
}
```

7. By using the license file, the developer is able to create the control on his machine and embed it in an app that he's building, but we don't want him to ship the license file with the app. That would allow the end users to use our expensive control to develop apps of their own, rather than simply running the control in apps purchased from licensed developers. Somehow the control needs to be able to verify its license from information supplied by the container app, rather than needing the license file. To accomplish this, the design tool has to get the license key from the control at design time and embed it within the container app's own file. It does this by calling the method IClassFactory2::RequestLicKey( ) . Thus:

Design Time: Saving New App

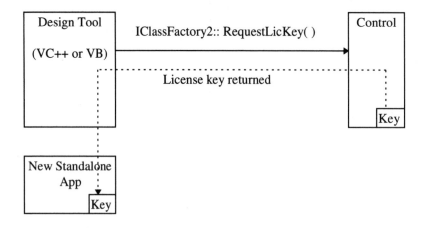

8. In the MFC, this functionality is obtained by calling the method **COleObjectFactory::GetLicenseKey( )**, which returns the license string in the form of a BSTR. The development environment must call this method when we embed a control in a dialog box or a VB form. The default implementation provided by the MFC simply hands over the hardwired license key string. In the case of a dialog box control, this is stored in the container app's .RC file and bound into the compiled app as a resource. Thus:

```
/*
This method is called by the dialog box editor when an ActiveX control
is placed in the dialog box.  Return the hard wired license string in
the form of a BSTR.
*/
```

```
BOOL CLicCtrl::CLicCtrlFactory::GetLicenseKey(DWORD dwReserved,
    BSTR FAR* pbstrKey)
{
    if (pbstrKey == NULL)
      return FALSE;

    *pbstrKey = SysAllocString(_szLicString);
    return (*pbstrKey != NULL);
}
```

```
<.RC file>

IDD_DIALOG1 DLGINIT
BEGIN
    IDC_LICOCXCTRL1, 0x376, 108, 0
0x002c, 0x0000, 0x0043, 0x006f, 0x0070, 0x0079, 0x0072, 0x0069, 0x0067,  // Copyrig
0x0068, 0x0074, 0x0020, 0x0028, 0x0063, 0x0029, 0x0020, 0x0031, 0x0039,  //ht (c) 19
0x0039, 0x0035, 0x0020, 0x0052, 0x006f, 0x006c, 0x006c, 0x0069, 0x006e,  //95 Rollin
0x0067, 0x0020, 0x0054, 0x0068, 0x0075, 0x006e, 0x0064, 0x0065, 0x0072,  //g Thunder
0x0020, 0x0043, 0x006f, 0x006d, 0x0070, 0x0075, 0x0074, 0x0069, 0x006e , //Computin
0x0067, 0x0000, 0x0001, 0x0634, 0x0000, 0x02ff, 0x0000, 0x0000, 0x0000,  //g
    0
END
```

9. When the finished container app wants to create a control at run time, it reads the control's license key from wherever it was stored when the app was compiled (the app's internal resources in the preceding example). The container then calls **CWnd::CreateControl( )** specifying the key in the form of a BSTR, which eventually passes the key to method IClassFactory2::CreateInstanceLic( ). Thus:

```
WCHAR key [256] ;
CLSID clsid ;

< read clsid and key from app's file>

BSTR bstrKey = SysAllocString (key) ;

CWnd NewWnd ;      CRect r ;

r.SetRect (100,0,200,50) ;

NewWnd.CreateControl ( clsid,      // class ID of control to create
    "",                           // control's text
    WS_CHILD | WS_VISIBLE,        // window style
      r,                          // window rectangle
      this,                       // parent
      2,                          // child ID
      NULL,                       // persistent state
      FALSE,                      // default
      bstrKey) ;                  // license key

SysFreeString (bstrKey) ;
```

202

Run Time: Creating Control

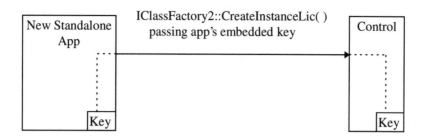

Compare key supplied by app with
control's embedded key. Allow run-
mode creation if successful.

NOTE: There are many wrapper functions in common use that query for the IClassFactory interface
which does not support licensing, rather than the IClassFactory2 interface which does. Examples of such
functions are CoCreateInstance( ) and OleLoad( ). If you care about backwards compatibility with these
widely used functions, you will not be able to use licensing for the components on which you want them
to operate.

Lab Exercises
Chapter 6
ActiveX Control Containers

Directory: \chap06\timeruser

1. As with the other MFC labs, this one also starts from an empty root directory. From the main menu of VC++ v4.0, pick "File — New". From the resulting dialog box, pick "Project Workspace", then select "MFC App Wizard .EXE". Continue with your App Wizard selections, picking "Multiple Documents" in step 1. In step 3, check the "OLE Controls" box. Select default options for all other settings. Build and run your app.

2. Start by adding a timer control from the previous lab to your container app's "About" dialog box. Open the dialog box in the resource editor, then click the right mouse button. From the resulting popup menu, pick "Insert OLE Control...". From the resulting dialog box, pick the timer control you created in the previous example, or the completed version of it in the \done directory. Choose "Layout -- Test" from the resource editor's menu. The dialog box will come up with your timer ticking away merrily inside it. Dismiss the test box.

3. In the resource editor, double-click on your timer control. You will see the property page(s) supported by the control, wrapped up between two different tabs supplied by the dialog box editor. Set the properties of the timer control to your satisfaction. Build and run your app, and try the dialog box. Note that the properties of the control are those that you set.

4. Now we want to use an ActiveX control as a regular window. To do this, we need to import it with a wrapper class. Select "Insert — Component" from VC++'s main menu. Pick the "OLE Controls" tab from the Component Gallery dialog box. Find your control and double-click it. Choose OK when the "Confirm Classes" dialog box come up. Note that new header and code files have been added for the generated class.

5. Add a member variable of the new ActiveX wrapper class to your app's CView-derived class. Using Class Wizard, process the WM_CREATE message in the view. In your OnCreate( ) handler, call the control's Create( ) method to create the control as a child of the view.

6. Now we want to use the methods and events of the control. Go to Class Wizard and select the "Member Variables" tab and your CAboutDlg class. Select the control ID for your timer control and pick "Add Variable". The resource editor will automatically add a variable of the wrapper class that has been generated for timer control. Add a button to your dialog box that calls the timer's SetAlarm( ) method with a delay of 5 seconds.

7. Go the "Message Maps" tab of Class Wizard, and in the "Object IDs" field, select the ID of your timer control. In the "Messages:" list, you will find the "AlarmExpired" event for it. Add a handler for this event popping up a simple message box. Build and run your app.

EXTRA CREDIT: Figure out a way to drag an ActiveX control around on a view. It's harder than it looks, because the control gets the mouse clicks rather than the CView that contains it.

Chapter 7

Structured Storage
Persistent Objects

A. CONCEPTS AND DEFINITIONS

1.   *Structured storage* is a storage architecture whereby logical divisions <u>within</u> a file can be created and used in a hierarchical manner, similar to the way in which the operating system distributes files among noncontiguous sectors of a disk while presenting a contiguous stream interface to the programmer. Structured storage provides the same tools for organizing the internal contents of your file that the operating system provides for organizing files on your disk, thereby making your life easier.

2. A *storage* is a division within a file analogous to a directory or subdirectory. A storage may contain any number of streams or substorages. A *stream* is a logically sequential block of data within a storage, analogous to a file. Each storage and stream has a name of up to 31 characters.

3. If an app uses structured storage for its files, then any other app has the potential of exploring the internal structure of those files. For example, Microsoft is encouraging apps to place in their data files a stream with the name "\005SummaryInformation", which is to contain a property set providing such information as a document's title, author, and list of keywords. Third-party browsers and the Windows 95 Explorer are able to open the file, read this stream, and present the information to the user without having to launch the app that created the file. You can examine the contents of any structured storage file by using the DocFile Viewer app DFVIEW.EXE that comes with your development environment.

4. Storages and streams may also be used for transferring data from one process to another, as OLE knows how to marshal them across process boundaries. This facility is used extensively in embedding and linking, where each embedded or linked object resides within its own storage in the container's document file. When transferring data via the IDataObject interface, the medium types TYMED_ISTORAGE and TYMED_ISTREAM are used to indicate a storage or a stream medium.

5. The code samples in the first half of this chapter refer to the sample app in directory \chap07\strucstr. In the picture below, the viewer is displaying the data file created and used by this app. Each storage is represented by a folder icon, and each stream by a page icon. The root storage has the name of the file itself, in this case "A". The root storage contains a single stream named "DisplayText", and a substorage called "SummaryInfo". The latter storage contains two streams, one named "Author" and one named "Title". In the bottom diagram, the viewer displays the contents of the "Title" stream.

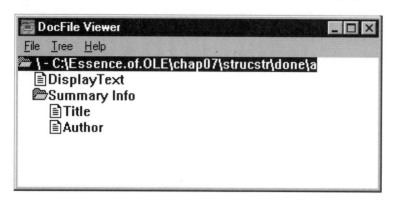

Note: The summary information storage and streams shown in this simple example are not the standard ones used by file viewers in Windows 95. That stream layout is actually quite complicated. You can find the description in Brockschmidt, pp. 789-791.

This page intentionally contains no text other than this sentence.

B. STORAGES

1. A storage is controlled via the *IStorage* interface. You do not have to write this interface or the IStream interface; it is provided by the operating system. All you have to do is obtain a pointer to it via an API function or an interface method and call the methods you want, as you did with the ITypeLib and ITypeInfo interfaces in Chapter 4.

The IStorage and IStream interfaces should seem familiar to you from your work in the API file system. For example, the method IStorage::CreateStream( ) is analogous to the function CreateFile( ), except that the former creates a stream within a structured storage file, while the latter creates a new separate file on the disk. The methods of the IStorage interface are:

IStorage::CreateStream	*// Create a new stream within this storage*
IStorage::OpenStream	*// Open existing stream within this storage*
IStorage::CreateStorage	*// Create new substorage within this storage*
IStorage::OpenStorage	*// Open existing substorage within this storage*
IStorage::CopyTo	*// Copy this storage into another storage*
IStorage::MoveElementTo	*// Move a substorage or stream to another storage*
IStorage::Commit	*// Commit changes made to this storage since last commit*
IStorage::Revert	*// Discard changes made to this storage since last commit*
IStorage::EnumElements	*// Enumerate substorages and streams contained in this storage*
IStorage::DestroyElement	*// Destroy a substorage or stream in this storage*
IStorage::RenameElement	*// Rename a substorage or stream in this storage*
IStorage::SetElementTimes	*// Set last modification time on substorage or stream*
IStorage::SetClass	*// Set Class ID associated with this storage*
IStorage::SetStateBits	*// Set state flags associated with this storage*
IStorage::Stat	*// Get statistics, such as name, for this storage*

2. You may obtain a pointer to a file's root IStorage interface via several API functions or interface methods. The function **StgCreateDocfile( )** creates a new structured storage file and returns a pointer to the IStorage object controlling that file. In the following example, the sample app creates an unnamed working file when it first starts up. Specifying NULL for the file name makes the system pick a unique one, thereby avoiding collisions. Specifying the STGM_DELETEONRELEASE flag means that the file will be automatically deleted when the pointer is released, thereby avoiding cluttering up the disk with a bunch of garbage files. If the user wants to keep the contents, he will do a "Save As" operation, writing the storage's contents into a new named storage. Thus:

```
LPSTORAGE pRootStg ;

case WM_CREATE:
{
    HRESULT hr ;
/*
Create a new structured storage file and get a pointer to the IStorage
interface controlling it.
*/
    hr = StgCreateDocfile (
        NULL,                              // system picks unique name
        STGM_CREATE | STGM_READWRITE |     // flags
        STGM_SHARE_EXCLUSIVE |
        STGM_TRANSACTED |
        STGM_DELETEONRELEASE,
        0,                                 // reserved
        &pRootStg) ;                       // output variable

/*
Create new internal structure in the file (code shown on facing page).
*/
    WriteNewStorageStructure (pRootStg) ;

    return 0 ;
}
```

NOTE: Getting the right combination of flags on calls to structured storage functions or methods can be tricky, and some of them aren't documented very well. If a structured storage function or method isn't working even though you think you have everything right, the odds are that you have the wrong combination of flags.

3. Once you have the initial storage open, you can create your file's internal structure. The method **IStorage::SetClass( )** marks the storage with your app's class ID so that your app can easily identify its own storages. The method **IStorage::CreateStream( )** creates a new stream within a storage, the method **IStorage::CreateStorage( )** creates a new substorage within the original storage. Note that the names of the storage elements, as with all strings passed to OLE, use wide characters. Thus:

```
extern CLSID MyCLSID ;

BOOL WriteNewStorageStructure (LPSTORAGE pNewStg)
{
    DWORD nActual ;        HRESULT hr  ;
/*
Mark the storage with our app's class ID so we can identify it later.
*/

    pNewStg->SetClass (MyCLSID) ;

/*
Create a stream for data in DisplayText[], then release it because we
don't need the pointer until and unless we are ready to save data to it.
*/

    LPSTREAM pStream ;

    pNewStg->CreateStream (L"DisplayText",// stream name
            STGM_CREATE | STGM_WRITE |      // flags
            STGM_SHARE_EXCLUSIVE,
            0, 0,                           // both reserved
            &pStream) ;                     // output variable

    pStream->Release( ) ;

/*
Create new substorage for summary info.
*/
    LPSTORAGE pSubStg ;

    pNewStg->CreateStorage (L"Summary Info", STGM_CREATE |
        STGM_DIRECT |STGM_READWRITE | STGM_SHARE_EXCLUSIVE,
        0, 0, &pSubStg) ;

/*
Create new stream in substorage. Write default data.
*/
    LPSTREAM pAuthor ;

    pSubStg->CreateStream (L"Author",
        STGM_CREATE | STGM_DIRECT |    STGM_WRITE | STGM_SHARE_EXCLUSIVE,
        0, 0, &pAuthor)    ;
    pAuthor->Write ("Some Bozo", 10, &nActual) ;
    pAuthor->Release ( ) ;
    pSubStg->Release ( ) ;
    return TRUE ;
}
```

4. If we want to open an existing file in response to the "File — Open" menu item, the function **StgOpenStorage( )** opens an existing structured storage file or optionally creates a new one. The function **StgIsStorageFile( )** tells you whether or not a given file is a structured storage file. The method **IStorage::Stat( )** fills in a structure of type **STATSTG** with statistics about a storage, one of which is the storage's class ID, set via the SetClass( ) method in the previous example. Thus:

```
extern CLSID MyCLSID ;

BOOL OpenFileByName (OLECHAR* pName, LPSTORAGE *ppStgOut)
{
    LPSTORAGE pNewStg ;
    LPSTREAM pStream ;

/*
Check to see if this is a structured storage file.  If not, complain and
quit.
*/
    if (StgIsStorageFile (pName) != S_OK)
    {
      MessageBox (NULL, "File is not a structured storage file",
            "Error", MB_OK | MB_ICONSTOP) ;
      return FALSE ;
    }

/*
It is a structured storage file; open it.
*/

    StgOpenStorage (pName, NULL,
      STGM_READWRITE | STGM_SHARE_EXCLUSIVE | STGM_TRANSACTED,
      NULL, 0, &pNewStg) ;

/*
If unable to open file, then complain and quit.  Must convert wide
character name to ANSI before passing it to MessageBox( ).
*/
    if (!pNewStg)
    {
      char AnsiName [256] ;
      WideCharToMultiByte (CP_ACP, 0,
            pName, -1, AnsiName, sizeof (AnsiName), NULL, NULL) ;
      MessageBox (NULL, AnsiName, "Couldn't open file",
            MB_OK | MB_ICONSTOP) ;

      return FALSE ;
    }

    <continued on next page>
```

212

```
/*
Check to see if the root storage's class ID is the one we gave it; i.e.,
it's one of our app's own files.  If not, complain and quit.
*/

    STATSTG stat ;

    pNewStg->Stat (&stat, STATFLAG_DEFAULT) ;

    if (MyCLSID != stat.clsid)
    {
      MessageBox (NULL, "File's class ID is different from ours",
            "Error", MB_OK | MB_ICONSTOP) ;

      pNewStg->Release ( ) ;
      return FALSE ;
    }


/*
Structured storage file successfully opened; fill output variable with
pointer to IStorage interface that controls the file.
*/
    *ppStgOut = pNewStg ;
    return TRUE ;
}
```

5. The method **IStorage::CopyTo( )** copies the contents of one storage to another storage. It is possible to exclude elements from the copy operation by filling in the first three parameters of this method. In the example shown below, which illustrates the "File -- Save As" operation, specifying NULL for the first three parameters causes all of the streams and substorages contained within the source storage to be copied in their entirety to the destination storage. Thus:

```
LPSTORAGE pRootStg ;
WCHAR WideFileName [256] ;

case ID_FILE_SAVEAS:
{

    <get wide-char file name from user>

/*
Create new storage for saved contents, with name specified by dialog
box.
*/
    LPSTORAGE pNewStg ;

    hr = StgCreateDocfile (WideFileName,
        STGM_READWRITE | STGM_SHARE_EXCLUSIVE |
        STGM_DIRECT | STGM_CREATE,
        0, &pNewStg) ;

/*
Copy the current main storage's contents into the new one.  Then release
the current main storage and make the newly created storage the main
document storage.
*/
    hr = pRootStg->CopyTo (
        NULL,               // number of elements to exclude, here none
        NULL,               // interface ID to exclude, here none
        NULL,               // array of elements to exclude, here none
        pNewStg) ;          // destination storage

    pRootStg->Release ( ) ;
    pRootStg = pNewStg ;

    return 0 ;
}
```

6. A storage may be opened in *transacted* mode by specifying the flag **STGM_TRANSACTED** in the function or method call that creates the storage. In this mode, changes made to any element within the storage are not written directly to the file, but rather are buffered until the storage is committed via the method **IStorage::Commit( )**. At any time you want to discard the changes, you can do so via the method **IStorage::Revert( )**. Streams do not yet support transacted mode, although this is promised for a future version of OLE. Currently, you must commit or revert all the streams within a storage with a single call. Thus:

```
/*
Save our data to a structured storage file.
*/
extern BOOL bSummaryChanged, bTextChanged ;
extern HWND hEdit ;

case ID_FILE_SAVE:
{

/*
Fetch text from edit control; write into the DisplayText stream.
*/
    LPSTREAM pStream ;
    char buf [4096] ;
    int length ;

    pRootStg->OpenStream (L"DisplayText",  NULL,
      STGM_READWRITE | STGM_SHARE_EXCLUSIVE, NULL,
      &pStream) ;

    length = GetWindowText (hEdit, buf, sizeof(buf)) + 1 ;
    pStream->Write (buf, length, NULL) ;
    pStream->Release ( ) ;

/*
Commit the root storage, thereby saving any changes that have been made
to it, including changes to the Author and Title streams in the Summary
Info substorage.
*/

    pRootStg->Commit (STGC_DEFAULT) ;

    bSummaryChanged = bTextChanged = FALSE ;
    return 0 ;
}
```

7. When you revert a storage, no further operations are possible on that pointer. All methods except Release( ) will fail with an error code. To continue operations on a reverted storage, it is necessary to release and reopen the storage. Thus:

```
extern WCHAR WideFileName [256] ;
extern IStorage *pRootStg ;

case ID_STORAGE_REVERT:
{

/*
Use the IStorage::Revert( ) method to roll back the uncommitted changes
made to any element contained at any level within the main storage.  In
this app, that means the Author and Title streams in the Summary Info
substorage.
*/

    HRESULT hr ;

    pRootStg->Revert( ) ;

/*
Reverted storage can no longer be used.  Release it and reopen storage
file.
*/

    pRootStg->Release ( ) ;

    hr = StgOpenStorage (WideFileName,  NULL,
            STGM_READWRITE | STGM_SHARE_EXCLUSIVE | STGM_TRANSACTED,
            NULL, 0, &pRootStg) ;

    <reload previous file contents>

    return 0 ;
}
```

8. You can enumerate the elements of a storage, conceptually similar to reading a directory, via the method **IStorage::EnumElements( )**. This gives you back an *IEnumSTATSTG* object, which you can step through to receive a STATSTG structure for each element in the storage. Thus:

```
case WM_INITDIALOG:
{
    LPSTORAGE pStg = (LPSTORAGE) lParam ;
    LPENUMSTATSTG pEnum ; STATSTG stat ;
    char out [256] ;

/*
Get a pointer to the IEnumSTATSTG object enumerating the storage that we
were passed in our initial lParam.
*/

    pStg->EnumElements(0, NULL, 0, &pEnum) ;

/*
Step through it until the end, getting a STATSTG structure for each
element contained in that storage.
*/

    while (pEnum->Next(1, &stat, NULL) == S_OK)
    {

/*
Compose a character string containing type, name, and length of the
element and put it in the dialog box's list box.
*/
        if (stat.type == STGTY_STORAGE)
        {
            wsprintf (out, "Strg: ") ;
        }
        else if (stat.type == STGTY_STREAM)
        {
            wsprintf (out, "Strm: ") ;
        }
        wsprintf (out+6, "%ls, %d bytes", stat.pwcsName,
            stat.cbSize.LowPart) ;
        SendDlgItemMessage (hDlg, IDC_LIST1, LB_ADDSTRING,0, (LPARAM)out);
    }

/*
Release the enumerator object.
*/
    pEnum->Release ( ) ;

    return TRUE ;
}
```

9. Streams and storages within a structured storage file may be constantly appearing and disappearing, expanding and contracting. The internal arrangement of the file may get fragmented, reducing efficiency. Standard file defragmenters do not work on the innards of a structured storage file. To defragment a file, use the **IStorage::CopyTo( )** method to copy the fragmented file to a temporary file. This operation will rewrite the internal structures in the most efficient manner possible. Then use the same method to copy it back to the original file, thus:

```
LPSTORAGE pRootStg ;

case ID_STORAGE_DEFRAGMENT:
{
    LPSTORAGE pTempStg ;


/*
Open new temporary storage for defragmenting file.
*/
    StgCreateDocfile (NULL,
      STGM_CREATE | STGM_READWRITE | STGM_SHARE_EXCLUSIVE |
      STGM_DELETEONRELEASE,
      0, &pTempStg) ;

/*
Copy existing storage to new temporary storage, which performs the de-
fragment.  Then copy it right back again and commit the changes.
*/
    pRootStg->CopyTo (NULL, NULL, NULL, pTempStg) ;
    pTempStg->CopyTo (NULL, NULL, NULL, pRootStg) ;
    pRootStg->Commit(STGC_DEFAULT) ;

    pTempStg->Release( ) ;

    return 0 ;
}
```

C. STREAMS

1. A stream is a logically contiguous sequence of bytes within a storage, analogous to a file within a file. The operations that are available for streams should remind you of the functions you are used to using to manipulate the contents of ordinary files. A stream is manipulated via the *IStream* interface, which contains the following methods:

IStream::Read   *// Read bytes from stream to memory*
IStream::Write   *// Write bytes from memory to stream*
IStream::Seek   *// Set position of stream pointer*
IStream::SetSize   *// Preallocate space for stream (streams are expandable anyway)*
IStream::CopyTo   *// Copy bytes from one stream to another*
IStream::Commit   *// Not yet implemented*
IStream::Revert   *// Not yet implemented*
IStream::LockRegion   *// Not yet implemented*
IStream::UnlockRegion   *// Not yet implemented*
IStream::Stat   *// Get statistics about this stream*
IStream::Clone   *// Create new stream pointer accessing same stream*

2. The IStream interface contains the methods Commit( ) and Revert( ), seeming to imply the availability of transacted mode as is supported for storages. It also contains the methods LockRegion( ) and UnlockRegion( ), seeming to imply the availability of this functionality. Both implications are wrong. Neither transacted mode nor region locking is available in the structured storage file implementation supplied with OLE, and these IStream methods don't do anything useful. I keep hearing rumblings about supporting them sometime in the future, but no firm plans have been announced at the time of this writing. Placing them in the interface now, even though they are not supported, means that code depending on this interface will not need to change if and when these methods are ever added.

3. The method **IStream::Read( )** reads in up to a specified number of bytes from a given stream. Here two streams are opened and read, and their contents put into edit controls in a dialog box for the user to examine and modify. Thus:

```
/*
Read them in and set them into the edit controls.  Hang on to objects
until done.
*/

static LPSTORAGE pSubStg ;
static LPSTREAM pTitle, pAuthor ;

case WM_INITDIALOG:
{
    char buf [256] ; DWORD nActual ;

/*
Open substorage and streams where author and title live.
*/
    pMainStg->OpenStorage (L"Summary Info", NULL,
      STGM_DIRECT | STGM_READWRITE | STGM_SHARE_EXCLUSIVE,
      NULL, 0,
      &pSubStg) ;

    pSubStg->OpenStream (L"Author", NULL,
      STGM_READWRITE | STGM_SHARE_EXCLUSIVE,
      0, &pAuthor) ;

    pSubStg->OpenStream (L"Title", NULL,
      STGM_READWRITE | STGM_SHARE_EXCLUSIVE,
      0, &pTitle) ;

/*
Read author and title from streams and set their text into edit
controls.
*/
    pAuthor->Read (buf, sizeof(buf), &nActual) ;
    SetDlgItemText (hDlg, IDC_EDIT1, buf) ;

    pTitle->Read (buf, sizeof(buf), &nActual) ;
    SetDlgItemText (hDlg, IDC_EDIT2, buf) ;

/*
Finish initialization of dialog box.
*/
    SetFocus (GetDlgItem (hDlg, IDC_EDIT1)) ;
    SendDlgItemMessage (hDlg, IDC_EDIT1, EM_SETSEL, 0, -1) ;
    return FALSE ;
}
```

4. Using separate streams allows you to save only the changed elements, not the whole thing — rewrite only the author, or only the title, but not both unless they both have changed. The method **IStream::Seek( )** positions the pointer of a stream. The method **IStream::Write( )** writes a specified number of bytes to the current position in the stream, updating the position when finished, extending the stream if necessary. The method **IStream::SetSize( )** sets the length of the stream. Thus:

```
case WM_COMMAND:
{
    if (LOWORD(wParam) == IDOK)      // OK button clicked
    {
      LARGE_INTEGER ZeroL = {0, 0} ;       ULARGE_INTEGER Size ;
/*
If contents of author edit control have changed, write new contents to
stream.
*/
      if (SendDlgItemMessage (hDlg, IDC_EDIT1, EM_GETMODIFY, 0, 0))
      {
            GetDlgItemText (hDlg, IDC_EDIT1, buf, sizeof(buf)) ;
            Size.LowPart = lstrlen (buf) + 1 ;
            Size.HighPart = 0 ;
/*
Find beginning of stream.  Write current contents fetched from edit
control.  Set stream length to size of current data, thereby truncating
stream in case new data is shorter than previous data.
*/
            pAuthor->Seek(ZeroL, STREAM_SEEK_SET, NULL) ;
            pAuthor->Write (buf, Size.LowPart, &nActual) ;
            pAuthor->SetSize (Size) ;
      }
/*
Do the same for the other edit control.
*/
      if (SendDlgItemMessage (hDlg, IDC_EDIT2, EM_GETMODIFY, 0, 0))
      {
            GetDlgItemText (hDlg, IDC_EDIT2, buf, sizeof(buf)) ;
            Size.LowPart = lstrlen (buf) + 1 ;
            Size.HighPart = 0 ;

            pTitle->Seek(ZeroL, STREAM_SEEK_SET, NULL) ;
            pTitle->Write (buf, Size.LowPart, &nActual) ;
            pTitle->SetSize (Size) ;
      }
/*
Release storage and streams.
*/
      pAuthor->Release( ) ;
      pTitle->Release( ) ;
      pSubStg->Release( ) ;

      EndDialog (hDlg, IDOK) ;
      return TRUE ;
    }
    < rest of WM_COMMAND case >
}
```

D. Persistent Objects

1. A *persistent object* is an object which knows how to save itself to a persistent storage device and then restore its exact state from that device during some later instantiation. Since an object's client has no idea how the object is organized internally, it is unable to perform this action without the object's assistance, which the object provides by supporting via QueryInterface( ) one or more of the following interfaces:

IPersistStream	*Save/restore object to/from a stream within a structured storage file*
IPersistStorage	*Save/restore object to/from a storage within a structured storage file*
IPersistFile	*Save/restore object to/from a separate file of any type the object recognizes*

2. The simplest persistent object interface is *IPersistStream*. In addition to IUnknown, the methods of the IPersistStream interface are:

IPersistStream::GetClassID	*// Get CLSID of object to be stored in stream*
IPersistStream::IsDirty	*// Ask object if it thinks it's dirty*
IPersistStream::Load	*// Load object's data from stream*
IPersistStream::Save	*// Store object's data to stream*
IPersistStream::GetSizeMax	*// Ask object how big its data might get*

3. A sample program that uses this interface is supplied for you in the directory \chap07\perstream. It is similar to the data3 sample provided in Chapter 2, except that in this sample, the data object representing the current time has been made persistent by having the data object support the IPersistStream interface. The menu selection "Save to Stream" uses this interface to save the object's state (the current time) into a stream provided by the client. The menu selection "Create from Stream" creates a new object and uses its IPersistStream interface to restore its previous state from the stream.

4. When you have an object which you want to save to a stream, you ask the object if it is capable of doing so by calling its QueryInterface( ) method, asking for the IPersistStream interface. If the object knows how to do this, it will supply a pointer to this interface.

Unless your client app only ever deals with one class of object, you will probably want to record in the stream the class ID of the stored object so you know which class to create when reconstituting the object. You can find the class ID via the method **IPersistStream::GetClassID( )**, and write it to the stream via the API function **WriteClassStm( )**. You then call the **IPersistStream::Save( )** method to tell the object to save its data to the stream. The layout of data in the stream looks like this:

Class ID (written by client)	Object state data written by object's IPersistStream::Save( ) method

```
0              16 17                    ...           N
```

```
extern IStream *pStream ;        // IStream with stream seek ptr at start

case ID_STREAM_SAVETOSTREAM:
{
    HRESULT hr ;
/*
Query the data object for the IPersistStream interface, to see if the
object is capable of saving itself to a stream.
*/
    IPersistStream *pPerStream ;

    hr = lpd->QueryInterface (IID_IPersistStream, (LPVOID*)&pPerStream);
    if (!SUCCEEDED(hr))
    {
      MessageBox (NULL, "Data object does not support IPersistStream",
            "Error", MB_ICONSTOP) ;
      return 0 ;
    }

/*
Ask the object for its class ID.  Write it into the stream.
*/
    CLSID clsid ;
    pPerStream->GetClassID (&clsid) ;
    WriteClassStm (pStream, clsid) ;

/*
Tell the object to save its data into the stream.
*/

    pPerStream->Save (pStream, TRUE) ;

/*
Release IPersistStream interface pointer when done.
*/
    pPerStream->Release ( ) ;
    return 0 ;
}
```

5. When the client wants to reload the object from its stream, it uses the API function **ReadClassStm( )** to read the class ID that the client wrote to the stream. This retrieves the class ID that the client needs to call CoCreateInstance( ), launching the server and creating a new object with whatever default data the server provides. We then query the newly created object for the IPersistStream interface, and use the **IPersistStream::Load( )** method to make the object read from the stream the state data that it saved in the previous session. Thus:

```
extern IStream *pStream ;        // IStream with stream seek ptr at start

case ID_STREAM_LOADFROMSTREAM:
{

/*
Read the class ID from the stream.  Attempt to create an object based
on it.
*/
    CLSID clsid ;
    ReadClassStm (pStream, &clsid) ;

    hr = CoCreateInstance (clsid, NULL, CLSCTX_LOCAL_SERVER,
            IID_IDataObject, (LPVOID *)&lpd) ;

    if (!SUCCEEDED(hr))
    {
      MessageBox (NULL, "Couldn't create object", "Error", MB_ICONSTOP);
      return 0 ;
    }

/*
Query the object for its IPersistStream interface.  If found, tell
object to load its data from the stream.
*/

    IPersistStream *pPerStream ;

    hr = lpd->QueryInterface (IID_IPersistStream, (LPVOID*)&pPerStream);

    if (!SUCCEEDED(hr))
    {
      MessageBox (NULL, "Data object does not support IPersistStream",
            "Error", MB_ICONSTOP) ;
      return 0 ;
    }

    pPerStream->Load (pStream) ;

/*
Release interface pointers when done.
*/
    pPerStream->Release ( ) ;
    return 0 ;
}
```

6. The objects used in this example support both the IDataObject and IPersistStream interfaces. The easiest way of writing an object that supports multiple interfaces is by multiple inheritance. You simply write a class that derives from both the desired interface definitions. Thus:

```
class CPersistTimeData : public IDataObject, public IPersistStream
{

    public:
      ULONG    m_RefCount ;
      BOOL     m_bIsDirty ;

    public:

        CPersistTimeData(void);
        ~CPersistTimeData(void);

    // IUnknown member functions

        STDMETHODIMP     QueryInterface(REFIID, LPVOID *);
        STDMETHODIMP_(ULONG)  AddRef(void);
        STDMETHODIMP_(ULONG)  Release(void);

    // IDataObject member functions

        STDMETHODIMP GetData (LPFORMATETC, LPSTGMEDIUM) ;
        STDMETHODIMP GetDataHere (LPFORMATETC, LPSTGMEDIUM) ;
        STDMETHODIMP QueryGetData (LPFORMATETC) ;
        STDMETHODIMP GetCanonicalFormatEtc (LPFORMATETC, LPFORMATETC) ;
        STDMETHODIMP SetData (LPFORMATETC, STGMEDIUM *, BOOL) ;
        STDMETHODIMP EnumFormatEtc (DWORD, LPENUMFORMATETC *) ;
        STDMETHODIMP DAdvise (FORMATETC *, DWORD, LPADVISESINK, DWORD *) ;
        STDMETHODIMP DUnadvise  (DWORD) ;
        STDMETHODIMP EnumDAdvise  (LPENUMSTATDATA *);

    // IPersistStream member functions

        STDMETHODIMP GetClassID(CLSID *) ;
        STDMETHODIMP IsDirty( void) ;
        STDMETHODIMP Load(IStream *) ;
        STDMETHODIMP Save(IStream *, BOOL) ;
        STDMETHODIMP GetSizeMax(ULARGE_INTEGER *) ;
};
```

7. The only GOTCHA! in this multiple inheritance operation is that every time you use the `this` pointer, you must cast it to specify which of the VTBLs it refers to. Don't worry, the compiler will remind you with an error if you forget. Thus:

```
HRESULT CPersistTimeData::QueryInterface(REFIID riid, LPVOID *ppv)
{

/*
Caller is asking for IUnknown or IDataObject interface.  Respond with a
pointer to our IDataObject VTBL.   IUnknown, as the root class of both
base classes, is available through either VTBL.
*/

    if (riid == IID_IUnknown || riid == IID_IDataObject)
    {
      *ppv = (LPDATAOBJECT) this ;
      AddRef();
      return S_OK ;
    }

/*
Caller is asking for the IPersistStream interface or the IPersist from
which it derives. Respond with a pointer to our IPersistStream VTBL.
*/

    else if (riid == IID_IPersist || riid == IID_IPersistStream)
    {
      *ppv = (LPPERSISTSTREAM) this ;
      AddRef();
      return S_OK ;
    }

/*
Caller is asking for an interface that we don't support.
*/

    else
    {
      *ppv = NULL;
      return  E_NOINTERFACE ;
    }
}
```

8. The methods of the IPersistStream interface are fairly simple. **IPersistStream::GetClassID( )** and **IPersistStream::IsDirty( )** are trivial, thus:

```
/*
Object has been asked for its class ID.  Return in the output variable.
*/

extern GUID GUID_PersistTimeData ;

STDMETHODIMP CPersistTimeData::GetClassID(CLSID * pClsID)
{
    *pClsID = GUID_PersistTimeData ;
    return S_OK ;
}

/*
Object has been asked whether it is dirty or not.  If it is, return
the success code S_OK (which has a numerical value of 0).  Otherwise,
return the error code.
*/

STDMETHODIMP CPersistTimeData::IsDirty( void)
{
    if (m_bIsDirty)
    {
      return S_OK ;
    }
    else
    {
      return S_FALSE ;
    }

}
```

9. **IPersistStream::GetSizeMax( )** is trivial to implement, but takes a little thinking about what you ought to say. The caller is asking how big a buffer is required to save the object in its current state. The estimate that you return should be conservative, because the caller's memory might not be expandable. This example is easy because the object's data is always the same size. Thus:

```
/*
This data object saves its size in a SYSTEMTIME structure.  That's
always exactly how much space we need.
*/

STDMETHODIMP CPersistTimeData::GetSizeMax(ULARGE_INTEGER *pLint)
{
    pLint->LowPart = sizeof (SYSTEMTIME) ;
    pLint->HighPart = 0 ;
    return S_OK ;
}
```

10. The method **IPersistStream::Save( )** instructs the object to save its data in its own native data format into the provided stream. The flag `bClearDirty` tells the object whether or not to clear its dirty flag. The client might be making a copy of the object, in which case this will be FALSE.

The saving object cannot depend on being the only owner of data in the stream. The client might have class ID or data format information stored in the stream ahead of the object's data, and might have other objects' data stored after it. The client is responsible for having the stream's seek pointer in the proper position, pointing to the beginning of the object's saved data before calling this method. The object is responsible for somehow detecting the end of its own data (in this example, the data is always of a fixed size) and leaving the stream's seek pointer positioned there at the end of this method. An object whose data size varied might write the length of its data as the first DWORD in the stream. Thus:

```
extern SYSTEMTIME LocalTime ;

STDMETHODIMP CPersistTimeData::Save (IStream *pStream, BOOL bClearDirty)
{

/*
If the clear flag is set by the caller, clear this object's dirty flag.
*/

    if (bClearDirty)
    {
      m_bIsDirty = FALSE ;
    }


/*
Write our own native data to the provided stream.
*/
    return pStream->Write ((LPVOID) &LocalTime, sizeof (SYSTEMTIME),
      NULL) ;
}
```

11. The method **IPersistStream::Load( )** tells the object to read its own native data from the provided stream. The client is responsible for providing a pointer to the stream in which data has been previously saved by the method IPersistStream::Save( ) of this object, with the stream pointer at the beginning of the area in which the object's data resides. Thus:

```
/*
Load our object's data from the provided stream.  Clear the dirty flag,
as the data is now new.
*/

extern SYSTEMTIME LocalTime ;

STDMETHODIMP CPersistTimeData::Load(IStream *pStream)
{
    m_bIsDirty = FALSE ;

    return pStream->Read ((LPVOID) &LocalTime,
      sizeof(SYSTEMTIME), NULL);
}
```

E. STRUCTURED STORAGE IN THE MFC

1. The MFC has its own architecture for persistent objects which was released at least two years before OLE structured storage. It does not use the persistence mechanism described in the latter part of this chapter.

The MFC uses structured storage as part of its prefabricated functionality for embedding and linking, with which this book does not deal. The MFC provides the *COleStreamFile* class which represents the IStream interface in a compound file.

Lab Exercises
Chapter 7
Structured Storage

Directory: \EssenceOfOLE\chap07\strucstr\templ

1.   Our app begins with a temporary working file. In the file MAINWIND.CPP, case WM_CREATE, use the function StgCreateDocfile( ) to create a new structured storage file with a unique name, using transacted mode. Store the pointer to this file's IStorage interface in the global variable pRootStg.

2. The next thing we need to do with our new file is to create its internal structure. The function WriteNewStorageStructure( ) is provided for you in the file STGUTIL.CPP, but it is an empty shell. First, use the method IStorage::SetClass( ) to write our app's class ID into the main storage so that we can identify our own files. The class ID is provided for you in the external variable MyCLSID. Then create a stream called "DisplayText" and a storage called "Summary Info" in the main storage using the methods IStorage::CreateStream( ) and IStorage::CreateStorage( ), respectively. In the Summary Info storage, create two streams, one named "Author" and another named "Title". Use the method IStream::Write( ) to put some default data into each of the streams. Make sure that you release all your interface pointers at the end of the function, except for the main IStorage pointer that you were passed as the function's parameter. Your new structured storage file now has an internal structure that the rest of the application expects. NOTE: When you write data in text string format, make sure you write the terminating NULL character into the stream. Write lstrlen(pString) + 1 characters, not lstrlen (pString) characters.

3. Now we have a file structure and some default data. We need to be able to save the file to disk. In the file MAINWIND.CPP, WM_COMMAND message, ID_FILE_SAVE case, use the method IStorage::Commit( ) to commit changes made to the file. This is what actually causes any changes that might have been made to the file to be physically written to the file's storage areas on the disk. The write of the DisplayText[ ] to the stream has already been done for you, as has the connection with the Save As... menu command. Use the DocFile Viewer in the OLE SDK to verify proper functionality.

4. We can now create a new file, edit its text, and save it. What we now need to do is to be able to open existing files through the File-Open menu command. The user interface has already been written for you. It calls a helper function called OpenFileByName( ), which lives in STGUTIL.CPP. Naturally, this function is an empty shell left for you to implement. You are passed a pointer to the file name and a pointer to an output variable in which to return the IStorage pointer that controls the file. You must return TRUE if you are able to open the file, FALSE if not. First, use the function StgIsStorageFile( ) to make sure that the requested file is a structured storage file. If it isn't, the skeleton app pops up a message box and returns FALSE. Next, open the file via the function StgOpenStorage( ) using transacted mode, then use the method IStorage::Stat( ) to get the class ID of this storage. If it is not the same as our class ID (MyGUID, see 2 above), the skeleton pops up a message box and returns FALSE. Once the file is opened, the code to read the data from the stream is provided for you.

5. When the user picks "File - Summary Info..." from the menu, a dialog box appears offering him the chance to edit the author and the title of the document. These items live in separate streams in a substorage, which you created in step 2. The dialog box response function lives in SUMMRDLG.CPP. In response to the WM_INITDIALOG message, open the substorage, open the two streams, read their contents, and set the title into the first edit control (IDC_EDIT1) and the author's name into the second (IDC_EDIT2). In response to the WM_COMMAND message from an OK button, each edit control checks to see if it has been modified. If it has, fetching the data from the edit control has been done for you; you must write it into the appropriate stream. I suggest that you keep open the streams that you opened in the first message, and only release them when you dismiss the dialog box. Position the stream pointer to the beginning via the method IStream::Seek( ), write the data via IStream::Write( ), and

231

truncate the length with IStream::SetSize( ). Make sure that you release all storages and streams before dismissing the dialog box.

6. Users occasionally change their minds and want to discard their changes. Since we are using transacted storage (you did set that flag in steps 1 and 4, didn't you ?), this is easily done via the method IStorage::Revert( ). In MAINWIND.CPP, case WM_COMMAND, subcase ID_STORAGE_REVERT, add a call to this method to discard any changes the user might have made. You must then release the root storage and reopen the file. The reopening has been done for you.

7. The user can pick the "Enumerate..." item from the menu and be shown a dialog box of the elements in the top storage. The dialog box response function lives in ENUMDLG.CPP. In the WM_INITDIALOG message, you are passed a pointer to the main storage in the lParam. Use this to call the method IStorage::EnumElements( ) to get a STATSTG enumerator. Step through this enumerator, calling its Next( ) method until it doesn't return S_OK, at which time you have seen every element in the storage. Each call fills in a STATSTG structure. Code already exists to pick elements of the structure and display them in a list box.

8. I've put a De-fragment option on the menu. By now, you'd probably rather just look at it. Be my guest. It's in MAINWIND.CPP, case WM_COMMAND, subcase ID_STORAGE_DEFRAGMENT. Examine it to make sure you understand what it does.

EXTRA CREDIT: When your app opens a file, it uses the function StgIsStorageFile( ) to check if the file uses structured storage or not. This means that our app can't open a simple text file. Modify your app so that if the user attempts to open a file that doesn't use structured storage, rather than simply rejecting it, you offer the user a choice to convert it. Use the function StgCreateDocfile( ) with the flag STGM_CONVERT to open the file. This will convert the plain vanilla file into a structured storage file, with the previous contents in a single stream called CONTENTS. Write the structure of one of our files into the root storage, then copy the contents into the DisplayText[ ] and then delete the stream.

EXTRA EXTRA CREDIT: Extend the enumeration dialog box. In the file ENUMDLG.CPP, add code to respond to a double-click on a line in the list box. If the user has clicked on a substorage, pop up another instance of the same type of dialog box, showing the elements in the substorage. If the user has double-clicked on a stream, pop up a dialog box showing the stream's contents, perhaps in a multiline edit control.

Chapter 8

Monikers

This page intentionally contains no text other than this sentence.

A. CONCEPTS AND DEFINITIONS

1. It is frequently useful in OLE for a client app to be able to connect to not just an object of a certain class (say, any old Excel spreadsheet), but rather one particular noninterchangeable object that belongs to that class (say, a particular range of cells in a particular sheet in a particular file). To provide this capability, OLE provides a general-purpose facility for the naming of objects. An object that wishes to provide its name to the world, so that a user of the object may at some later time recreate that specific object and no other, identifies itself by supplying a *moniker*, which is an object that supports the *IMoniker* interface.

2. A moniker is an intelligent name. It contains all the code and data necessary to locate the original object's server and instruct the server to recreate the original object. The moniker does not contain the object's data, but rather a reference to it (such as a file name) that is understood by the server. The process by which an object is recreated from its moniker is called *binding*, and is accomplished via the method **IMoniker::BindToObject( )**. Once the client has used the moniker to bind to the object, the client generally has no further use for the moniker and will release it. Thus:

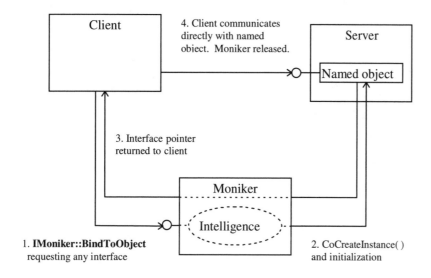

3. Since monikers are used to recreate a specific object at some later time, it is necessary to have some mechanism for storing them from one session to another. OLE accomplishes this by deriving the IMoniker interface from IPersistStream. Therefore, every moniker ever created knows how to save itself into a stream provided by the client app. This will generally live in the client app's data file.

4. Implementing the IMoniker interface can be quite complicated, so we aren't going to do it ourselves. Rather, the portions of this chapter that deal with sourcing monikers will confine themselves to the standard types provided by the operating system and created via simple API functions. We will treat them as atomic, occasionally combining them into molecules. This will suffice for over 95 percent of all applications. See Brockschmidt, pp. 461-470 for notes on implementing your own custom monikers.

B. CLIENT USE OF MONIKERS

1. When a client app opens a file containing a moniker, it first needs to load the moniker from its stream within the file. The stream contains the moniker's class ID followed by the moniker's private data, thus:

Class ID	Moniker's private data ...

The API function **OleLoadFromStream( )** will recreate any class of object that supports the IPersistStream interface and has been saved in the above format. This function reads the class ID from the stream and calls CoCreateInstance( ) to create an object of that class, asking for the IPersistStream interface. It then calls IPersistStream::Load( ) to make the object read its data from the stream. Finally, it calls QueryInterface( ) on the object for the interface ID specified by the caller. Thus:

```
extern IMoniker * pMoniker ;

case ID_MONIKER_OPENMONIKERFILE:
{
    HRESULT hr ;
    IStream *pStream ;

    <get file name from user, open file and stream containing moniker>

/*
Load moniker from the stream in which it was stored.
*/

    hr = OleLoadFromStream (
      pStream,                        // stream containing moniker's data
      IID_IMoniker,                   // interface ID wanted on new object
      (void **) &pMoniker) ;          // output variable

    if (!SUCCEEDED(hr))
    {
      MessageBox (NULL, "Couldn't load moniker from stream",
            "Error", 0) ;
    }
    pStream->Release( ) ;


    <continued on facing page>
```

NOTE: The sample client and server apps referred to in this section can be found in the directory \chap08\monikers. Use of these samples is less obvious than usual, so see the lab exercise instructions at the end of this chapter for directions on how to register and run them.

2. Having reconstituted the moniker, we now want to bind to the object that it names. We do this via the method **IMoniker::BindToObject( )**. This requires us to create a *bind context* object, essentially a memory scratchpad used by the moniker during the binding operation. Direct creation and use of the bind context are shown in the section on the URL moniker on page 254. The API function **BindMoniker( )** combines these operations into a single function call, creating the bind context, calling IMoniker::BindToObject( ), and releasing the bind context. This tells the moniker to do whatever it needs to do to reconstitute the object that it names and return a pointer to the specified interface on the new object. If it succeeds, we can then use the new object to our heart's content. Whether it succeeds or fails, we have no further use for the moniker, so we release it. Thus:

```
<continued from previous page>

/*
Bind to the object named by the moniker. The bind context will be
created and released internally.
*/
    if (pMoniker)
    {
      hr = BindMoniker (
            pMoniker,                // moniker naming desired object
            0,                       // reserved
            IID_IDataObject,         // interface ID wanted on new object
            (void **) &lpd) ;        // output variable

      if (!SUCCEEDED(hr))
      {
            MessageBox (NULL, "Couldn't bind to moniker", "Error", 0) ;
      }
      else
      {
            <use new object>
      }

/*
Release moniker as we no longer need it.
*/
      pMoniker->Release( ) ;
      pMoniker = NULL ;
    }

    return 0 ;
}
```

Note: If the client is able to directly handle the raw data in the file named by the moniker, it can bypass the server and fetch that data directly into a storage or a stream via the method **IMoniker::BindToStorage( )**. This is shown in more detail in the section dealing with the URL moniker on page 254.

3. How does the client app get and save the moniker in the first place? There are a number of ways. If you start with the object whose name you want, you can call its QueryInterface( ) method asking for the IMoniker interface. If the object supports naming, it will return its moniker. Monikers may also be supplied by other mechanisms, such as the method IOleObject::GetMoniker( ) method used in embedding and linking.   Monikers may also be transferred via data objects, such as from the Clipboard or drag-and-drop. The data transfer operation for a moniker uses the private Clipboard format "Link Source" and a stream storage medium.   The stream will look and behave exactly like the ones on the previous pages; the only difference is that it came out of a data object instead of from a file. The function OleLoadFromStream( ) will recreate the moniker as in the previous example. Thus:

```
UINT cfLinkSource ;
case WM_CREATE:
{
    cfLinkSource = RegisterClipboardFormat ("Link Source") ;
    return 0 ;
}


case ID_MONIKER_PASTEFROMCLIPBOARD:
{
    HRESULT hr ;     LPDATAOBJECT pClip ;
    FORMATETC fe ;   STGMEDIUM stg ;
/*
Get clipboard data object.  Get its data in link source format in
an IStream medium.
*/
    OleGetClipboard (&pClip) ;
    fe.cfFormat = cfLinkSource ;
    fe.tymed = TYMED_ISTREAM ;
    fe.lindex = -1 ;
    fe.dwAspect = DVASPECT_CONTENT ;
    fe.ptd = NULL ;
    hr = pClip->GetData (&fe, &stg) ;

/*
Seek the stream to its beginning. Load the moniker from the stream.
*/

    LARGE_INTEGER li = {0, 0} ;
    stg.pstm->Seek (li, STREAM_SEEK_SET, NULL) ;

    hr = OleLoadFromStream (stg.pstm,       // stream containing object
      IID_IMoniker,                         // interface ID desired
      (void **)&pMoniker);                  // output variable

    if (hr != S_OK)
    {
      MessageBox (NULL, "Couldn't load moniker", "", 0) ;
    }
    ReleaseStgMedium (&stg) ;

    <use moniker to our heart's content>
    pClip->Release ( ) ;
    return 0 ;
}
```

4. Once the client app obtains a moniker, it saves the moniker into a stream via the API function **OleSaveToStream( )**, which operates on any object that supports the IPersistStream interface. This function first obtains the object's class ID via the method IPersistStream::GetClassID( ) and writes it to the stream via the function WriteClassStm( ). It then tells the moniker to write its private data into the stream by calling the method IPersistStream::Save( ), thereby producing the stream layout detailed previously. Thus:

```
extern IMoniker *pMoniker ;

case ID_MONIKER_SAVEMONIKERAS:
{
    HRESULT hr ;

    IStream *pStream ;

    <open stream for moniker to live in>
/*
Tell the moniker to save its data into the stream.
*/
    hr = OleSaveToStream (
            pMoniker,              // IPersistStream-derived object
            pStream) ;            // stream to save object in

    if (!SUCCEEDED(hr))
    {
      MessageBox (NULL, "Couldn't save moniker", "Error", 0) ;
    }

/*
Release interface pointers when done.
*/
    pStream->Release ( ) ;

    return 0 ;
}
```

C. SERVER SUPPORT OF SIMPLE MONIKERS

1. Suppose I have the simplest server app I can think of. The server is so simple that it makes its objects' data available to clients only in text format via the IDataObject interface. Its objects are files containing text that the user enters.

In addition to simply transferring text, the server app also wants to make it possible for a client to preserve not the server object's data itself, but rather a reference the server's object. At some later time, the client wants to be able to reconstitute the object representing that data. In order to accomplish this, the server has to do two things. First, it has to provide to the client a moniker naming its objects. Second, it has to be able to reconstitute the named objects when asked to do so by the monikers. In this manner, if the user runs the server app and makes a change in a file, then the next time a user runs the client app and recreates the object, the object will reflect the changes that have been made by the user of the server.

2. This app has two classes of data objects. The first, CFileTextData, is the data object that contains the actual contents of the file. The second, CMonikerData, is used only for transferring a moniker to a client app via the Clipboard or drag-and-drop. The moniker naming the file object is a *file moniker*, one of OLE's standard types, which you create via the API function **CreateFileMoniker( )**. Thus:

```
#include "cmonikerdata.h"
/*
User picked "Edit -- Copy File Link" from the menu.
*/


WCHAR WideFileName [256] ;

case ID_EDIT_COPYFILELINK:
{
    LPMONIKER pFileMoniker ;    LPDATAOBJECT pData ;

/*
Create moniker naming currently open file.
*/


    CreateFileMoniker (WideFileName, &pFileMoniker) ;

/*
Create a data transfer object that knows how to transfer monikers and
place it on the Clipboard. This object maintains a reference count on
the moniker.
*/
    pData = new CMonikerData (pFileMoniker) ;
    OleSetClipboard (pData) ;

/*
No further business with any of these objects, so release them here.
Final release from Clipboard will destroy them.
*/
    pFileMoniker->Release( ) ;
    pData->Release ( ) ;
    return 0 ;
}
```

3. The method CMonikerData::GetData( ) has to provide the moniker to a client app using "Link Source" Clipboard format in a stream storage medium. We could create a disk file to contain this stream, but that would be slow. It is fastest to create a stream in global memory via the API function **CreateStreamOnHGlobal( )**. The function OleSaveToStream( ) is then used to save the moniker into the global memory stream. Finally, the stream is returned in the STGMEDIUM structure that transfers data in this operation. Thus:

```
extern UINT cfLinkSource ;

STDMETHODIMP CMonikerData::GetData (LPFORMATETC lpfe, LPSTGMEDIUM lpstg)
{

/*
We support link source format, transferred through an IStream, with
aspect content.
*/
    if (lpfe->cfFormat == cfLinkSource &&
      lpfe->dwAspect == DVASPECT_CONTENT &&
      lpfe->tymed == TYMED_ISTREAM)
    {
/*
Create a new stream in global memory.
*/
        CreateStreamOnHGlobal (
            NULL,               // allocate new memory block
            TRUE,               // automatically free when stream released
            &lpstg->pstm) ;     // output variable

/*
Save the moniker into the stream.  Moniker provided in class constructor
on previous page, kept in member variable.
*/

        OleSaveToStream (m_pMoniker, lpstg->pstm) ;

/*
Set elements of STGMEDIUM structure for transfer.
*/

        lpstg->tymed = TYMED_ISTREAM ;
        lpstg->pUnkForRelease = NULL ;

        return S_OK ;

    }
/*
User asked for a format that we couldn't supply.  Return error code.
*/
    return DATA_E_FORMATETC ;
}
```

241

4. When the client binds to the file-based moniker, the OLE-supplied implementation of the file moniker looks for the file whose name is encoded in the moniker and attempts to launch a server based on it. The search for the server of a given file is performed internally via the API function **GetClassFile( )**. The procedure followed by this function is as follows:

A. If the file is a structured storage file, then the moniker will look for the class ID with which the root storage was marked.

B. Failing that, it will look in the registry section HKEY_CLASSES_ROOT\FileType for an entry. The file's contents are checked against each of the class ID subkeys in this section. Each class ID entry has one or more subkeys specifying the byte pattern that a file must contain to be identified as belonging to the server of that class ID. In the example shown below, the file's contents beginning at offset 0, continuing for the next 8 bytes, combined with the mask 0xFF00F9FF0000FFFF using the logical AND operation, must produce the result 0x0900000000002000 to be identified with the server whose class ID is {00020811-0000-0000-C000-000000000046}, which is Microsoft Excel. If the entry contains more than one subkey, a file must match all of them.

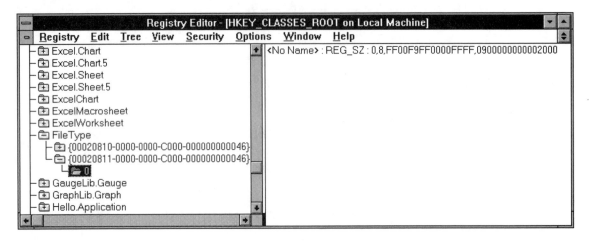

C. Failing that, it will look in the registry for a key that corresponds to the file's extension. If found, this key will contain the name of the object that a file with the specified extension contains. The moniker will then look up the class ID associated with that named object, and launch the server of that class. In the following example, a file with the extension .XLS is thought to contain an Excel.Sheet.5 object.

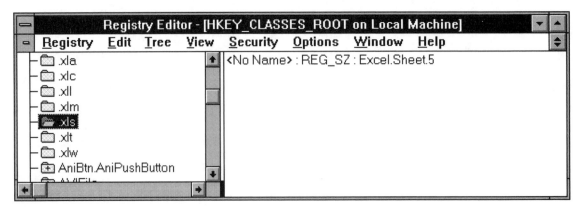

242

5. When the moniker locates the class ID of the server that handles the file, the moniker will call CoCreateInstance( ) to create an object of this class, asking for the IPersistFile interface, discussed on the following page. Obtaining this, the moniker calls IPersistFile::Load( ) to make the object read its data from the file specified in the moniker. Finally, the moniker calls QueryInterface( ) for the interface specified by the client in the call to BindMoniker( ). A failure at any point terminates the binding operation with an error. The sequence of events is shown graphically below:

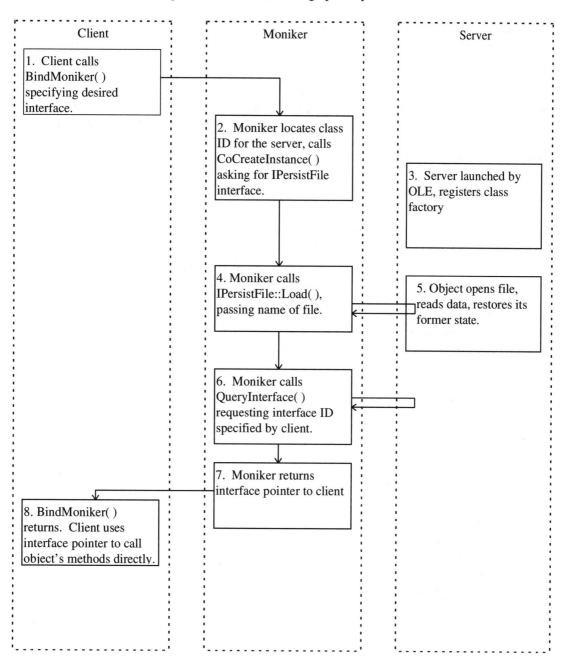

6. The *IPersistFile* interface is somewhat similar to the IPersistStream interface seen in the previous chapter. It tells an object to load its data from a standalone file rather than a stream. The methods of this interface are:

GetClassID( )   // *Get class ID of object saved in file.*
IsDirty( )   // *Ask object if it has changed since it was last saved to its current file.*
Load( )   // *Open specified file and initialize object from the file contents.*
Save( )   // *Save object's data to specified file.*
SaveCompleted( )   // *Notify object that it can revert from NoScribble mode to Normal mode.*
GetCurFile( )   // *Get the current name of the file.*

In the sample program, when the moniker calls CoCreateInstance( ), the server's class factory manufactures an object of class CFileTextData, which supports both the IDataObject and IPersistFile interfaces. After creating the object, the moniker will then call the **IPersistFile::Load( )** method, passing it the name of the file contained in the moniker. It is up to the object to open the file and properly reconstitute the object's previous state from the contents of that file. Thus:

```
STDMETHODIMP CFileTextData::Load(LPCOLESTR pFileName, DWORD grfMode)
{

    HRESULT hr ;
/*
Open storage file we are passed. Open stream that contains data within
the storage file.
*/

    IStorage *pStor ;
    IStream *pStream ;

    hr = StgOpenStorage (pFileName, NULL,
      STGM_READWRITE | STGM_SHARE_EXCLUSIVE,
      NULL, 0, &pStor) ;

    if (!SUCCEEDED(hr))
    {
      return E_FAIL ;
    }

    hr = pStor->OpenStream (L"Text", 0,
      STGM_READWRITE | STGM_SHARE_EXCLUSIVE,
      0, &pStream) ;

    if (!SUCCEEDED(hr))
    {
      return E_FAIL ;
    }
```

```
/*
Find length of stream, allocate enough memory to hold its contents.
*/
    ULARGE_INTEGER ul ; LARGE_INTEGER l_zero = {0, 0} ;

    pStream->Seek (l_zero, STREAM_SEEK_END, &ul) ;
    pStream->Seek (l_zero, STREAM_SEEK_SET, NULL) ;

    m_length = ul.LowPart+1   ;
    m_cp = (char *)GlobalAlloc (GMEM_FIXED, m_length) ;
    if (!m_cp)
    {
       return E_OUTOFMEMORY;
    }

/*
Read file text from stream. Make sure it is NULL-terminated.
*/

    pStream->Read (m_cp, m_length-1, NULL) ;
    *(m_cp + ul.LowPart) = 0 ;

/*
Release storage and stream.
*/
    pStor->Release ( ) ;
    pStream->Release ( ) ;

}
```

D. COMPOSITE MONIKERS

1. File monikers are fine, but their granularity is too large for most applications. Suppose the object named by the moniker has a finer granularity, such as a range of cells in a spreadsheet. In our server example, if the user selects a block of text with the mouse, he wants to be able to provide a moniker that refers to only the selected text. The server in this case must supply a *composite moniker*, which is a moniker made up other monikers.

2. A composite moniker is composed from left to right. Each moniker narrows down the field until the desired granularity and determinism are reached. A composite moniker generally begins with a file or URL moniker specifying the root file, then contains one or more *item monikers*. An item moniker is an intelligent persistent name object supporting the IMoniker interface, but whose contents only have meaning to the server application. An item moniker does not know how to stand alone. In the supplied server example, the selected text block is named by an item moniker consisting of the first and last selected characters, separate by a colon. Thus:

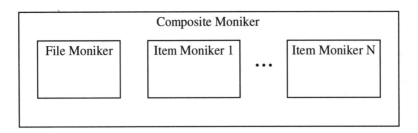

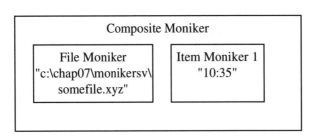

3. When the user chooses "Edit -- Copy File!Item" from the main menu, the server constructs a composite moniker based on the current text selection and places it on the Clipboard as before. The API function **CreateItemMoniker( )** makes an item moniker for us. The delimiter character in its first parameter specifies a character that we promise OLE will never appear in this item's name. The item moniker uses it to separate its strings internally. The choice of the bang ('!') character as shown below is customary but not required.

The obtusely named function **CreateGenericComposite( )** takes two monikers and binds them together into a single composite moniker. The left-hand moniker, here the file moniker, is specified first in its parameter list. If you wanted to, you could take the resulting composite moniker, bind another one to its right, and go on to create composite monikers of staggering complexity. Thus:

```
case ID_EDIT_COPYFILEITEMLINK:
{
    LPMONIKER pFileMoniker, pItemMoniker, pCompositeMoniker ;
    LPDATAOBJECT pData ;  char out [256] ; WCHAR wout [256] ;

/*
Create moniker for currently open file.
*/
    CreateFileMoniker (WideFileName, &pFileMoniker) ;

/*
Get selection of text, convert to wide chars, and create item moniker
naming it.
*/
    DWORD dwSel = SendMessage (hEdit, EM_GETSEL, 0, 0) ;
    wsprintf (out, "%d:%d", LOWORD(dwSel), HIWORD(dwSel)) ;
    MultiByteToWideChar (CP_ACP, 0, out, -1, wout, 80) ;

    CreateItemMoniker (L"!",     // delimiter character
      wout,                      // object name
      &pItemMoniker) ;           // output variable

/*
Combine file and item moniker into composite. Place composite moniker in
data transfer object.  Place on Clipboard.
*/
    CreateGenericComposite (
      pFileMoniker,              // leftmost moniker
      pItemMoniker,              // right-hand moniker to add
      &pCompositeMoniker) ;      // output variable

    pData = new CMonikerData (pCompositeMoniker) ;
    OleSetClipboard (pData) ;

/*
Release everything.
*/
    pFileMoniker->Release ( ) ;
    pItemMoniker->Release ( ) ;
    pCompositeMoniker->Release( ) ;
    pData->Release ( ) ;
    return 0 ;
}
```

4. The client that uses the moniker doesn't know or care whether the moniker is simple or composite. All it does is call BindMoniker( ) as shown in the first example. It is up to the server to properly decompose the composite moniker and reconstruct the named object in accordance with the names contained therein.

Composite monikers are decomposed from right to left. When the client calls the composite moniker's BindToObject( ) method, the composite delegates that call to the rightmost moniker in the composite, passing a pointer to the remaining composite to the left of rightmost moniker. The rightmost moniker attempts to recreate the object that it names, but is usually unable to do so without the assistance of the moniker on its left. In the text server example shown previously, the item moniker on the right which indicates the range of selected text is meaningless without the file in which the range resides. The item moniker knows this, so it calls the BindToObject( ) method on the moniker to its left, asking for the IOleContainerItem( ) interface. When this returns, the rightmost moniker calls the method IOleItemContainer::GetObject( ), passing its own item name. This method is where the intelligence resides to create an object based on the file and item names. This process is shown graphically on the facing page:

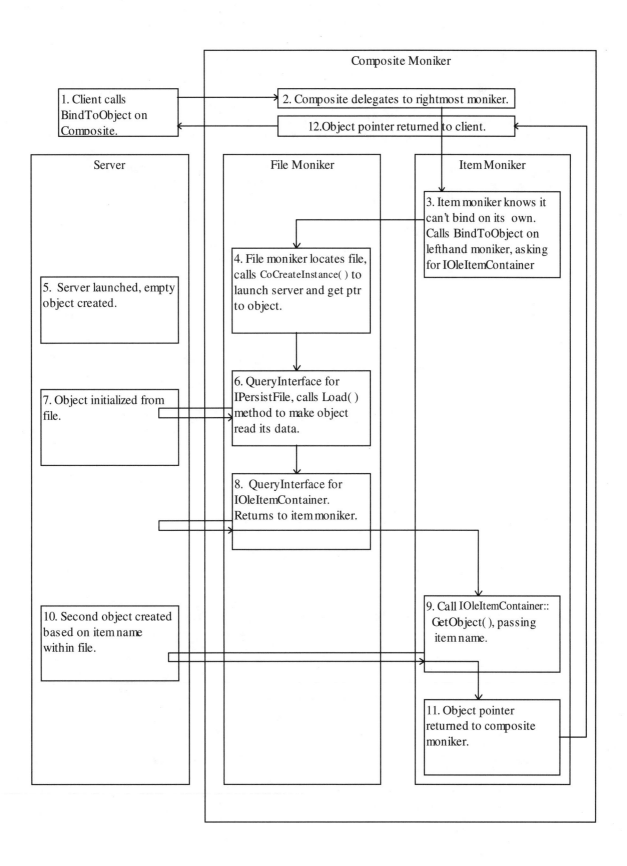

Composite Moniker

1. Client calls BindToObject on Composite.

2. Composite delegates to rightmost moniker.

12.Object pointer returned to client.

Server

File Moniker

Item Moniker

3. Item moniker knows it can't bind on its own. Calls BindToObject on lefthand moniker, asking for IOleItemContainer

4. File moniker locates file, calls CoCreateInstance( ) to launch server and get ptr to object.

5. Server launched, empty object created.

6. QueryInterface for IPersistFile, calls Load( ) method to make object read its data.

7. Object initialized from file.

8. QueryInterface for IOleItemContainer. Returns to item moniker.

9. Call IOleItemContainer:: GetObject( ), passing item name.

10. Second object created based on item name within file.

11. Object pointer returned to composite moniker.

249

5. To properly decompose and bind to composite moniker, the server must support the interface *IOleItemContainer*. The methods of this interface are:

ParseDisplayName( )	*// Parses object's display name to form moniker.*
EnumObjects( )	*// Enumerates objects in a container.*
LockContainer( )	*// Keeps container running until explicitly released.*
GetObject( )	*// Returns a pointer to a specified object.*
GetObjectStorage( )	*// Returns a pointer to an object's storage.*
IsRunning( )	*// Checks whether an object is running.*

The one with which we are most concerned is **IOleItemContainer::GetObject( )**, shown below. In it, we are passed the name of the item from the item moniker. It is up to this code to make sense of the name and create an object based on it. Thus:

```
STDMETHODIMP CFileTextData::GetObject(LPOLESTR pWideItemName,
    DWORD dwSpeed, LPBINDCTX pbc, REFIID riid, VOID **ppv)
{

    HRESULT hr ;
    char ItemName [256] ;

/*
Convert item name from wide to the ANSI that we use internally.
*/

    WideCharToMultiByte (CP_ACP, 0, pWideItemName, -1,
      ItemName, sizeof(ItemName), NULL, NULL) ;

/*
Parse first and last digit out of item name
*/

    char *pColon  = strchr (ItemName, ':') ;
    *(pColon) = 0x00 ;
    int first = atoi (ItemName) ;
    int last = atoi (pColon+1) ;

/*
Instantiate new CFileTextData object, using the overloaded
constructor that allows us to specify a data pointer and an
extent.
*/

    CFileTextData *pNewTextData = new CFileTextData (m_cp+first,
      last-first) ;

/*
Query new object for requested interface.  Return result code.
*/
    hr = pNewTextData->QueryInterface(riid, ppv);
    pNewTextData->Release();

    return hr ;
}
```

This page intentionally contains no text other than this sentence.

E. URL MONIKERS

1. With the advent of Internet support in most apps, the *URL moniker* has been added to the standard types supported by the operating system. This is a standalone moniker that may also be used as the root of composite monikers. It is similar in operation to the file moniker, except a URL moniker binds to an object named by an Internet URL rather than a local file name. You create a URL moniker via the API function **CreateURLMoniker( )**. A sample app that uses the URL moniker to download information from the Internet is provided for you in the directory \chap08\urlmoniker. Thus:

```
void CUrlmonikerDlg::OnBind()
{
    char name [256] ;
    HRESULT hr ;

/*
Get name from combo box control.
*/

    m_URLCombo.GetWindowText (name, sizeof(name)) ;


/*
Use name to create an URL moniker. Store moniker in a member variable.
This function, as do all OLE functions, requires a wide character
string.  The macro A2W( ) is an MFC macro that performs this conversion.
The macro USES_CONVERSION must be inserted prior to it as shown.
*/

    USES_CONVERSION ;
    hr = CreateURLMoniker (NULL, A2W(name), &m_pUrlMoniker) ;

    <continued on facing page>
```

252

2. You generally want to bind to a URL moniker asynchronously. Downloading data over the Internet may take a long time or fail completely, and you probably don't want to hang your main app while waiting for it. In the synchronous binding operation shown in the beginning of this chapter, you created a bind context and called IMoniker::BindToObject( ) or IMoniker::BindToStorage( ). When that method returned, the object had been fully reconstituted and you could use it freely.

In asynchronous binding, you create the same bind context and call the same IMoniker method; however, this merely starts the binding process. When the function returns, the object has not been fully reconstituted. The object's data will be retrieved over the Internet and the binding process completed at some later time, possible never.

To bind asynchronously, you must provide the moniker with an *IBindStatusCallback* object, which receives notifications as the binding operation proceeds. This interface is described in more detail on the following pages. You place this object in the bind context via the API function **RegisterBindStatusCallback( )**.

In the first example in this chapter, we used the method IMoniker::BindToObject( ) to launch the server associated with the object named by the moniker and have the server read the object's data and present it to us. In this example, our client knows how to use the raw data of the object named by the moniker without the mediation of a server, so we call **IMoniker::BindToStorage( )** rather than IMoniker::BindToObject( ). This retrieves the data named by the moniker and presents it to us in a stream. Thus:

```
<continued from previous page>

/*
Create a new IBindStatusCallback operation to control the asynchronous
binding operation.
*/

    m_pBindStatusCallback = new CBindStatusCallback (this) ;

/*
Create a bind context.  Register the IBindStatusCallback with it,
*/

    hr = CreateBindCtx (0, &m_pBindCtx) ;

    hr = RegisterBindStatusCallback (
      m_pBindCtx,
      m_pBindStatusCallback,
      BSCO_ALLONIBSC,
      NULL) ;

/*
Tell the moniker to bind to the storage.  This returns the data named by
the moniker.
*/

    hr = m_pUrlMoniker->BindToStorage (
      m_pBindCtx,                // bind context
      0,                         // not used
      IID_IStream,               // interface ID on returned data
      (void **)&m_pStream) ;     // output variable

}
```

3. The IBindStatusCallback is used by the moniker to get information from the client about the binding operation and to inform the client about important events in the binding operation as it takes place. Its methods are

GetBindInfo( )	*// provide control information to moniker .*
GetPriority( )	*// provide priority of download operation.*
OnDataAvailable( )	*// provide downloaded data to client.*
OnLowResource( )	*// signals client of low resources.*
OnObjectAvailable( )	*// provide requested interface pointer to client*
OnProgress( )	*// tell client about current progress of this bind operation .*
OnStartBinding( )	*// tells client that bind operation has started.*
OnStopBinding( )	*// tells client that bind operation has completed.*

When binding to the storage, as shown in the supplied example, there are two choices for how the data is downloaded. In the example provided, the moniker downloads data when the client explicitly requests it to do so by reading from a provided data stream. If the client stops reading, the moniker will stop downloading until the client starts reading again. This is called the "data-pull" model and is analogous to the IDataObject::GetData( ) method. Its primary advantage is that the client knows that it will never miss data because of an overrun. The primary disadvantage is that it requires the data to be copied twice, once by the moniker from the net into a buffer, and again by the client from the buffer into the client's own storage.

The other alternative is to use the "data-push" operation, in which the client provides a buffer to the moniker and the moniker downloads data continuously into the stream until the operation completes. This is analogous to the IDataObject::GetDataHere( ) method. It saves the extra copy operation. On the other hand, if the moniker downloads data faster than the client can handle it, you can run into trouble and coding to handle this error may be more trouble than its worth. Implementing this mechanism is left as an extra-credit exercise to the student.

4. Our implementation of the IBindStatusCallback object looks like this. The constructor and destructor don't do anything interesting.

```
class CBindStatusCallback : public IBindStatusCallback
{
  public:

    // Data members

    DWORD              m_RefCount ;
    DWORD              m_LastSize ;
    CUrlmonikerDlg*    m_pDlg ;
    char *             m_pBuf ;
    IBinding *         m_pBinding ;
    BOOL               m_BeganDownload ;

    // constructor/destructor

    CBindStatusCallback(CUrlmonikerDlg *);
    ~CBindStatusCallback();

    // IUnknown methods

    STDMETHODIMP       QueryInterface(REFIID, void **);
    STDMETHODIMP_(ULONG)    AddRef() ;
    STDMETHODIMP_(ULONG)    Release() ;

    // IBindStatusCallback methods

    STDMETHODIMP    OnStartBinding(DWORD, IBinding*);
    STDMETHODIMP    GetPriority(LONG*);
    STDMETHODIMP    OnLowResource(DWORD dwReserved);
    STDMETHODIMP    OnProgress(ULONG, ULONG, ULONG, LPCWSTR);
    STDMETHODIMP    OnStopBinding(HRESULT, LPCWSTR);
    STDMETHODIMP    GetBindInfo(DWORD*, BINDINFO*);
    STDMETHODIMP    OnDataAvailable(DWORD, DWORD, FORMATETC *,
                        STGMEDIUM*);
    STDMETHODIMP    OnObjectAvailable(REFIID riid, IUnknown* punk);
} ;
```

5. The first method that the URL moniker will call is **IBindStatusCallback::GetBindInfo( )**. The moniker is asking us for detailed information describing the binding operation that we have just instructed it to perform. We provide this information by filling out the fields of a structure of type **BINDINFO**, which is passed to us in the parameter list. The flag **BINDF_PULLDATA** signifies the use of data-pull mode.

```
/*
Moniker is asking us to fill in a BINDINFO structure describing the
binding operation that is about to occur.
*/


STDMETHODIMP CBindStatusCallback::GetBindInfo (DWORD* pgrfBINDF,
    BINDINFO* pbindInfo)
{

/*
Fill out flags calling for asynchronous binding using the data-pull
mode.
*/

    *pgrfBINDF = BINDF_ASYNCHRONOUS|BINDF_ASYNCSTORAGE|BINDF_PULLDATA ;

/*
Clear out STGMEDIUM structure in BINDINFO, signifying that the moniker
should allocate its own.
*/

    memset(&pbindInfo->stgmedData, 0, sizeof(STGMEDIUM));

/*
Set other elements to their default values.
*/
    pbindInfo->cbSize = sizeof(BINDINFO);
    pbindInfo->szExtraInfo = NULL;
    pbindInfo->grfBindInfoF = 0;
    pbindInfo->dwBindVerb = BINDVERB_GET;
    pbindInfo->szCustomVerb = NULL;

    return S_OK;
}
```

6. Once it has retrieved the BINDINFO structure describing the operation, the moniker will signal the start of the binding operation by calling the method **IBindStatusCallback::OnStartBinding( )**. We put in this method whatever code we want to initialize our downloading operation, in this case allocating a buffer and displaying information to the user. In the parameter list is a pointer to an object of type *IBinding*. This object provides methods giving us control over the download operation, allowing us to suspend or abort it. It is described in more detail on page 262.

The URL moniker does not provide an automatic timeout for the location of the desired resource, and there is no central agency to say that a specified page does not exist. The only way to tell if a resource is unavailable is if the download does not begin within an interval that you feel is reasonable. In this example, we read the interval specified by the user in an edit control on the parent dialog box, and start a timer for that duration. If the download does not begin within that length of time, we will abort the operation as shown on page 262. Thus:

```
STDMETHODIMP CBindStatusCallback::OnStartBinding(DWORD grfBSCOption,
    IBinding* pbinding)
{

/*
Show status to user.
*/

    m_pDlg->SetDlgItemText (IDC_STATUS, "Starting to bind ...") ;

/*
Allocate a large buffer for incoming text.
*/
    m_pBuf = (char *) GlobalAlloc (GMEM_FIXED | GMEM_ZEROINIT, BUFSIZE);

/*
AddRef the IBinding and store for later use.
*/
    m_pBinding = pbinding ;
    m_pBinding->AddRef ( )  ;

/*
Start the timeout interval for beginning the download.
*/
    UINT TimeoutSec = m_pDlg->GetDlgItemInt (IDC_TIMEOUTSEC) ;
    SetTimer (m_pDlg->m_hWnd, (UINT)this, TimeoutSec * 1000, TimerFunc);

    return S_OK;
}
```

7. During the download operation, the moniker will periodically call the **IBindStatusCallback::OnProgress( )** method to provide us with some idea of the progress of the operation. The first two parameters are unsigned longs, giving us the number of bytes downloaded and total number of bytes expected. In this sample program, we use these to set a progress indicator control on the parent dialog box. The ulStatusCode contains flags telling us the current state of the operation, which we use to choose a status string to show the user. The final parameter is a pointer to a text string containing the name of the data location. Thus:

```
STDMETHODIMP CBindStatusCallback::OnProgress(ULONG ulProgress,
    ULONG ulProgressMax, ULONG ulStatusCode, LPCWSTR szStatusText)
{

/*
Set state of progress indicator bar.  Since its range is only 0-64K,
scale it by factor of 1000.
*/
    m_pDlg->m_Progress.SetRange (0, ulProgressMax/1000) ;
    m_pDlg->m_Progress.SetPos (ulProgress/1000) ;

/*
Find character string that corresponds to status flag.  Place in
edit control for user to look at.
*/
    char *cp ;
    switch (ulStatusCode)
    {
      case BINDSTATUS_FINDINGRESOURCE: cp = "Finding resource"; break;
      case BINDSTATUS_CONNECTING: cp = "Connecting"; break ;
      case BINDSTATUS_REDIRECTING: cp = "Redirecting"; break ;
      case BINDSTATUS_BEGINDOWNLOADDATA: cp ="Beginning download";break;
      case BINDSTATUS_DOWNLOADINGDATA: cp = "Downloading"; break ;
      case BINDSTATUS_ENDDOWNLOADDATA: cp = "Download complete"; break ;
      default: cp = "Unknown progress flag" ;
    }
    m_pDlg->SetDlgItemText (IDC_STATUS, cp) ;


/*
Put status string with data location into status edit control.
*/
    USES_CONVERSION ;
    m_pDlg->SetDlgItemText (IDC_PROGSTRING, W2A(szStatusText)) ;

    return S_OK ;
}
```

8. As the data is downloaded, the moniker makes it available to us by calling our **IBindStatusCallback::OnDataAvailable( )** method. The data is provided in a storage medium structure using the medium that we requested in the call to IMoniker::BindToStorage( ), in this example a stream. We use the method IStream::Read( ) to read the data from the stream into a buffer. In the data-pull model being used in this example, we must also perform a second IStream::Read( ) operation to signal the moniker to download the next block of data. This will not actually fetch any more data. The return code should be E_PENDING if there is more data to come, or E_FALSE if we have reached the end of the file.

```
STDMETHODIMP CBindStatusCallback::OnDataAvailable(DWORD grfBSCF,
    DWORD dwSize, FORMATETC* pfmtetc, STGMEDIUM* pstgmed)
{

/*
If more data has arrived, read it into our local buffer and place it in
the parent dialog box's edit control for the user to look at.
*/
    DWORD nBytesToRead = dwSize - m_LastSize ;
    DWORD nActual ;

    if (dwSize > m_LastSize)
    {
      pstgmed->pstm->Read (m_pBuf + m_LastSize, nBytesToRead, &nActual);
      m_pDlg->SetDlgItemText (IDC_DATAEDIT, m_pBuf) ;
      m_LastSize = dwSize ;
/*
Set flag saying download has started.
*/
      m_BeganDownload = TRUE ;
    }


/*
Since we are using the data-pull mode, we must do another read to keep
the flow of data coming.
*/
    HRESULT hr = pstgmed->pstm->Read (m_pBuf + m_LastSize, 1, NULL) ;

    return S_OK;
}
```

9. The moniker signals the end of the download operation by calling our **IBindStatusCallback::OnStopBinding( )** method.   We use this to do any cleanup that might be required, in this case only signaling the parent dialog. All the deallocation of resources is done in our object's destructor, thereby ensuring that it is not done until the final release of our object. Thus:

```
STDMETHODIMP CBindStatusCallback::OnStopBinding (HRESULT hrStatus,
    LPCWSTR pszError)
{
    if (pszError)
    {
      USES_CONVERSION ;
      m_pDlg->SetDlgItemText (IDC_STATUS, W2A(pszError)) ;
    }
    else
    {
      m_pDlg->SetDlgItemText (IDC_STATUS, "Completed") ;
    }


/*
Signal the parent dialog box that the operation has finished. It will
take care of all the UI stuff.
*/
    m_pDlg->BindFinished( ) ;

    return S_OK;
}
```

10. When it called OnStartBinding( ), the moniker provided us with an IBinding object as a means of controlling the download operation while it is in progress. The methods of the IBinding interface are:

Abort( )	// Permanently aborts the bind operation.
Suspend( )	// Suspends the bind operation until further notice.
Resume( )	// Resumes a suspended bind operation.
SetPriority( )	// Establishes the priority for the bind operation.
GetPriority( )	// Retrieves the current priority of this bind operation.

In the example shown below, the timer created in our OnStartBinding( ) method has expired. If the download operation has begun by this time, the flag m_BeganDownload will have been set to TRUE in the OnDataAvailable( ) method. If not, we figure that the requested resource can't be found and abort the operation via the method **IBinding::Abort( )**. This causes the moniker to call our OnStopBinding( ) method, thereby cleaning up nicely. Thus:

```
void CALLBACK TimerFunc(HWND hWnd, UINT msg,  UINT idEvent,
    DWORD dwTime)
{
    CBindStatusCallback *pThis =  (CBindStatusCallback*) idEvent ;


/*
Didn't begin download in time, abort the operation. This should generate
a call to OnStopBinding( ) ;
*/
    if (pThis->m_BeganDownload == FALSE)
    {
      pThis->m_pBinding->Abort( ) ;
    }

    KillTimer (hWnd, idEvent) ;
}
```

F. RUNNING OBJECT TABLE

1. If the object that the moniker names is currently active when a binding operation is performed, it would be nice to be able to connect directly to it, without requiring a new server to start up and a new instance of the object to be created. OLE provides the *Running Object Table* to enable exactly this sort of optimization.

2. The ROT is a global table that matches objects with their monikers. You obtain a pointer to the running object table via the function **GetRunningObjectTable( )**. This function returns a pointer the interface *IRunningObjectTable*, by which the ROT is read and manipulated. The member functions of this interface are:

```
Register( )                  // Place object and associated moniker in ROT.
Revoke( )                    // Remove object and its moniker from ROT.
IsRunning( )                 // Check whether an object is in ROT.
GetObject( )                 // Return a pointer to the object named by specified moniker.
NoteChangeTime( )            // Notify the ROT of time at which an object last changed .
GetTimeOfLastChange( )       // Return the time at which an object last changed.
EnumRunning( )               // Return an enumerator of objects in ROT .
```

3. An object is placed in the ROT via the method **IRunningObjectTable::Register( )**, passing a pointer to the object and to the moniker which names the object. In the following example, the object itself performs the registration in its IPersistFile::Load( ) method, as this is where the object finds out its file name and becomes useful. Thus:

```
STDMETHODIMP CFileTextData::Load(LPCOLESTR pFileName, DWORD grfMode)
{

    <open file and read contents as in previous example>

/*
Create new moniker based on current file name.
*/

    CreateFileMoniker (pFileName, &m_pFileMoniker) ;

/*
Make entry for new file in Running Object Table.
*/
    LPRUNNINGOBJECTTABLE pROT ;

    GetRunningObjectTable (0, &pROT) ;

    pROT->Register (0,              // flags
        (LPDATAOBJECT)this,         // running object
        m_pFileMoniker,             // moniker of running object
        &m_dwRegisterROT) ;         // output variable

    pROT->Release ( ) ;

    return S_OK ;
}
```

4. An object is removed from the ROT via the method **IRunningObjectTable::Revoke( )**. In this example, this is performed in the class destructor.

```
CFileTextData::~CFileTextData(void)
{

/*
Remove ourselves from the running object table.
*/
    if (m_dwRegisterROT != 0)
    {
      LPRUNNINGOBJECTTABLE pROT ;

      GetRunningObjectTable (0, &pROT) ;
      pROT->Revoke (m_dwRegisterROT) ;
      pROT->Release ( ) ;
    }
/*
Release moniker.
*/
    if (m_pFileMoniker)
    {
      m_pFileMoniker->Release ( ) ;
    }

/*
Free data storage.
*/
    GlobalFree (m_cp) ;

    return;
}
```

Lab Exercises
Chapter 8
Moniker Client

Directory: \EssenceOfOLE\chap08\monikers\templ\monikercl

In this lab, we'll create the moniker client discussed in the first part of this chapter. It gets a moniker from the Clipboard and uses it to bind to a data object at a later time.

1. To develop and test the client, it is necessary to have a server to interact with. Go to the root directory of this example and run the registry file MONIKERSV.REG. This will make the necessary entries in the system registry to connect the server MONIKERSV.EXE in the directory chap08\monikers\done\monikersv as the automation server for the object whose human-readable name is "EssenceOfOle.Monikersv". If the root directory you are using for your samples is anything other than C:\EssenceOfOLE, you will need to edit the .REG file to make the LocalServer32 entry point to the exact path location of the server file.

2. Run the server app MONIKERSV.EXE mentioned in the previous paragraph. It will come up with an empty edit control in its main window. Type some text of your choosing into the edit control, then use the "File – Save As" menu item to save your text into a named file that the server app knows how to use. The server directory already contains one such with the name 'a'. (That way it appears first on the list). Pick "Edit – Copy File Link" from the server's menu to create a moniker and place it on the Clipboard.

3. In the file MAINWIND.CPP, case WM_COMMAND, subcase ID_MONIKER_PASTEFROMCLIPBOARD, we have to get from the Clipboard the stream containing the moniker that the server has placed there and reconstitute the moniker from the stream. Use the API function OleGetClipboard( ) to get a data object representing the Clipboard contents. Use the method IDataObject::GetData( ) to get the moniker from the Clipboard. Use the Clipboard format cfLinkSource, which has been registered for your in the WM_CREATE case of the client app, and the TYMED_ISTREAM. Once you have gotten the data, use the API function OleLoadFromStream( ) to reconstitute the moniker.

4. Having reconstituted the moniker, use the API function BindMoniker( ) to get the object which the moniker names. Ask for the IDataObject interface, storing it in the global variable pMoniker. After this call succeeds, the template app contains code that will call IDataObject::GetData( ), thereby transferring the data from the server to the client.

5. Now the client needs to save the moniker into a data file. One is constructed for you in the subcase ID_MONIKER_SAVEMONIKERAS which contains a stream named "Moniker". Use the API function OleSaveToStream( ) to save your moniker into this stream. Paste a moniker into the client app from the Clipboard as before, then choose "File – Save As" from the menu and save your file. Then use the DocFile viewer shown in the previous chapter to examine the contents of this file and the "Moniker" stream. You will find that it begins with the class ID of the file moniker, which is 00000303-0000-0000-C000-000000000046, and the contains the name of the server file in wide characters. You don't have to worry about that, it is entirely the moniker's responsibility. Close the client app and the server app.

6. Now the client needs to reconstitute the moniker from its data file. In the subcase ID_MONIKER_OPENMONIKERFILE, the client app opens the file and the "Moniker" stream. Use the API function OleLoadFromStream( ) to load the moniker from this stream, then use the API function BindMoniker( ) to create the object that it names. This should launch the server and make it open the specified file. The template app contains code to transfer the data from the file. Everything is cool. Shut down client and server.

7. Now start the server app again and either open one of its previously saved files or type in new text and save it. Select a range of characters with the mouse, then pick "Edit – Copy File!Item Link" from the menu. Run the client app, paste the link, and save the client file as before. Note that only the selected characters from the server were copied by the paste operation.

8. Save the client file and look at it with the DocFile viewer as before. Note how much larger and more complicated the moniker has become. Note that the client doesn't give a damn, its moniker loading, saving, and binding code works unchanged. The new contents of the moniker are entirely the moniker's problem. That's what we mean when we say that the moniker is an intelligent name.

Directory: \EssenceOfOLE\chap08\monikers\templ\monikersv

This app is the server side for the moniker client you did in the preceding lab.

1. Now that your controller is working, you have something to test the server with. Before starting to work on the server, you must change the entries in the registry so that the controller will use the new server that you are developing rather than the finished one supplied in the \done directory. You can do this either by editing the .REG file to point to new server's path (in the directory \templ\debug) and reregistering the whole thing, or by using the registry editor and changing only the path itself.

2. The IPersistFile interface has been written for you. You can find it in the file CPERFILE.CPP. Examine it until you feel comfortable with it.

3. When the user picks "Copy File Link" from the menu, we need to create a moniker and place it on the Clipboard for the use of a potential client. In the file MAINWIND.CPP, case WM_COMMAND, subcase ID_EDIT_COPYFILELINK, use the API function CreateFileMoniker( ) to create a file moniker. You will find the name of the currently open file in the variable pFileDataObj->m_wFileName, and you must store the resulting moniker pointer in the local variable pFileMoniker. Note that the moniker is released at the end of the message case.

4. In order to transfer the moniker to the Clipboard, we instantiate an object of class CMonikerData, passing it a pointer to the moniker in its constructor, which calls AddRef( ) on the moniker pointer. In the file CMONIKERDATA.CPP, modify the GetData( ) method. Create a stream on an HGLOBAL via the API function CreateStreamOnHGlobal, place it in the output STGMEDIUM structure. Use the API function OleSaveToStream( ) to instruct the moniker to save itself into the stream. Build and run your server app, paste a link into the client app and save the client's file. Use the DocFile viewer to look at the client's file. You should see a stream named "Moniker" whose contents are similar to those in step 5 of the client example lab.

5. Now we want to do transfer a composite moniker based on a partial selection in the server's edit control. In the subcase ID_EDIT_COPYFILEITEMLINK, create a file moniker as before. Create an item moniker using the string wout, which is a wide character string containing the beginning and ending characters selected by the user. Use the API function CreateGenericComposite( ) to combine the file and item monikers together into a composite moniker. The code to put the composite moniker on the Clipboard has already been written for you.

6. When the client binds to the composite moniker, the IOleItemContainer interface comes into play. It has been written for you in the file ITEMCONT.CPP. Examine it until you feel comfortable.

This page intentionally contains no text other than this sentence.

Chapter 9

Custom Interfaces

A. WHY USE CUSTOM INTERFACES ?

1. Why would you want to expose your app's capabilities to the world by writing your own COM interfaces? What's wrong with just using DLLs, which were touted as the magic bullet of component software for the first seven or eight years of Windows' existence?

- When a client app links to a DLL, the DLL's name is hard coded inside the client app. The DLL must be located in the client app's directory or in the system path. With a custom COM interface, the name and location of the server are found in the registry, so servers can be moved or changed without changing the client.

- A DLL exposes all of its functions in a flat programming model. There is no notion of hierarchy of functions within a DLL. This makes it hard for a single DLL to provide more than one set of functions to the world. The interface-oriented COM programming model makes it easier to combine several groups of functions within the same DLL without them stepping on each other's toes.

- Versioning becomes much, much easier because each new version of an interface has its own ID. A new release of a server can contain within it the code to support any previous versions, thereby eliminating the proliferation of DLLs for each version (VBRUN100.DLL, VBRUN200.DLL, etc.). Because a client app queries at runtime for the interfaces it wants, the server can load code for outdated features only if requested. Conversely, a new client that can use the latest features but finds an old server can gracefully degrade to use only those features supported by the server rather than crashing with an "undefined dynlink" error.

- DLL functions by definition had to live in a DLL on the same machine as the client app. A COM object's server can live in an .EXE file as well as a DLL, and even on a different machine somewhere on a network.

Kraig Brockschmidt expounded on these points in much more detail (for example, four full pages on versioning) in two articles entitled "How OLE and COM Solve the Problems of Component Software Design" and "How COM Solves the Problems of Component Software Design, Part II" in the May and June 1996 issues of *Microsoft Systems Journal*.

2. When writing your own interfaces, why would you choose a VTBL-based custom interface over an IDispatch interface as shown in the OLE Automation chapter? The primary drawback of a VTBL-based interface is that it is harder to use from an interpreted language such as VB; however, a VTBL interface has three main advantages:

- The overhead of a VTBL function call is much lower than that of a dispinterface function call. The client doesn't have to pack up all the parameters into a bunch of VARIANT structures. The server doesn't have to check the number of parameters or their types. All of this gets compiled away instead of being performed at runtime on every function call. The sample app in \chap09\eliza provides an easy way for you to measure this overhead. On a Pentium 120, a call to an in-proc server VTBL interface passing a single string and receiving a single string took 1.8 microseconds, while a call to the same method on an IDispatch interface took 94 microseconds. This doesn't sound like much, but who has microseconds to waste? Also, the IDispatch overhead will get much worse as more and larger parameters are added, whereas the VTBL will not degrade as much, particularly if large parameters are passed by reference.

- In a call to a dispinterface function, you can only pass the types of parameters that are contained in a VARIANT structure. The most annoying part of this restriction is that you cannot pass a structure of any type. A VTBL function call does not have this restriction. Think about even a very simple interface such as IDataObject, with its FORMATETC and STGMEDIUM structures. You will have to work hard to implement a workaround for passing these via a dispinterface, costing more performance, and worst of all, delaying ship dates by taking longer to develop.

- Unless you are using the MFC, a dispinterface takes much longer to write and debug, at least a couple of weeks even cutting and pasting code.

3. Which do you choose? In practice, an in-proc server with a VTBL interface is easiest for you to write and easiest for your compiled clients to use. If your client apps are going to be compiled, or if you need the last scrap of performance, you probably want a VTBL interface. If your clients are interpreted, marketing considerations will probably require that you provide a dispinterface.

4. If you can't make up your mind, you can supply both a dispinterface and a VTBL interface. You can supply them separately, with different class factories. Or you can use the much-touted dual interface, which is a custom interface derived from IDispatch, allowing interpreted clients to use the dispinterface and compiled clients to use the VTBL interface (see Brockschmidt pp. 670-675). I find very few of my customers going this route, however. They find that if they need a dispinterface for marketing reasons, compiled clients can use it fairly easily by generating a wrapper class as shown in Chapter 4, and that providing a VTBL interface in addition is not worth even the small amount of extra development time it takes.

B. ACCESSING AN INTERFACE

1. As shown in the diagram below, when a client process creates or receives an object from an in-proc (DLL) server, the object resides completely within the address space of the client process. Calls made to an object's functions are thus direct VTBL calls with parameters passed on the stack, which makes for very fast, very efficient execution and easy development.

When an object server is a local server (different process, same machine) or remote server (different machine connected via network), the client cannot simply make direct calls to the object's interface methods, as the object's code resides in a different process and possibly a different machine. Rather, when the object is created, COM creates an *object proxy* in the client's address space. The proxy exposes the same functions and accepts the same parameters as the object, but the proxy does not contain the object's actual functionality. Instead, the proxy communicates via remote procedure calls with a *stub* in the server's address space. The stub actually calls the object's methods in the server's address space and passes the results back to the proxy, which in turn passes them back to the client.

When a client calls an object's methods via this proxy/stub mechanism, the transfer of data between client and server is known as *marshaling*. COM provides marshaling support for all of its standard interfaces. If you want to write your own custom interface that can be used from local and remote servers, you must provide marshaling support for this interface. Strangely enough, it isn't that hard.

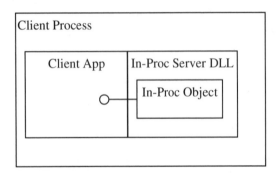

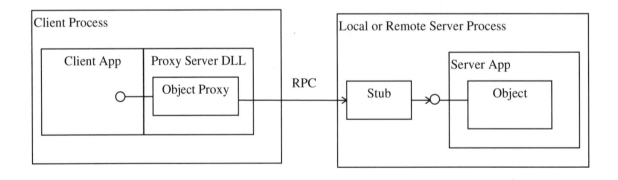

C. SIMPLE CUSTOM INTERFACE, IN-PROC SERVER

1. Implementing a custom interface in an in-proc server is quite simple. Suppose we have a sample of the old "Eliza" psychotherapy program that we want to provide to the world via COM. Let's create a custom interface called *IEliza*, derived (as all COM interfaces must be) from IUnknown. Our interface will contain a single member function called IEliza::Complain( ), which takes the patient's complaint as an input string, and returns Eliza's response as a string in a caller-supplied buffer.

We use the GUIDGEN.EXE utility program to generate a 16-byte GUID to identify this interface. We then write a C++ class definition file similar to those provided by Microsoft for the standard interfaces. The keyword **interface** is used to denote a COM interface; it is actually #defined as **struct**. Each member function must return an HRESULT, must use the **__stdcall** calling convention, and must be declared as pure virtual. The interface's definition file looks like this:

```
<file IELIZA.H>

#include <windows.h>

/*
Interface ID for the IEliza interface.   Generated via the utility app
GUIDGEN.EXE.
*/

static const GUID IID_IEliza = {0x35fc0c40, 0xc4fa, 0x11ce,
    {0xad, 0x55, 0x0, 0x60, 0x8c, 0x86, 0xb8, 0x9c}} ;

/*
Our custom interface, which only has one method. It is derived, as are
all COM interfaces without exception, from IUnknown.
*/

interface IEliza : public IUnknown
{
    virtual HRESULT __stdcall Complain (LPOLESTR pIn, LPOLESTR pOut) =0;
} ;
```

2. To implement the IEliza interface, we will write our own class called CEliza that provides the member functions required by the definition of IEliza. This is similar to what we did in Chapters 1 and 2, writing our own classes which implemented the IDropTarget and IDataObject interfaces. Our CEliza header file looks like this:

```
<file CELIZA.h>

#include <windows.h>
#include "ieliza.h"

class  CEliza : public IEliza
{
    protected:
        ULONG              m_RefCount;


    public:
        CEliza  (void);
        ~CEliza (void);

        //IUnknown members

        STDMETHODIMP          QueryInterface(REFIID, LPVOID*);
        STDMETHODIMP_(ULONG) AddRef(void);
        STDMETHODIMP_(ULONG) Release(void);

        //IEliza members

        STDMETHODIMP          Complain (LPOLESTR, LPOLESTR);
};
```

3. The implementation of the methods is similar to those we have seen before. In a DLL, it's not that complicated. If you've understood the book to this point, it works like you think it ought to. The QueryInterface( ) and other IUnknown methods look almost identical to those we have seen before, the only difference being the inclusion of our own custom interface ID **IID_IEliza**, in QueryInterface( ). We then implement the methods of our own interface as in the **IEliza::Complain( )** example shown here. The code for faking the responses of a shrink lives in the sample code file "eliza.c", for anyone interested. Thus:

```
#include <celiza.h>

/*
Standard query interface method, only new thing is our custom interface
GUID IID_IEliza.
*/

STDMETHODIMP CEliza::QueryInterface(REFIID riid, LPVOID *ppv)
{
    if (riid == IID_IUnknown || riid == IID_IEliza)
    {
      *ppv = (LPVOID)this;
      AddRef( ) ;
      return NOERROR;
    }
    else
    {
      *ppv = NULL ;
      return E_NOINTERFACE;
    }

}

/*
This is the only new method in the IEliza custom interface.  The
function Eliza( ), which fakes the role of a psychotherapist, lives in
the file "eliza.c".  The caller's complaint is in the character array
pIn.  Eliza considers it, and places her reply in the buffer pointed to
by pOut.
*/

STDMETHODIMP CEliza::Complain (LPOLESTR pIn, LPOLESTR pOut)
{
    Eliza (pIn, pOut) ;
    return NOERROR ;
}
```

This page intentionally contains no text other than this sentence.

D. CUSTOM INTERFACE CLIENT

1. The client who uses the custom interface does not do anything different at all, that's the whole point of COM. The operating system jumps through a few hoops to arrange the connection between the object's client and server, then gets out of the way while they talk to each other. The following code should look almost identical to the IDataObject client code shown in Chapter 2, because it IS almost identical:

```
IEliza *pEliza = NULL ;          // ptr to custom IEliza interface
CLSID CLSID_Eliza ;              // class ID of Eliza object
extern HWND hInWnd, hOutWnd ;

/*
Ask COM to create us an object of the class CLSID_Eliza, and give us
back a pointer to the IEliza interface on the object.
*/

case ID_ELIZA_CREATEINPROC:
{
    HRESULT hr ;

    hr = CoCreateInstance (
      CLSID_Eliza,                // Eliza object ID from registry
      NULL,                       // standalone object, no aggregation
      CLSCTX_INPROC_SERVER,       // in-proc server
      IID_IEliza,                 // IEliza custom interface ID
      (LPVOID *) &pEliza) ;       // output variable

    return 0 ;
}

case IDC_SEND:
{
    char WinText [256], in [256]  ;

/*
Get user's complaint from the edit control where he enters it.  Call the
method IEliza::Complain( ) to pass it on to Eliza and get her response.
Place response in the output window.
*/
    if (pEliza)
    {
      GetWindowText (hOutWnd, WinText, sizeof(WinText)) ;

      pEliza->Complain (WinText, in) ;

      SendMessage (hInWnd, EM_SETSEL, (WPARAM) -1, (LPARAM)-1) ;
      SendMessage (hInWnd, EM_REPLACESEL, 0, (LPARAM) in) ;
    }

    return 0 ;
}
```

E. LOCAL SERVER, STANDARD MARSHALING

1. Suppose we can't or don't want to place the Eliza server in a DLL. Perhaps we have an existing ELIZA.EXE app that has its own user interface, and we now want to expose its functionality via COM so that other programs can use it. Our 10 year old spaghetti code can't be easily extracted into a DLL, so we have to somehow provide a custom interface directly from our .EXE. Writing the IEliza interface is the same as it was for the DLL in the previous example, but because we now live in an .EXE, we need to provide the proxies and stubs shown on page 273.

2. Proxies and stubs are created by COM when the client calls a function or method that returns an interface pointer, such as CoCreateInstance( ) or IUnknown::QueryInterface( ). After the server returns the interface pointer to COM, but before COM returns the interface pointer to the client, COM creates the proxy and stub for the specified interface and returns to the client a pointer to the proxy. This process is called *marshaling the interface pointer*.

3. COM uses the operating system's RPC mechanism to create proxies and stubs for marshaling its standard interfaces. Suppose a client calls the API function CoGetClassObject( ), which returns a pointer to the class factory object that manufactures a specified class of object. If the class factory is provided by a local or remote server, COM will need to create a proxy and stub and return to the client a pointer to the proxy. In other words, COM needs to marshal the IClassFactory interface pointer into the client's address space. How does COM accomplish this?

After obtaining the pointer to the class factory from the server, but before returning it to the client, COM looks in the HKEY_CLASSES_ROOT\Interface section of the registry for a key containing the interface's IID. Under that key COM will find a subkey "ProxyStubClsid32", containing the class ID of the server that produces the proxies and stubs. In the example below, the IClassFactory interface has the class ID {00000001-0000-0000-C000-000000000046}. Looking in the registry, we see that the proxy and stub for this interface are produced by the server whose class ID is {00000320-0000-0000-C000-000000000046}. Before returning from CoGetClassObject( ), COM will wake up the proxy/stub server registered for the IClassFactory interface, make it create a proxy and stub, and return the proxy pointer to the client.

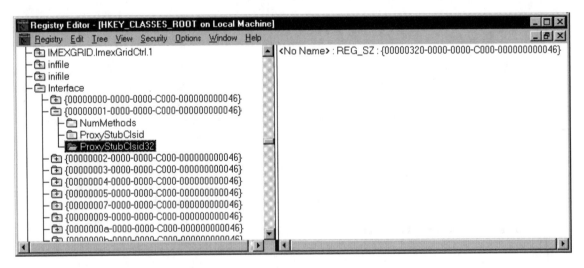

4. The proxies and stubs are produced at runtime by an object that supports the barely documented interface *IPSFactoryBuffer*. Its member functions are:

CreateProxy( )   *// create client-side proxy for marshaling specified interface*
CreateStub( )   *// create server-side stub for marshaling specified interface.*

As you can see from the registry below, the server that produces the proxies and stubs for the IClassFactory interface is the system DLL OLE32.DLL.

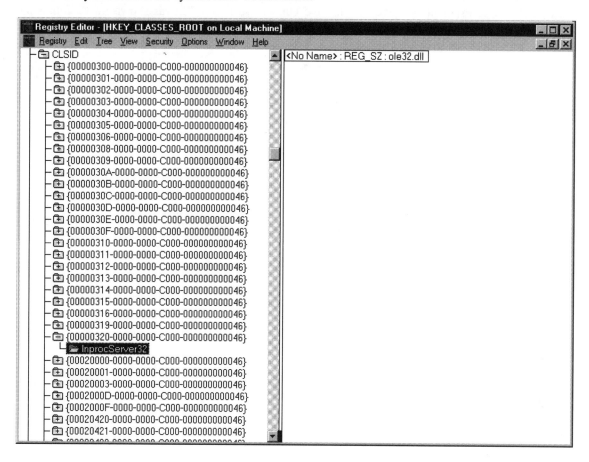

5. To marshal our custom IEliza interface, we need to provide a proxy/stub factory server in a manner similar to that used for the standard interfaces. We could do it the hard way by writing all the code ourselves, but that would be extremely bloody (more than it looks from the simple example shown here, see Brockschmidt, pp. 290-295). Or we could do it the (relatively) easy way by using the programming tools supplied for the operating system's RPC mechanism to generate the server for us.

The tool used in RPC is the MIDL compiler, which comes with the Win32 SDK but not with VC++. We write a source file in Microsoft's *Interface Descriptor Language* (.IDL). We run the MIDL compiler over it, which produces C language source files containing the proxy and stub code. We than add a .DEF file to export the required names and build these into a DLL as shown in the following diagram. We make a few registry entries, and off we go. Sounds simple ? It mostly is.

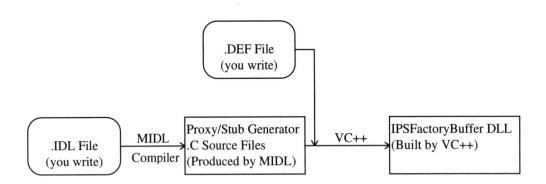

6. IDL language is a strongly typed language used for the description of RPC operations. The ODL language used for type libraries can be considered a subset of it. The .IDL file describing the IEliza interface is shown below. The .IDL for IUnknown is incorporated by reference via the keyword `import`, you will find this file in the directory "mstools\include." The uuid specified is the interface ID for the IEliza interface. The IDL directives for the Complain( ) method describe the type and direction of the data marshaling to be performed. See the .IDL reference manual for further details.

```
<file eliza.idl>

/*
IEliza interface ID
*/

[uuid(35FC0C40-C4FA-11ce-AD55-00608C86B89C), object]

interface IEliza:IUnknown
{

/*
IUnknown methods incorporated by reference.
*/
    import "unknwn.idl" ;

/*
IEliza custom methods.   IDL directives describe the direction of data
marshaling required.
*/

    HRESULT  Complain ([in] LPOLESTR pIn,
      [out, size_is(256)] LPOLESTR pOut) ;
}
```

7. Once you have the .IDL file, you run the MIDL compiler on it. A batch file that does this for the file shown is:

```
<file midlme.bat>

midl /ms_ext /app_config /c_ext eliza.idl
```

8. Running MIDL as shown will produce the .C files "dlldata.c", "eliza_i.c", and "eliza_c.c". The latter is where most of the code resides. You make a new .DLL project in VC++, using these three files. You must also add the import library RPCRT4.LIB, which contains references to the operating system's RPC functions, to the linker input list. Thus:

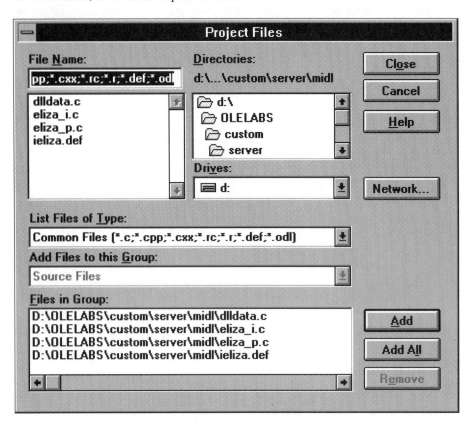

9. You must also create and include in your project a .DEF file which tells the linker to export by name the functions DllGetClassObject( ), DllCanUnloadNow( ), and GetProxyDllInfo( ), as shown below. You do not have to write any code, all of it is in the proxy/stub code generated for you by MIDL. The first two you have seen before, the last one is new here. It provides the IPSFactoryBuffer interface to COM in the same way that DllGetClassObject( ) provided the IClassFactory interface. The DLL produced by building this project is the proxy/stub generator.

```
LIBRARY      ELIZAPRX
DESCRIPTION  IEliza Interface Proxy/Stub DLL

EXPORTS      DllGetClassObject
             DllCanUnloadNow
             GetProxyDllInfo
```

10. Now that we have our custom proxy/stub generator DLL, we need to tell COM where to look for it and how to use it. Once you have done this, COM will support standard marshaling for this interface for the use of any local or remote server. This is exactly the same mechanism as COM uses for its standard interfaces.

As you saw for the standard interfaces, we must make entries in the HKEY_CLASSES_ROOT\Interface section of the registry specifying the server that produces the proxy and stub for marshaling this interface. The requisite keys and values are:

```
HKEY_CLASSES_ROOT
    Interface
      <interface IID>
            BaseInterface = <IID of interface from which this one derives, IUnknown assumed if
absent>
            NumMethods  = <Total # of methods in your interface, including any base interface(s)>
            ProxyStubClsid32 = <class ID of server providing IPSFactoryBuffer for this interface>
```

In our IEliza example, these entries are:

```
HKEY_CLASSES_ROOT
    Interface
      {35FC0C40-C4FA-11ce-AD55-00608C86B89C} = IEliza Custom Interface
      {35FC0C40-C4FA-11ce-AD55-00608C86B89C}\NumMethods = 4
      {35FC0C40-C4FA-11ce-AD55-00608C86B89C}\ProxyStubClsid32 =
        {35FC0C40-C4FA-11ce-AD55-00608C86B89C}  ;(sic)
```

Note that the interface ID and the proxy/stub server's class ID are identical. This is necessary when using MIDL to generate the proxy/stub code. The last line above is not a typo. They do not conflict because they are used in completely different contexts. See Brockschmidt, pg. 328.

You also need to make the standard InProcServer32 entry in the CLSID section of the registry so that COM can find the IPSFactoryBuffer server. A human-readable app name with a CLSID key is not necessary. Note that the server's CLSID and the interface's IID are the same.

```
HKEY_CLASSES_ROOT
    CLSID
      {35FC0C40-C4FA-11ce-AD55-00608C86B89C} = IEliza Proxy/Stub Factory
      {35FC0C40-C4FA-11ce-AD55-00608C86B89C}\InProcServer32 =
        C:\EssenceOfOle\chap09\eliza\localsv\done\midl\elizaprx.dll
```

F. LOCAL SERVER, CUSTOM MARSHALING

1. In the previous section of this chapter, we created standard marshaling support for our IEliza interface in a local server. It works, it's simple, it wasn't that hard to write, but the problem is that it is slow, about a factor of 100 slower than an in-process server which requires no marshaling at all. Suppose we want to try to speed up our local server. Instead of using the standard marshaling that MIDL gives us, we can use our intimate knowledge of the conversation between the client and server to write our own proxies and stubs which will be much faster than the lowest common denominator provided by MIDL. By doing this, we will be able to speed it up by a factor of about 10 compared to standard marshaling, leaving it still about a factor of 10 slower than an in-proc server.

2. Every COM object server has the right to control its own data marshaling if it prefers, rather than accept the standard marshaling that COM provides. You may provide custom marshaling for your own custom interfaces, or even for standard COM interfaces such as IDataObject. You may choose to provide custom marshaling in order to optimize throughput, or to provide features that COM doesn't yet support.

3. The whole point of custom marshaling is that the server vendor provides both proxy and stub. Because these are both written by the same source, they can use their intimate knowledge of their communication mechanism to optimize throughput.

4. Custom marshaling consists of two parts. First, the server app must create and establish communication with the object proxy that resides in the client's address space (marshaling the interface pointer, as explained on page 279). This is done via the *IMarshal* interface, which both server and proxy must support. The use of the IMarshal interface is shown in the diagram on page 287. Whenever a server provides an object pointer to COM, such as in the methods IClassFactory::CreateInstance( ) or IUnknown::QueryInterface( ), before setting up standard marshaling, COM will call that object's QueryInterface( ) method to see if it supports IMarshal. If not, COM will attempt to provide standard interface marshaling as described in the previous section. If the object wants to perform its own marshaling, it does so by returning a pointer to the IMarshal interface, whose methods are:

GetUnmarshalClass ( )	*// get class ID of client-side in-process proxy object*
GetMarshalSizeMax ( )	*// get size of marshaling data packet*
MarshalInterface ( )	*// fill packet with marshaling data and send to proxy*
UnmarshalInterface ( )	*// proxy receives marshaling data from server*
ReleaseMarshalData ( )	*// proxy signals completion of marshaling process*
DisconnectObject ( )	*// inform client that server has disconnected*

5. Once the IMarshal interface establishes communication between the proxy and the object server, it falls out of the picture. The proxy and server communicate via whatever inter-process communication mechanism you decide to write. In the provided example, the IEliza::Complain( ) method is implemented by means of a shared memory-mapped file. The two apps place their data in a shared RAM bank and signal each other by means of events, as shown in the diagram below.

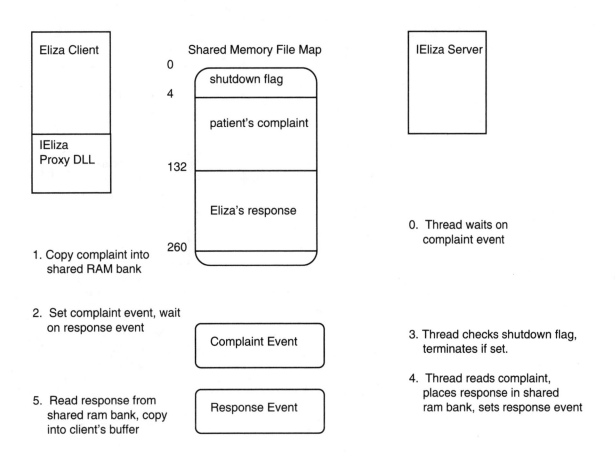

6. The process of marshaling the interface pointer is controlled by the methods of the IMarshal interface. The sequence of events is shown in the following diagram:

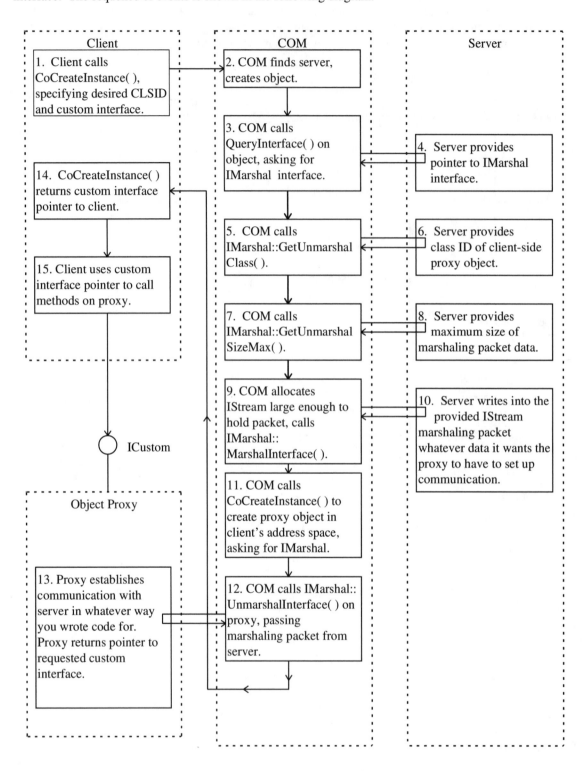

7. To implement our custom marshaling server, we create a class that supports both the IMarshal and IEliza interfaces. It contains member variables for performing the marshaling operation. In this sample app, the stub shown on page 273 is built into the server for simplicity, rather than being a separate entity. Thus:

```
#include <windows.h>
#include "ieliza.h"

/*
Class ID for client-side proxy.
*/

static const GUID CLSID_ElizaProxy =
    { 0x402f6bd0, 0xcb37, 0x11ce, { 0x84, 0x9c, 0xca, 0x8d, 0xf3, 0x9c,
    0x7d, 0x1b } };

class  CElizaServer : public IEliza, public IMarshal
{
    protected:
        ULONG            m_RefCount ;
    public:
      TCHAR        m_ShareName [128] ;
      HANDLE       m_hMap ;
      HANDLE       m_hComplaintEvent ;
      HANDLE       m_hResponseEvent ;
      HANDLE       m_hThread ;
      LPTSTR       m_pSharedMem ;
      DWORD        m_ThreadID ;

      CEliza  (LPOLESTR);
        ~CEliza (void);

    //IUnknown members

    STDMETHODIMP          QueryInterface(REFIID, LPVOID*);
    STDMETHODIMP_(ULONG) AddRef(void);
    STDMETHODIMP_(ULONG) Release(void);

    //IEliza members

    STDMETHODIMP          Complain (LPOLESTR, LPOLESTR);

    // IMarshal members

    STDMETHODIMP GetUnmarshalClass (REFIID, VOID*, DWORD, VOID*, DWORD,
      CLSID *) ;
    STDMETHODIMP GetMarshalSizeMax (REFIID, VOID*, DWORD, VOID*, DWORD,
      DWORD *) ;
    STDMETHODIMP MarshalInterface (IStream *, REFIID , VOID * , DWORD,
      VOID *, DWORD) ;
    STDMETHODIMP UnmarshalInterface (IStream *, REFIID, VOID **) ;
    STDMETHODIMP ReleaseMarshalData (IStream * ) ;
    STDMETHODIMP DisconnectObject ( DWORD ) ;
};
```

8. The first thing that COM will do after getting your object's IMarshal interface pointer is to call the method **IMarshal::GetUnmarshalClass( )**. COM is asking for the class ID of the in-proc server that provides the proxy object. This must be a standard in-proc server DLL with standard registry entries that implements the client side of the custom marshaling interface. Thus:

```
static const GUID CLSID_ElizaProxy =
{ 0x402f6bd0, 0xcb37, 0x11ce, { 0x84, 0x9c, 0xca, 0x8d, 0xf3, 0x9c,
0x7d, 0x1b } };

STDMETHODIMP CElizaServer::GetUnmarshalClass (REFIID riid, VOID* pVoid,
    DWORD dwDestCtx, VOID*, DWORD, CLSID *pClsid )
{

/*
Custom marshaling is provided on a per-interface basis, signaled by the
first parameter.  A different proxy can be used for each interface. This
object only knows how to marshal the IEliza interface.  Anything else is
an error, in which case COM will try to set up standard marshaling for
the requested interface.
*/
    if (riid != IID_IEliza)
    {
      *pClsid = IID_NULL ;
      return E_FAIL ;
    }
/*
The supplied context flags describe the relation between the processes.
The particular scheme we have implemented here depends on the two
objects running on the same machine.  If they aren't, fail with an
error.
*/

    if (dwDestCtx != MSHCTX_LOCAL)
    {
      *pClsid = IID_NULL ;
      return E_FAIL ;
    }

/*
Return the class ID of the server that provides our proxy DLL
*/

    *pClsid = CLSID_ElizaProxy ;
    return S_OK ;

}
```

9. COM will next transmit a block of data from the server to the client proxy. This data block is called the *marshaling packet*, and is transmitted by means of a stream. Its contents can be anything that the server wants the client to know so that they can establish communication. In this example, it is the base name from which the server has generated the names it uses for the shared memory file map and related events.

COM will first call the method **IMarshal::GetMarshalSizeMax( )** to find the maximum amount of memory it needs to allocate for the marshaling packet. Thus:

```
STDMETHODIMP CElizaServer::GetMarshalSizeMax (REFIID riid, VOID* pv,
    DWORD dwDestCtx, VOID* pvReserved, DWORD dwFlags, DWORD *pSize)
{

/*
COM is asking for the maximum size of the marshaling packet.  In this
case, it is the size of the name we are using for the shared file map
and the events.
*/

    *pSize = sizeof(m_ShareName) ;
    return S_OK ;
}
```

10. Next, COM calls the method **IMarshal::MarshaInterface( )**, passing it a pointer to the marshaling packet stream which will be sent to the proxy. The server uses the method IStream::Write( ) to write into the stream whatever data it wants to send to the proxy so that the latter knows how to set up the custom marshaling. In this example, we also use this method to actually create the file mapping, events, and thread that we will use to perform the custom marshaling.

Note that an additional **AddRef( )** is required on the server's object. A standard COM stub keeps a reference count on its object. We need to provide this code in our custom marshaling case.

```
STDMETHODIMP CElizaServer::MarshalInterface (IStream *pStream,
    REFIID riid, void* pv, DWORD dwDestCtx, void *pvReserved,
    DWORD dwFlags)
{

/*
Write the name we will use for the file mapping and event into the
stream provided.  This is the marshaling packet that will be passed
to the client proxy.
*/

    pStream->Write (m_ShareName, sizeof(m_ShareName), NULL) ;

/*
Additional AddRef( ) on this object to make up for the lack of
a system-supplied stub.
*/

    AddRef( ) ;

/*
Create file mapping and map it into our address space
*/

    char out [256] ;
    wsprintf (out, "%sMap", m_ShareName) ;
    m_hMap = CreateFileMapping ((HANDLE)-1, NULL, PAGE_READWRITE,
      0, 1000, out) ;
    m_pSharedMem = (LPTSTR) MapViewOfFile (m_hMap, FILE_MAP_ALL_ACCESS,
      0, 0, 0) ;

/*
Create events that the client proxy will set to signal us that
data has been placed in the shared RAM buffer.  Create a thread to
wait on the event.
*/

    wsprintf (out, "%sComplaintEvent", m_ShareName) ;
    m_hComplaintEvent = CreateEvent (NULL, FALSE, FALSE, out) ;
    wsprintf (out, "%sResponseEvent", m_ShareName) ;
    m_hResponseEvent = CreateEvent (NULL, FALSE, FALSE, out) ;

    m_hThread = CreateThread (NULL, 0, ThreadFunc,
      (LPVOID)this, 0, &m_ThreadID) ;
    return S_OK ;
}
```

290

11. These three methods are the only ones that COM will call on the server. The others may be stubbed out, thus:

```
STDMETHODIMP CElizaServer::UnmarshalInterface (IStream *pStream,
    REFIID riid, VOID **ppv)
{
    MessageBox (NULL, "Unexpected UnmarshalInterface", "Server", 0) ;
    return S_OK ;
}


STDMETHODIMP CElizaServer::ReleaseMarshalData (IStream *pStream)
{
    MessageBox (NULL, "Unexpected ReleaseMarshalData", "Server", 0) ;
    return S_OK ;
}


STDMETHODIMP CElizaServer::DisconnectObject (DWORD dwReserved)
{
    MessageBox (NULL, "Unexpected DisconnectObject", "Server", 0) ;
    return S_OK ;
}
```

This page intentionally contains no text other than this sentence.

12. Having received all it needs from the server, COM will now call CoCreateInstance( ) and create this proxy in the client's address space, asking for the IMarshal interface. COM knows that the proxy was provided for the purpose of custom marshaling, so if it can't get that interface, the object creation must fail. Once COM has the IMarshal pointer, it will call the method **IMarshal::UnmarshalInterface( )**, passing a pointer to the marshaling packet provided by the server. The proxy reads the data from the marshaling packet's stream and does whatever it needs to do to initialize the custom marshaling. In the provided example, the proxy reads from the marshaling packet the name that the server used to create the shared file mapping and events that are to be used for communication between proxy and server. The proxy provides the target interface pointer (here IEliza) back to COM in the output parameter. Thus:

```
STDMETHODIMP CElizaProxy::UnmarshalInterface (IStream *pStream,
    REFIID riid, VOID **ppv)
{

/*
Read file mapping name from pStream.  Create file mapping and map memory
pointer for that name.  Also open the events that the server should have
already created.
*/

    pStream->Read (m_ShareName, sizeof(m_ShareName), NULL) ;

    char out [256] ;

    wsprintf (out, "%sMap", m_ShareName) ;
    m_hMap = OpenFileMapping (FILE_MAP_ALL_ACCESS, FALSE, out) ;
    m_pSharedMem = (LPTSTR) MapViewOfFile (m_hMap, FILE_MAP_ALL_ACCESS,
      0, 0, 0) ;

    wsprintf (out, "%sComplaintEvent", m_ShareName) ;
    m_hComplaintEvent = OpenEvent (EVENT_MODIFY_STATE, FALSE, out) ;

    wsprintf (out, "%sResponseEvent", m_ShareName) ;
    m_hResponseEvent = OpenEvent (EVENT_ALL_ACCESS, FALSE, out) ;
/*
If we couldn't open the file map or the events, fail construction of the
object.
*/

    if (!m_pSharedMem || !m_hComplaintEvent || !m_hResponseEvent)
    {
      *ppv = NULL ;
      return E_NOINTERFACE ;
    }
/*
Return pointer to IEliza interface.
*/

    return QueryInterface (riid, ppv) ;
}
```

13. The proxy implements its methods that are called directly from the client. Instead of providing the actual object functionality, the proxy communicates with the server in whatever way the writer of both of these has decided to use. In this case, the proxy copies the patient's complaint into a specified area of the shared file memory map and signals the server of a new complaint by setting an event on which the server is waiting. The proxy then waits on a second event with a timeout of 1second. The server will think about the patient's complaint and place its response in another area of the shared memory and signal the proxy by setting this event. The proxy will then copy the response from the shared memory to the buffer provided by the caller. If the server does not respond in time, the proxy's wait will time out, causing the proxy to try to cover up. Thus:

```
STDMETHODIMP CElizaProxy::Complain (LPOLESTR pIn, LPOLESTR pOut)
{

/*
Copy client's complaint into shared ram buffer.  Signal server by
setting an auto-reset event that the server ought to be waiting for.
*/

    lstrcpyn (m_pSharedMem+4, pIn, 128) ;
    SetEvent (m_hComplaintEvent) ;

/*
Wait for server to respond, timeout interval 1 second.  If found, copy
into output buffer.
*/
    if (WaitForSingleObject (m_hResponseEvent, 1000) == WAIT_OBJECT_0)
    {
      lstrcpyn (pOut, m_pSharedMem+132, 128) ;
    }

/*
Otherwise, hem and haw.
*/
    else
    {
      lstrcpy (pOut, "I'm sorry, I spaced out.  What did you say ?") ;
    }

    return NOERROR ;
}
```

14. The proxy knows how to handle internally all the methods of IUnknown, so we don't need to marshal their calls to the server. This is another case of how custom marshaling can save performance, by preventing an unnecessary context switch. The server doesn't care if the proxy's reference count goes from 5 to 6; it only cares when it touches zero, so these calls are handled internally on the proxy. When the proxy object gets its final release, we use its class destructor to signal the server to finally destroy its object. Thus:

```
STDMETHODIMP_(ULONG) CElizaProxy::AddRef(void)
{
    return ++m_RefCount;
}



STDMETHODIMP_(ULONG) CElizaProxy::Release(void)
{
    m_RefCount -- ;

    if (m_RefCount == 0)
    {
        delete this;
      return 0 ;
    }

    return m_RefCount ;
}



CElizaProxy::~CElizaProxy (void)
{

/*
Object being destroyed, signal final release to the server.
*/

    *(DWORD *) m_pSharedMem = 1 ;
    SetEvent (m_hComplaintEvent) ;

/*
Clean up.
*/

    UnmapViewOfFile (m_pSharedMem) ;
    CloseHandle (m_hMap) ;
    CloseHandle (m_hResponseEvent) ;
    CloseHandle (m_hComplaintEvent) ;

    return;
}
```

G. CUSTOM INTERFACES IN THE MFC

1. The MFC also supports custom interfaces. Implementing one may feel painful at first compared to the easy point-and-click support that the MFC provides for OLE automation. It took me a few tries to figure it out, but if you read through this section a few times and let it settle, it ought to make sense. In any event, the code is provided here for you to cut and paste. As you remember from Chapter 2, implementing an interface is identical for a local or in-proc server except the mechanism by which the class factory is exposed to the world, and this holds true in the MFC as well. Exposing the class factory is demonstrated on pages 303 and 304. Samples of the IEliza custom interface can be found in the directories \chap09\mfcipsv for an in-proc server and \chap09\mfclosv for a local server.

2. When you use App Wizard to generate your project, select no OLE support. Otherwise you will wind up with a bunch of stuff that doesn't help you and only gets in the way. As shown in previous chapters, include the header file <afxdisp.h> in your stdafx.h, and add a call to AfxOleInit( ) in your CWinApp::InitInstance( ) method.

3. All COM interfaces must derive from IUnknown. In the MFC, IUnknown is built into the class CCmdTarget. So, to write a custom interface in the MFC, begin by using Class Wizard to derive a class from CCmdTarget, leaving the "OLE Automation" selection at "None". Thus:

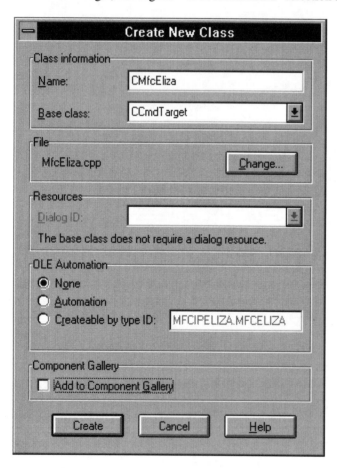

4. You must manually add several elements to your new class's header file. First, you must include the header file which defines the custom interface that you are implementing, in this case "**ieliza.h**". You must also include the macros **BEGIN_INTERFACE_PART** and **END_INTERFACE_PART**. Between these, you place the declaration of your custom interface's methods, omitting the IUnknown methods which are automatically declared by the former macro. This macro creates inside your CCmdTarget object a nested class which implements the member functions required by your custom interface. The name of the nested class is the first name specified in the macro with the letter 'X' prepended to it. The expansion of these macros is shown in the comment block of the source code sample below.

You must also include the macro **DECLARE_INTERFACE_MAP**, which declares an array of structures that IUnknown::QueryInterface( ) will use to keep track of the IDs and locations of the interface(s) you support. Finally, you must also declare a static variable of class *COleObjectFactory*, which is the MFC implementation of the class factory for your new COM class. Thus:

```
<file mfceliza.h>

#include "ieliza.h"

static const GUID GUID_MfcEliza = {0x963a0c60, 0x1a2c, 0x11cf,
    {0x89, 0xe1, 0x0, 0xaa, 0x0, 0xa5, 0x80, 0x97}} ;

class CMfcEliza : public CCmdTarget
{
    <standard header contents omitted>

/*
Declaration of the member functions used in the IEliza interface. When
expanded by the preprocessor, it becomes:

    class XEliza : public IEliza
    {
      public:
        STDMETHOD_(ULONG, AddRef)();
        STDMETHOD_(ULONG, Release)();
        STDMETHOD(QueryInterface)(REFIID iid, LPVOID* ppvObj);
        HRESULT virtual __stdcall Complain (LPOLESTR, LPOLESTR) ;
    } m_xEliza ;
    friend class XEliza ;

*/
    BEGIN_INTERFACE_PART (Eliza, IEliza)
        HRESULT virtual __stdcall Complain (LPOLESTR, LPOLESTR) ;
    END_INTERFACE_PART (Eliza)

/*
Declaration of array of structures used by IUnknown::QueryInterface to
determine which interface(s) this object supports.
*/
    DECLARE_INTERFACE_MAP ( )
/*
Declaration of class factory object, one per class.
*/
    static COleObjectFactory ms_ElizaFactory ;
};
```

5. The base class CCmdTarget contains an implementation of IUnknown, so you don't have to write any of the code for it. What you do have to provide is an array of data structures that the inherited QueryInterface( ) can use to determine which interfaces your object supports and which nested classes contain the VTBLs used for accessing the methods of these interfaces. This is conceptually and operationally similar to the message and dispatch maps used in the MFC. You provide this array of structures via the macros **BEGIN_INTERFACE_MAP** and **END_INTERFACE_MAP**. Between these two macros, you place one **INTERFACE_PART** macro for each interface you support. If you look at the expansion of the macro in the comment block below, you will find that it contains simply the interface ID and the offset of the nested object within the CCmdTarget. Thus:

```
<file mfceliza.cpp>

///////////////////////////////////////////////////////////////////////////
/////
// CMfcEliza message handlers

/*
On expansion, the INTERFACE_PART macro becomes:

    { &IID_IEliza, offsetof(CMfcEliza, m_xEliza) }

*/


BEGIN_INTERFACE_MAP (CMfcEliza, CCmdTarget)
    INTERFACE_PART (CMfcEliza, IID_IEliza, Eliza)
END_INTERFACE_MAP( )
```

6. When you used the BEGIN_INTERFACE_PART macro, it expanded as shown in the previous example to create a nested class with the letter X prepended onto the specified name. You must implement your interface's methods as member functions of the nested class. The linker will produce an error if you omit any of them. The IEliza::Complain( ) method is implemented as follows:

```
HRESULT CMfcEliza::XEliza::Complain (LPOLESTR pIn, LPOLESTR pOut)
{
    Eliza (pIn, pOut) ;
    return S_OK ;
}
```

7. The nested class's COM interface methods are called directly from the client application. Therefore, the implied C++ `this` pointer on the stack points to the nested class XEliza object itself, not the outer CMfcEliza object that contains it. The nested class's methods will almost certainly want to access the outer class's data or functions, but if you try to write code that does this directly, you will get a compiler error. The macro **METHOD_PROLOGUE** produces a pointer called **pThis** that points to the outer class and may be used to access its members.

8. You must provide function shells in the interface's VTBL for the nested class's QueryInterface( ), AddRef( ), and Release( ) methods; however, you don't have to write their actual code. The CCmdTarget base class contains an intelligent implementation of these methods, all you have to do is delegate to them as shown below. The MFC CCmdTarget is quite smart, even supporting a client request for aggregation (not discussed in this book; see Brockschmidt, pp. 101-105). The CCmdTarget methods **ExternalQueryInterface( )**, **ExternalAddRef( )**, and **ExternalRelease( )** will work properly whether your object is aggregated or not. The base class also contains internal versions of these functions, but the external versions shown are the ones you want. Thus:

```
/*
Implementation of nested class AddRef( )method.
*/

ULONG CMfcEliza::XEliza::AddRef( )
{
/*
Set up pThis pointer to access outer object.
*/
    METHOD_PROLOGUE (CMfcEliza, Eliza)

/*
Use pThis pointer to delegate to outer object's AddRef( ) method.
*/
    return pThis->ExternalAddRef( ) ;
}

ULONG CMfcEliza::XEliza::Release( )
{
    METHOD_PROLOGUE (CMfcEliza, Eliza) ;
    return pThis->ExternalRelease( ) ;
}

long CMfcEliza::XEliza::QueryInterface (REFIID riid, LPVOID *ppv)
{
    METHOD_PROLOGUE (CMfcEliza, Eliza) ;
    return pThis->ExternalQueryInterface (&riid, ppv) ;
}
```

9. You must also construct the class's **COleObjectFactory** static member variable, passing its constructor the parameters it needs to do its job. This creates the class factory object that produces CMfcEliza objects and sets the class factory's initial state. The first parameter is the class ID of the object manufactured by the class factory. Since App Wizard didn't generate it for you, you must use GUIDGEN.EXE to create a new one, which I have placed in the class header file which you saw on page 298. Thus:

```
AFX_DATADEF COleObjectFactory CMfcEliza::ms_ElizaFactory (
    GUID_MfcEliza,                      // class ID manufactured by this CF
    RUNTIME_CLASS(CMfcEliza),           // class to instantiate
    FALSE,                              // multi-instance ?
    TEXT("EssenceOfOle.Eliza.MfcCustomInProc")) ;    // human-readable
                                        //name of object for registry
```

10. You must also call the static function **COleObjectFactory::RegisterAll**( ), which does the internal MFC bookkeeping that connects the class factory to the MFC object that it manufactures. This probably wants to be done in the CWinApp::InitInstance( ) method. Thus:

```
BOOL CMfcipelizaApp::InitInstance()
{

/*
Initialize OLE in the MFC.
*/
    AfxOleInit ( ) ;

/*
Do internal bookkeeping that binds class factory to the MFC object that
it manufactures.
*/

    return COleObjectFactory::RegisterAll( ) ;

}
```

11. As shown in Chapter 2, in-proc servers must export the functions DllGetClassObject( ) to expose their class factories to the world and DllCanUnloadNow( ) to allow COM to monitor their internal states. You will probably also want to add the function DllRegisterServer( ) to perform self-registration of your in-proc server, as described in Appendix A. These are included automatically by App Wizard if you specify an OLE Automation in-proc server, but not if you specify a non-OLE DLL as we have done in the custom interface sample code. In this case, you must add them manually to your source code and export them from a .DEF file as shown below. All of these external entry points may simply delegate to internal MFC functions that perform the necessary operations. You will find the original code in the MFC source file DLLOLE.CPP. Thus:

```
<file mfceliza.cpp>

/*
Export class factory to COM.
*/

STDAPI DllGetClassObject(REFCLSID rclsid, REFIID riid, LPVOID* ppv)
{
    AFX_MANAGE_STATE(AfxGetStaticModuleState());

    return  AfxDllGetClassObject(rclsid, riid, ppv);
}

/*
Export internal state to COM.
*/

STDAPI DllCanUnloadNow(void)
{
    AFX_MANAGE_STATE(AfxGetStaticModuleState());
    return AfxDllCanUnloadNow();
}

/*
Export self-registration function to COM.
*/

STDAPI DllRegisterServer(void)
{
    AFX_MANAGE_STATE(AfxGetStaticModuleState());
    COleObjectFactory::UpdateRegistryAll();
    return S_OK;
}

<file mfcipeliza.def>
; mfcipeliza.def : Declares the module parameters for the DLL.

LIBRARY        "MFCIPELIZA"
DESCRIPTION    'MFCIPELIZA Windows Dynamic Link Library'
EXPORTS
    DllRegisterServer
    DllGetClassObject
    DllCanUnloadNow
```

12. Since you generated the custom interface local server without App Wizard OLE support, you must add the code shown below to initialize your app. The local server app first checks its command line to see if was launched as an OLE server. As you recall from Chapter 2, in this case a local server provides its class factory by calling the API function CoRegisterClassObject( ). In the MFC, this is wrapped up in the method **COleObjectFactory::RegisterAll( )**. If the app was not launched as an OLE server, it then calls the method COleObjectFactory::UpdateRegistryAll( ) to perform self-registration, as discussed in Appendix A.

This local server uses the IEliza interface. Since the marshaling code for the interface was set up in the standard marshaling local server example, you don't have to do anything else to get it to work.

```
BOOL CMfclosvApp::InitInstance()
{
/*
Initialize OLE.
*/
    AfxOleInit ( ) ;

/*
Check command line to see if launched as an OLE server.  If so, then
register class factories and return before showing the main window,
which is customary behavior in a server. The sample app has the return
line commented out, causing it to show itself for illustrative purposes.
*/
    if (cmdInfo.m_bRunEmbedded || cmdInfo.m_bRunAutomated)
    {
      COleObjectFactory::RegisterAll();
      return TRUE ;
    }

/*
If not, then update the registry with the app's current settings.
*/
    COleObjectFactory::UpdateRegistryAll();

    if (!ProcessShellCommand(cmdInfo))
      return FALSE;

    return TRUE;
}
```

13. An MFC custom interface app does not know to shut itself down after the last object has been destroyed. If you want this to happen, you must write your own code to make it so. In the supplied example, when an object is created, we increment a global counter in the class constructor. When an object is destroyed, we decrement the counter, and when the object count reaches 0, we shut down the app. Thus:

```
/*
Global count of all objects in the app.
*/

UINT g_ObjectCount = 0 ;

///////////////////////////////////////////////////////////////////////////
/////
// CMfcEliza

IMPLEMENT_DYNCREATE(CMfcEliza, CCmdTarget)

/*
Eliza object constructed, increment global object counter.
*/

CMfcEliza::CMfcEliza()
{
    g_ObjectCount ++ ;
}


/*
Eliza object destroyed, decrement global object counter.  Shut down app
if object count reaches 0.
*/

CMfcEliza::~CMfcEliza()
{
    g_ObjectCount -- ;

    if (g_ObjectCount == 0)
    {
      PostQuitMessage (0) ;
    }
}
```

This chapter contains more sample apps than the others. They are arranged as follows:

\EssenceOfOLE
  \chap09
    \Eliza

\client	client app for all IEliza samples
\inprocsv	in-proc server for IEliza interface
\localsv	local server for IEliza interface, standard marshaling
\marshprox	client-side proxy for IEliza interface, custom marshaling
\marshsv	local server for IEliza interface, custom marshaling
\mfcipau	MFC in-proc server for IEliza dispinterface, for comparison
\mfcipsv	MFC in-proc server for IEliza interface
\mfclocau	MFC local server for IEliza dispinterface, for comparison
\mfclosv	MFC local server for IEliza interface, standard marshaling

Because of the volume and interrelatedness of these apps, this chapter does not contain a prefabricated lab exercise. Instead, this section contains detailed instructions for getting the sample code up and running, and provides suggestions for experiments you might like to make with it. The non-MFC apps all use Unicode; the MFC apps do not.

1. First you must register all the servers. The root directory \Eliza contains a registry file ELIZA.REG. Run this file from the Explorer; it will register the IEliza in-proc server and local server. It also registers the standard marshaling of the IEliza interface and the custom marshaling proxy and server apps.

2. The MFC apps register contain MFC support for self-registration. Running the two local servers from the Explorer will cause them to make their own entries in the registry. The two MFC DLLs require the assistance of the system utility app REGSVR32.EXE. Running this app passing the name of the server DLL on the command line will load the DLL and cause it to make its own registry entries.

3. Run the client app.

4. The Time Test menu item makes a number of repeat calls. If "Perform Eliza Processing" box is checked, then Eliza will think about your response. If it is cleared, then Eliza will ignore it, allowing you to measure only the function call overheads.

This page intentionally contains no text other than this sentence.

Chapter 10
Distributed COM (DCOM)

A. CONCEPTS AND DEFINITIONS

1. Consider the model of OLE shown in the diagram below (see Chapter 9 if you need a refresher). One of the major strengths of OLE to date is that neither client nor server need particularly concern itself with whether the other party is in a .EXE file or a .DLL. With the release of Windows NT 4.0, this transparency is extended to apps running on different machines connected by a network. The component of the operating system that performs this function is Distributed COM (DCOM).

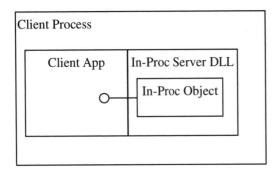

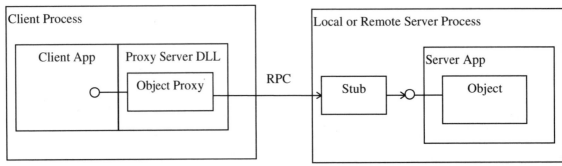

2. When a client creates an object which lives on a remote server, the client doesn't do much different than when it connects to an object on a local server. The functions to create the object might change a little (see page 311) or possibly not at all (see page 310). All object functions appear to the client to reside in a DLL in the client's address space. Sometimes the functions contain the object's actual functionality (in-proc server), and sometimes they contain only proxy functions that communicate with the actual object functionality that lives in another process (local server) or another machine (remote server). The client neither knows nor cares nor could easily find out which case it is.

3. The server of a remote object generally doesn't do anything different at all. Exposing its capability to clients on different machines is primarily an administrative task performed by the system administrator. The server generally doesn't know or care if its clients are local or remote.

WARNING: The sample programs in this chapter were developed with the Beta 2 version of Windows NT 4.0. There will probably be significant changes between these samples and the release of the final operating system. Don't be surprised if you have to recompile the sample apps or rebuild their projects. The TCP/IP network protocol needed to be installed and running for any of these functions to work.

B. USING EXISTING CLIENT APPS WITH DCOM

1. Existing client apps that were developed without knowledge of DCOM may still use objects provided by remote servers. Remember that when a client app calls CoCreateInstance( ), OLE reads the registry looking for the InProcServer32 or LocalServer32 entries in order to find the server for the specified class ID. With the addition of DCOM to the operating system, if this search fails, then OLE will look for the registry key "**RemoteServerName**" under the object's CLSID entry. In the following example, the data3 sample from Chapter 2 will look for its server on the remote machine \\SAMADAMS. For this operation to succeed, a server .EXE or .DLL for the specified class ID must be registered on the named remote system, and the client must have permission from the server machine's security system to launch that app (see page 315). Thus:

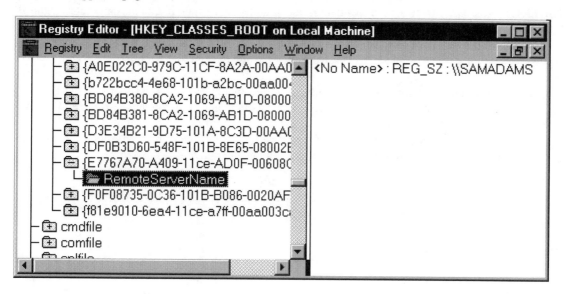

C. REMOTE OBJECT CREATION

1. You may explicitly create an object on a remote system via the API function **CoCreateInstanceEx( )**. An example of the use of this function is shown on the facing page. The flag **CLSCTX_REMOTE_SERVER** specifies that the object is to be created on a remote machine which may be anywhere on the network that is visible to the calling app. The server name is specified in a structure of type **COSERVERINFO**.

OLE object method calls over a network are slow compared to calls made on the same machine. To improve performance, CoCreateInstanceEx( ) allows you to query for more than one interface when the object is created. In this way, you incur the network overhead of only a single function call when obtaining all the interface pointers you want to use. You pass a pointer to an array of structures of type **MULTI_QI** as the last parameter to CoCreateInstanceEx( ). Each structure contains a pointer to the ID of the requested interface, which you must set before making the call. Each structure contains an HRESULT and an interface pointer which are filled on output. When the function returns, these will be filled with the result of the request for the specified interface and a pointer to that interface.

2. A sample app containing the code fragment on the facing page may be found in the directory \chap10\data4\client. It contains an upgraded version of the client app from the data3 example in Chapter 2. I have added menu choices to the app which allow you to specify a remote server for an object and create an object from the remote server. The performance test menu items and advise loop functionality have been left in, allowing you to compare local versus remote operation.

```
extern WCHAR wServerName ;
extern CLSID GUID_TimeData ;
extern LPDATAOBJECT lpd ;

case ID_DATAOBJECT_CREATEFROMREMOTESERVER:
{
    HRESULT hr ;

/*
Set up COSERVERINFO structure specifying name of remote server.
*/
    COSERVERINFO si ;
    si.dwSize = sizeof (si) ;
    si.pszName = wServerName ;

/*
Set up array of MULTI_QI structures to specify requested interfaces and
hold returned pointers. Here we only have one.
*/

    MULTI_QI mqi [1] ;
    CLSID ido = IID_IDataObject ;

    mqi [0].pIID = &ido ;
    mqi [0].pItf = NULL ;
    mqi [0].hr = 0 ;

/*
Create instance of object on remote machine.
*/
    hr = CoCreateInstanceEx (
      GUID_TimeData,               // class ID of requested object
      NULL,                        // no aggregation
      CLSCTX_REMOTE_SERVER,        // remote server required
      &si,                         // name of remote server
      1,                           // # of interfaces to query for
      mqi) ;                       // array of MULTI_QI for each
                                   //   requested interface

/*
If call succeeded, use returned interface pointer.  Otherwise signal
error.
*/
    if (SUCCEEDED(mqi[0].hr))
    {
      lpd = (LPDATAOBJECT) mqi [0].pItf ;
    }
    else
    {
      MessageBox (hWnd, "Couldn't create object", "Error", MB_ICONSTOP);
    }
    return 0 ;
}
```

3. The function **CoGetClassObject( )**, which gets the class factory that manufactures a specified class of object, has also been upgraded to support DCOM. The third parameter to this function, which previously was reserved, now may contain a pointer to a COSERVERINFO structure which specifies the remote machine from which the class factory is to be obtained. Thus:

```
LPCLASSFACTORY lpcf ;
extern WCHAR wServerName ;
extern CLSID GUID_TimeData ;

case ID_DATAOBJECT_GETREMOTECLASSFACTORY:
{
    HRESULT hr ;

/*
Set up COSERVERINFO structure specifying name of remote server.
*/
    COSERVERINFO si ;
    si.dwSize = sizeof (si) ;
    si.pszName = wServerName ;

/*
Get class factory that manufactures objects of class GUID_TimeData. We
might use it later to create an instance of the object.
*/

    hr = CoGetClassObject (
       GUID_TimeData,            // class ID made by requested factory
       CLSCTX_REMOTE_SERVER,     // remote server required
       &si,                      // server on which to get class factory
       IID_IClassFactory,        // interface ID wanted on class factory
       (LPVOID *) &lpcf) ;       // output variable

    if (!SUCCEEDED(hr))
    {
       MessageBox (NULL, "Couldn't get remote cf", "", 0) ;
    }

    return 0 ;
}
```

Note: The preceding code fragment does not appear in the data4cl sample program. Implementing it is left as an exercise to the student.

D. CONFIGURING DCOM

    1. Most of the work in setting up the server side of DCOM is a matter of administration, not programming. DCOM is configured using the utility app DCOMCNFG.EXE, which is still in its infancy at the time of this writing. It's so new that it doesn't even have its own icon, it still uses the generic MFC icon. You use this app to specify which users are allowed to perform which operations on which apps. You enable DCOM and specify its default connection information with the "Default Properties" tab. Thus:

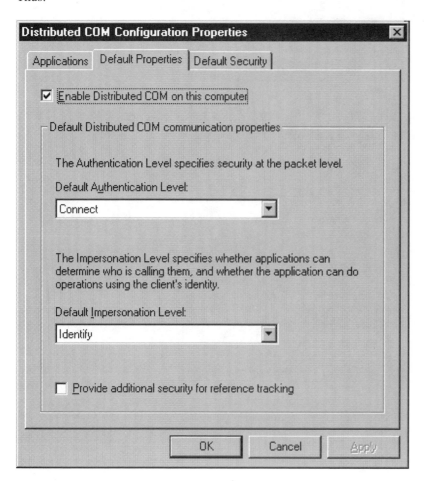

2. On the "Default Security" tab, you specify which users are allowed to access applications and which users are allowed to launch server apps. Individual apps may override these settings as shown on subsequent pages. Thus:

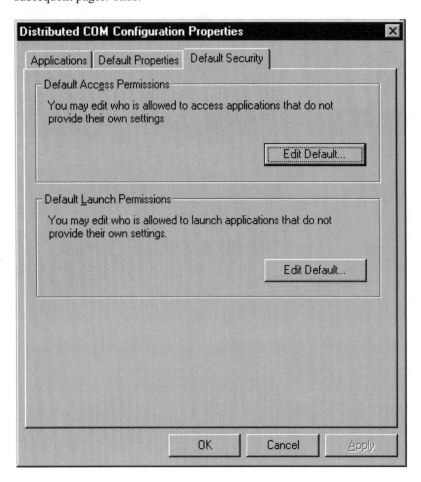

3. When you pick the "Edit Default" button, you see the following dialog box with which you allow or deny launch permission to various users or groups of users. This process is similar to setting permissions for other security features. The actual security information is stored in the system registry. Thus:

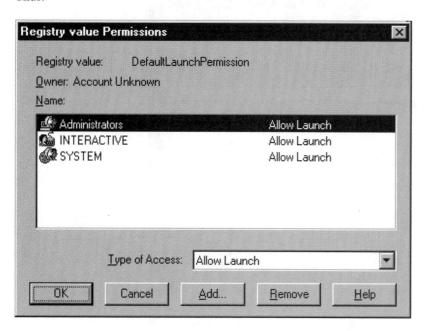

4. When you start DCOMCNFG, it reads the registry and shows you a list of the registered object servers on the system. Thus:

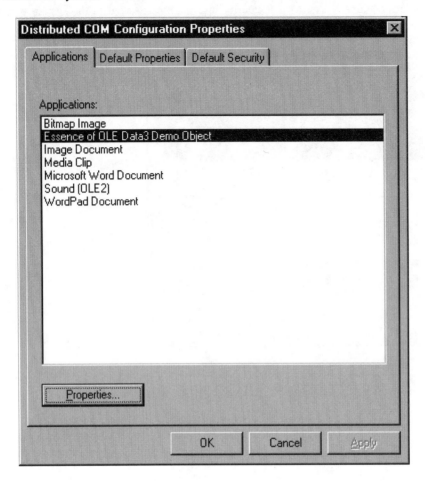

5. For each object, you can specify that it uses the default access permissions that you set systemwide. Or you can specify different access permissions for different servers. Thus:

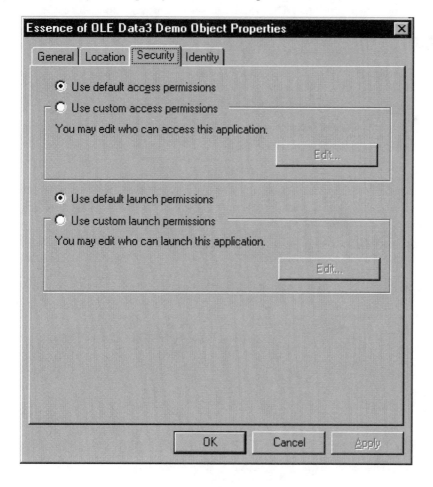

6. You may also specify the identity of the user with which a server is launched. A server may change this via the API functions CoImpersonateClient( ) and CoRevertToSelf( ) (not shown), which operate in a similar manner to the named pipe and DDE security impersonation functions. Thus:

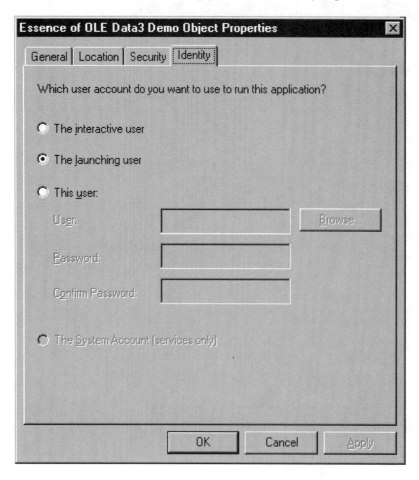

Chapter 11
ActiveX Controls on the Internet

A. COMPONENT DOWNLOAD SERVICE

    1. To operate in an Internet environment, container apps need to be able to download ActiveX controls from the Internet and install them on the user's local system. In addition, container apps need some form of security checking to allow the user to download only controls from trusted sources and ensure that they have not been tampered with. This functionality is provided by the *component download service*.

    The control download service is not restricted to downloading only ActiveX controls. It can download and use any OLE server, in-proc or local, provided that the server is self-registering as specified in Appendix A. It is also fully backwards compatible – the downloaded server need not contain any extra functionality in order to make it downloadable.

    The examples shown in this section use the sample app found in the directory \CHAP11\CLIENT. For maximum flexibility and transparency, this app does not read its parameters from an HTML page. Instead, the user enters them through a dialog box. The app creates a single control of any class that you specify, downloading the control from the Internet if necessary. The app also allows you to specify the name and value of a single property. When the app finishes creating the control, it will set the named property to the specified value. Thus:

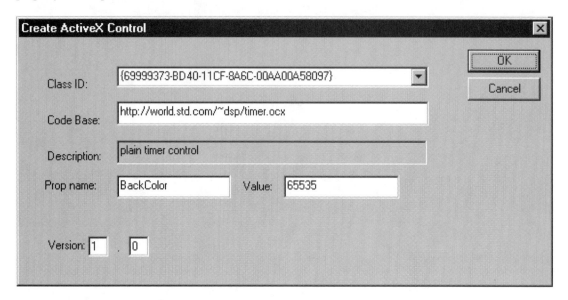

    Note: This sample app was generated using App Wizard with "OCX Controls" box checked. However, to get CoGetClassObjectFromURL( ) to work, it was necessary to add a call to AfxOleInit( ) in the CWinApp::InitInstance( ) method. Otherwise, it came back with an error saying that OLE hadn't been initialized.

2. In HTML, an ActiveX control is signaled via the **<OBJECT>** tag, added to the HTML 3.2 specification by Microsoft. When you use the ActiveX Control Pad utility app (shown on next page) to add a timer control of the type built in Chapter 5 to an HTML page, you get the following HTML code, which may be found in the directory \CHAP11\DOWNLOAD\TIMER.HTM:

```
<OBJECT
    ID="Timer1" WIDTH=100 HEIGHT=51
    CLASSID="CLSID:69999373-BD40-11CF-8A6C-00AA00A58097"
    CODEBASE="http://www.rollthunder.com/timer.ocx">
    <PARAM NAME="_Version" VALUE="65536">
    <PARAM NAME="_ExtentX" VALUE="2646">
    <PARAM NAME="_ExtentY" VALUE="1341">
    <PARAM NAME="_StockProps" VALUE="1">
    <PARAM NAME="ShowSeconds" VALUE="-1">
</OBJECT>
```

The **CLASSID** attribute specifies the class ID of the OLE object to create. This is the same OLE/COM class ID that we've used throughout this book. The **CODEBASE** attribute specifies the URL from which the object's server (the .OCX DLL) can be downloaded if it isn't already on the user's system.

Each **<PARAM>** tag specifies the name and value of a property of the control. The properties that begin with an underscore, such as "_Version" in the above example, are not properties exposed by the control itself, but instead are for the use of the HTML browser. In the example shown above, the control's "ShowSeconds" property is set to -1 (TRUE).

3. You can place ActiveX controls on an HTML document using the ActiveX Control Pad, an HTML utility app available free from Microsoft's Web site. When you run the app and select "Edit – Insert ActiveX control", it reads the registry and shows you the following dialog box containing the names of all the controls registered on your system. As far as I can tell, it detects controls by looking for the "Control" registry key that OCX and now ActiveX controls place in their registry entries. Thus:

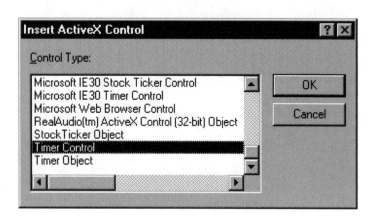

4. When you insert a control, the Control Pad loads the control's DLL, creates an instance of the control, and displays a window for editing the control's properties in a manner similar to Visual Basic. When you close the control's window, the Control Pad writes the appropriate HTML statements into its file. Thus:

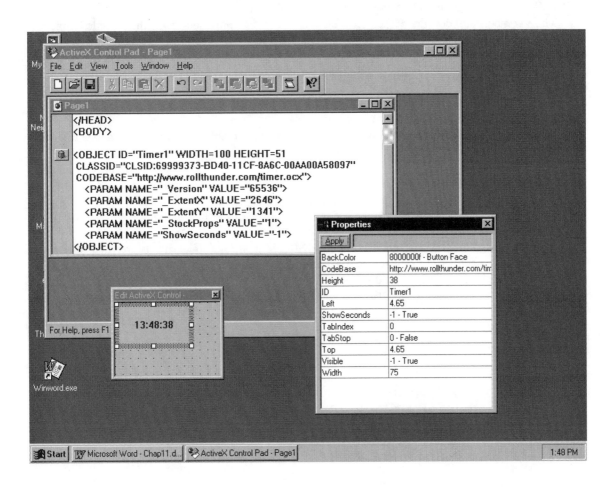

5. Your container app will eventually need to create a new ActiveX control, either from reading an HTML file or, as in the sample app, because the user makes entries in a dialog box. The control might already be on your machine, or you might have to download it from the Internet. Even if a version of the control already exists on your system, the Web page may specify a newer version, so any time you see an <OBJECT> tag, you might need to download it or you might not.

The component download service of ActiveX is provided by the single function **CoGetClassObjectFromURL( )**. This function does its level best to return a pointer to the requested object's class factory.

The function first attempts to retrieve from the user's machine the class factory for the specified class ID and version of object. If this is successful, the function returns immediately with the success code S_OK and the output parameter contains a pointer to the class factory. In this case, the behavior is identical to the API function CoGetClassObject( ).

If this is not successful, the function attempts to download the control from the Internet using the specified URL. This process uses the asynchronous URL moniker with an IBindStatusCallback object, as discussed in the last section of Chapter 8. In this case, the function returns the code **MK_S_ASYNCHRONOUS**, meaning that the download has been successfully started. Further notifications of progress and final success or failure are signaled through the IBindStatusCallback interface's methods. The URL may indicate a single .EXE or .DLL, or it may point to compressed .CAB and .INF files.

After the download is successfully completed, the control's integrity is verified using the WinTrustVerify( ) mechanism discussed on page 333. The control is registered on the user's machine using the self-registration mechanism discussed in Appendix A. Finally, the control is loaded and the class factory returned in the method IBindStatusCallback::OnObjectAvailable( ) shown on page 328. Thus:

```
class CClientView : public CView
{
public:
    CBindStatusCallback *m_pCallback ;      IUnknown*    m_pUnknown ;
    IBindCtx*       m_pBindCtx ;            CProgressCtrl m_Progress ;

    <rest of class declaration>
}


void CClientView::OnControlCreate()
{
/*
Pop up dialog box asking user which control to create.
*/
    CCreateControlDlg dlg ;
    if (dlg.DoModal( ) == IDOK)
    {
      m_clsid = dlg.m_clsid ;
/*
Create a new bind status callback for asynchronous notifications during
the download. Create a bind context. Register the IBindStatusCallback
with it.
*/
        m_pCallback = new CBindStatusCallback (this) ;
        HRESULT hr = CreateBindCtx (0, &m_pBindCtx) ;

        IBindStatusCallback *pPrev = NULL ;
        hr = RegisterBindStatusCallback (m_pBindCtx, m_pCallback, &pPrev,
            NULL);
```

```
/*
Get class factory for specified control, downloading from the Internet
if necessary. Parameters entered by user via dialog box.
*/
      hr = CoGetClassObjectFromURL (
                  dlg.m_clsid,               // class ID of control
                  dlg.m_wUrlString,          // URL to download from
                  dlg.m_VersionMajor,        // major version number
                  dlg.m_VersionMinor,        // minor version number
                  NULL,                      // mime type
                  m_pBindCtx,                // bind ctx with IBindStatusCallback
                  CLSCTX_INPROC_SERVER,      // server context
                  NULL,                      // reserved
                  IID_IUnknown,              // interface ptr wanted on class f'y
                  (LPVOID *) &m_pUnknown) ;     // output variable

/*
Return code was S_OK, meaning control already existed on the user's
machine.  Create the control.
*/
      if (hr == S_OK)
      {
            ReallyCreateControl ( ) ;
            Cleanup ( ) ;
      }
/*
Return code was MK_S_ASYNCHRONOUS, meaning control must be downloaded.
Show progress control to user.
*/
      else if (hr == MK_S_ASYNCHRONOUS)
      {
            m_Progress.ShowWindow (SW_NORMAL) ;
            m_StatusText = "Control download Pending" ;
            Invalidate ( ) ;
      }
/*
Error condition.  Signal and abort.
*/
      else
      {
            AfxMessageBox ("Couldn't download control") ;
            Cleanup ( ) ;
      }
   }
}
```

6. The IBindStatusCallback object used in component download is a little different than that shown in Chapter 8. It must also support the interface *ICodeInstall*, which provides access to the UI for the component installation services. Supporting this interface is easily done via multiple inheritance. Its methods are pretty trivial. Thus:

```
class CBindStatusCallback : public IBindStatusCallback,
    public ICodeInstall
{
  public:

    < remainder of IBindStatusCallback declaration omitted, see page N>

    // ICodeInstall methods

    STDMETHODIMP GetWindow (REFGUID , HWND *) ;
    STDMETHODIMP OnCodeInstallProblem (ULONG, LPCWSTR, LPCWSTR, DWORD) ;
} ;


/*
Provide window handle used by OLE as parent for dialog boxes that OLE
will show relating to code installation.
*/

STDMETHODIMP CBindStatusCallback::GetWindow (REFGUID riid, HWND *phWnd)
{
    if (phWnd)
    {
      *phWnd = m_pView->m_hWnd ;
    }
    return S_OK;
}


/*
OLE has signaled a code installation problem.  Tell the user about it,
and return the code E_FAIL to abort the installation.
*/

STDMETHODIMP CBindStatusCallback::OnCodeInstallProblem (ULONG uiStatus,
    LPCWSTR pExistFile, LPCWSTR pSource, DWORD dwReserved)
{
    AfxMessageBox ("OnCodeInstallProblem") ;
    return E_FAIL ;
}
```

7. When CoGetClassObjectFromURL has downloaded, verified, and registered the specified control, it will call the method **IBindStatusCallback::OnObjectAvailable( )**. This is your signal that the object now exists and may be used. In the sample app, we create the control and clean up. Thus:

```
STDMETHODIMP CBindStatusCallback::OnObjectAvailable(REFIID riid,
    IUnknown* punk)
{

/*
Component download finished, control should now be installed. Use helper
function, shown on next page, to create it.
*/

    m_pView->ReallyCreateControl( ) ;

/*
Clean up after the control creation.
*/

    m_pView->Cleanup ( ) ;
    return S_OK;
}
```

8. Once you have the control's server installed on your system, you create the control exactly like any other OLE control, via the method CWnd::CreateControl( ). Why don't we use the IClassFactory interface pointer that we got from CoGetClassObjectFromURL( )? Because the CWnd proxy model used by control containers in the MFC requires so much other auxiliary setup, which is built into the CreateControl( ) method, that we can't skip it.

Once the control is created, you need to set its properties. In the MFC, it's dead easy to work with a control if you know at compile time which control you will be using. Class Wizard just generates a wrapper class based on the control's type info. It's much more difficult if you don't know until run time which control you will be using. The control in the sample app lives within a class called *CCtrlHolder*, which provides auxiliary functions for manipulating an arbitrary control.

If the <OBJECT> HTML tag contains an attribute with the name <DATA>, it represents a property stream saved by the control. You can query the control for the IPersistStream interface and pass the <DATA> stream to it. But you can't depend on this being present, so you need to be able to set the control's properties individually via its IDispatch interface, as represented by the **CCtrlHolder::SetPropByName( )** function called below and discussed on the following pages. Thus:

```
BOOL CClientView::ReallyCreateControl (void)
{

/*
Delete previous CWnd proxy that held our control, if there was one.
Then create CWnd proxy to hold new control.
*/
    if (m_pCtrlHolder)
    {
      delete m_pCtrlHolder ;
    }
    m_pCtrlHolder = new CCtrlHolder (m_clsid) ;

/*
Create the control as usual.
*/
    CRect r (10, 10, 200, 200) ;
    BOOL bOK = m_pCtrlHolder->CreateControl (
      m_clsid, "", WS_CHILD | WS_VISIBLE | WS_BORDER,
      r, this, 1, NULL, FALSE, NULL) ;

    if (!bOK)
    {
      AfxMessageBox ("Couldn't create") ;
    }
    else
    {
      m_pCtrlHolder->ShowWindow (SW_SHOWNORMAL) ;
      m_pCtrlHolder->BringWindowToTop( ) ;
    }
/*
Set property specified in dialog box.
*/
    m_pCtrlHolder->SetPropByName (m_PropName, m_PropVal) ;
    return bOK ;
}
```

9. The method **CCtrlHolder::SetPropByName( )** takes the name of a property and its value in the form of strings and sets it. First, we get the dispatch ID of the name and the type of the property via auxiliary functions shown on the following pages. To convert the string value of the property into whatever type is required, we instantiate an object of the MFC class *COleVariant* and use the method **COleVariant::ChangeType( )**.

The actual setting of the property is done via the method **COleControlSite::SetPropertyV( )**. The member variable m_pCtrlSite, introduced in Chapter 6, is a member of the CWnd class, which you have to include the header file "**occimpl.h**" in order to acces. Thus:

```
HRESULT CCtrlHolder::SetPropByName (CString PropName, CString PropVal)
{

/*
Get dispatch ID of named property via helper function shown on next
page.
*/
    DISPID id ;
    HRESULT hr = GetIDOfName (PropName, &id) ;

    if (hr != S_OK)
    {
      return hr ;
    }

/*
Get type of named property using helper function shown on subsequent
page.
*/
    VARTYPE vt ;
    hr = GetTypeOfProperty (id, &vt) ;

/*
Convert string value of property into requested type.
*/
    COleVariant var (PropVal) ;
    var.ChangeType (vt) ;

/*
Set the actual property. The method requires a pointer to the data
element of the VARIANT structure, which is 8 bytes from the start.
*/

    VARIANT *pv = (LPVARIANT)(&var) ;
    m_pCtrlSite->SetPropertyV (id, vt, ((char *)pv) + 8) ;

    return S_OK ;
}
```

10.   The   method   **CCtrlHolder::GetIDOfName( )**   is   a   simple   wrapper   for IDispatch::GetIDsOfNames( ). The IDispatch interface is present in the m_pControlSite's **m_dispDriver** element. Thus:

```
HRESULT CCtrlHolder::GetIDOfName (CString &Name, DISPID *pDispIdOut)
{
    DISPID id ;

/*
Convert property name into wide char.
*/
    WCHAR wName [256], *pNames ;

    MultiByteToWideChar (CP_ACP, 0, (LPCTSTR)Name, -1,
      wName, sizeof(wName)/sizeof(WCHAR)) ;

    pNames = wName ;

/*
Call IDispatch::GetIDsOfNames( )on the IDispatch that lives inside the
COleControlSite that lives inside the CWnd.
*/
    HRESULT hr = m_pCtrlSite->m_dispDriver.m_lpDispatch->GetIDsOfNames(
      IID_NULL, &pNames, 1, LOCALE_SYSTEM_DEFAULT, &id) ;

    *pDispIdOut = id ;
    return hr ;
}
```

11. The helper function **CCtrlHolder::GetTypeOfProperty( )** looks in the object's type info to read the type of the property associated with the specified dispatch ID. This is fairly simple using the principles shown in Chapter 4. The only tricky part is the types of stock properties. If you look them up in the type library, you will find that they have the value VT_USERDEFINED, so this method needs to special case them. Thus: :

```
HRESULT CCtrlHolder::GetTypeOfProperty (DISPID id, VARTYPE *pvt)
{
    ITypeInfo *pti ;

/*
Get type info describing this IDispatch.
*/
    HRESULT hr = m_pCtrlSite->m_dispDriver.m_lpDispatch->GetTypeInfo (0,
        LOCALE_SYSTEM_DEFAULT, &pti) ;

    if (hr != S_OK)
    {
      return hr ;
    }

/*
Check for stock property dispatch IDs. The type library does not tell us
what they are, but the Microsoft spec does.
*/
    switch (id)
    {
      case DISPID_BACKCOLOR:
      case DISPID_FORECOLOR:
      {
          *pvt = VT_I4 ;
          return S_OK ;
      }
    }

/*
Iterate through all the properties until we find the specified one.
*/
    int i = 0 ;   VARDESC *pVarDesc ;

    while (pti->GetVarDesc  (i, &pVarDesc) == S_OK)
    {
      if (pVarDesc->memid == id)
      {
          *pvt = (pVarDesc->elemdescVar).tdesc.vt ;
          pti->ReleaseVarDesc (pVarDesc) ;
          return S_OK ;
      }
      i++ ;
      pti->ReleaseVarDesc (pVarDesc) ;
    }
    return E_FAIL ;
}
```

331

B. ActiveX Control Security

1. Downloading and running code from the Internet raises obvious concerns about security. How do you know that the full-motion belly dancer control that a page promises isn't a Trojan horse for code that formats your hard drive and cancels your subscription to the automatic backup service?

Microsoft had two options for designing control security. Internet controls could have been run in a heavily restricted space with a low level of privileges, for example, not allowing them to delete files. This "sandbox" design approach was rejected because it would have severely limited the usefulness of code from the net, and would have been impossible to implement on Windows 95.

The selected design approach uses a verification system, not a restriction system. It provides accountability, not safety. The operating system does not restrict the actions of a control once it has been installed. It doesn't keep a control from formatting your hard drive. It ensures that you know whom to kill if it does. The relatively few things you can do to protect against malicious controls that slip through are described at the end of this section.

A control from a responsible vendor will contain a digital signature, allowing the operating system to verify that it really does come from the vendor that it says it does. The control will also contain an encrypted hash value, allowing the operating system to detect if it has been altered since the vendor signed it. With this knowledge, you may decide intelligently whether or not to allow the control to be installed on your system. The process of generating a signature and placing it on a control is discussed in more detail on page 337.

2. CoGetClassObjectFromURL( ) uses the API function WinVerifyTrust( ) to inspect the newly downloaded control and check for the presence of the encrypted signature block. This signature block is decoded by a public key provided by a commercial security company such as VeriSign or GTE CyberTrust. The decoded signature block ensures that the file comes from a vendor that has registered with a security company, and contains a hash code that ensures it hasn't been tampered with since it was signed by its vendor.

When the function determines that the control contains a valid signature and hasn't been changed, it will pop up the following dialog box, thereby allowing the user to accept or reject the component. All the dialogs shown on this page and the next are shown directly by WinVerifyTrust( ). Thus:

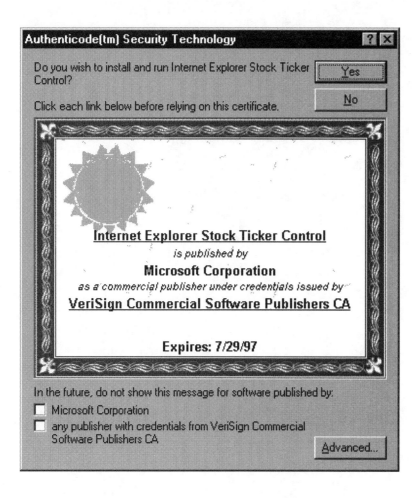

3. If the downloaded control does not contain a verifiable signature block, the user will see one of the following two dialog boxes. The first box is shown even if the control has in fact been signed but has later been tampered with, thereby invalidating the hash code. It is up to you to decide whether or not to allow the control to be installed. Good luck.

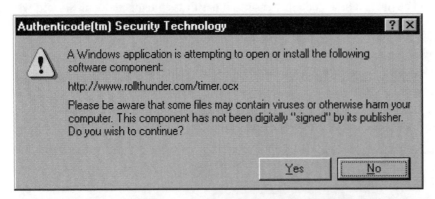

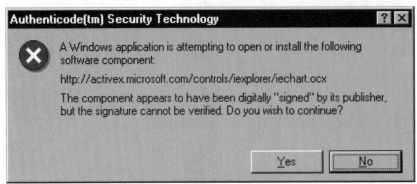

4. The user has the choice of designating certain vendors as trusted. In this case, any future downloaded component from any of the designated sources is automatically installed and the user not queried as on the previous page, provided that the control hasn't been tampered with. Thus:

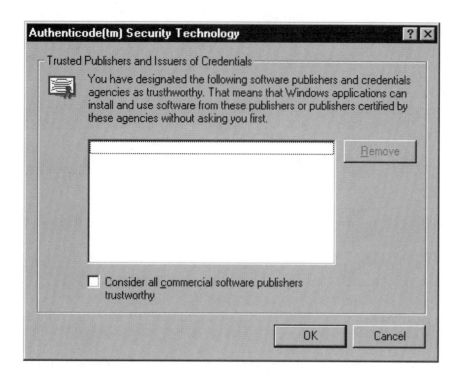

Note: Checking the bottom box to allow any commercial software vendor is not quite as stupid as it initially appears. Think what you do today in a software store. You don't worry about security problems because the boxes are shrink wrapped from commercial vendors. I still wouldn't check it myself.

5. The algorithm used by WinVerifyTrust( ) is based on the RSA public key encryption system. This system relies on two large prime number keys. A message encoded with one key can only be decoded with the other. The keys are large enough that one cannot reasonably be calculated from the other. You publish one, the public key, and keep the other, the private key, secret.

Suppose you are a vendor. You generate a private/public key pair and publish the latter half of it. Anyone wanting to send you a secure message encodes it using your public key before sending it to you. If someone intercepts the message, he will not be able to read it because decoding requires your private key. Conversely, if you encode a message with your private key and post the message on the Internet, anyone who downloads the message can be statistically sure that it came only from you if they can successfully decode it with your public key.

This works fine as long as the public keys are trustworthy. Suppose I were to post a malicious control on the Internet and claim that it came from Microsoft, and post a public key with which it could be decoded. You would take the control, decode it successfully with the key, and think everything was OK. The problem was that the public key didn't really come from Microsoft; instead it came from Trojan Horse Software and your hard disk is toast. You need a trustworthy repository of public keys for this scheme to work.

Enter the *certification authority* (CA), such as VeriSign GTE's or CyberTrust. These companies, for an annual fee, will verify your identity and provide a digital certificate that contains your public key. WinVerifyTrust( ) looks for such a certificate when it validates the control's signature.

You can sign up with a CA over the Internet, at www.verisign.com and www.cybertrust.gte.com. During the sign-up process, your browser will use the operating system's cryptography API to generate a private and public key pair. The private key will be saved on your machine in a file with the extension ".PVK". The public key will be sent to the CA. This outfit will do whatever verification of your identity it thinks it ought to, and if successful, send you a digital certificate, a file with the extension ".SPC". You need both of these files to sign a control.

Most certifying agencies provide several levels of authentication. In researching this book, I got an individual developer certificate from VeriSign, which costs $20 per year. To authenticate your existence, VeriSign looks you up in the Equifax credit bureau files. If your information matches theirs, you're in. Equifax had my age wrong and I wasn't able to sign up until I got a copy of my credit report from Equifax and signed up with VeriSign using the incorrect information. So much for trusting the individual certificate. A commercial developer's certificate costs $400 per year and requires a Dun & Bradstreet number or similar reference.

6. Once you get the key from a certifying agency, you sign your control using the utility app SignCode. This performs a hash of your control and encrypts it with your private key. It then places the encryted hash result and the CA certificate into your control.

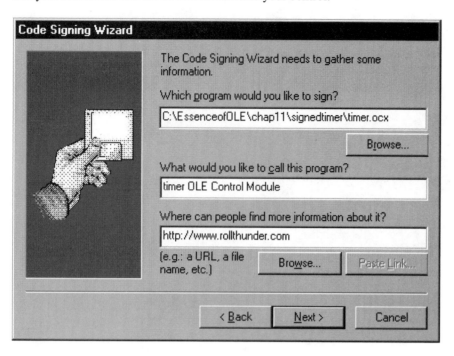

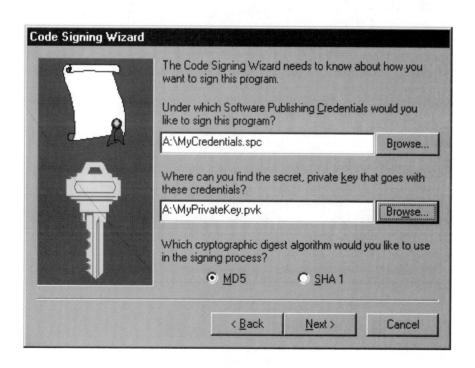

7. The final dialog box looks like this. The directory \CHAP11\SIGNEDTIMER contains a version of the timer control from Chapter 5 which has been signed. When you download it from the Internet, you will see the dialog box at the bottom of the page.

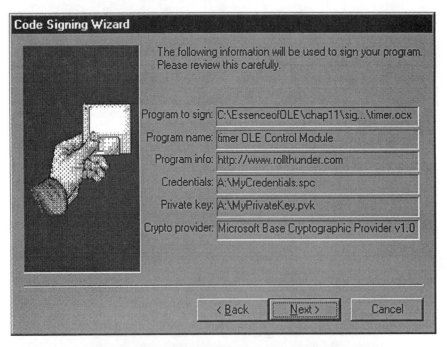

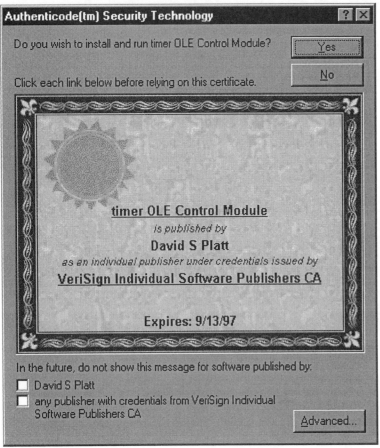

8. There is a limit to the amount of safety that the code signing approach can provide. If you're not comfortable with it, there are a couple of things that you can do. The first is to restrict the locations from which controls can be downloaded to places that you trust. This is accomplished via the code base search path. In the registry, there is a value called:

```
HKEY_CURRENT_USER\Software\Microsoft\Windows\CurrentVersion\
    InternetSettings\CodeBaseSearchPath
```

as shown in the screen shot below:

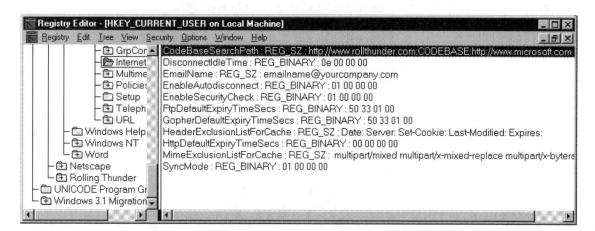

When an app running on this machine calls CoGetClassObjectFromURL( ), the function will attempt to download the code from the servers specified in this registry setting, in the order in which they appear. In the example above, the function will first attempt to download from www.rollthunder.com, then from the URL passed as a parameter to the function, then from www.microsoft.com. If you leave out the CODEBASE keyword, then downloads will only be possible from servers specified in the registry list regardless of what parameters are passed to the function. This is probably the first line of defense for a corporate intranet.

9. Anyone wanting more security and running Windows NT can use the NTFS file system. You make a separate account with no privileges that you use only for Internet surfing. If a malicious control tries to access or modify a disk file owned by another account, it will be blocked by the operating system. You still have the problem of it planting a malicious document and infecting global files such as a WinWord document template, but at least you've raised the intelligence and effort a vandal needs to damage your system.

C. ADVANCED FEATURES OF ACTIVEX CONTROLS

1. With the release of MFC 4.2, Microsoft added advanced properties to ActiveX controls. While these properties were originally inspired by the design needs of controls on HTML pages, they may be used any place you think they make sense. These are accessed via the "Advanced..." button in Control Wizard. Thus:

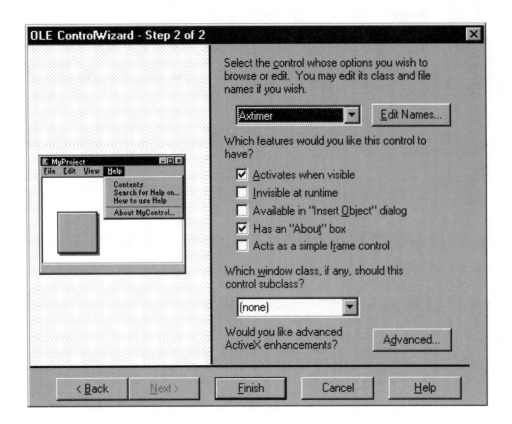

2. When you select the "Advanced..." button, Control Wizard shows you the following dialog box allowing you to select the advanced properties that you want. Loading properties asynchronously is a very useful property for an Internet control and the balance of this chapter discusses it in detail.

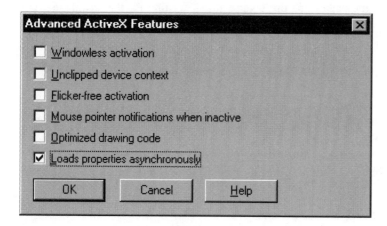

The other features are today mostly red herrings. You make little or no profit, and possibly incur a loss, from implementing them. They all depend on the active support of their container. At the time of this writing no container supports them, not even IE3 or the VC++ Test Container, so you can't tell if they work or not. I have to think that it will be a long time before Netscape supports them, if it ever does. This means that even if you want your control to use windowless activation if available, you will still have to support windowed activation as well in order to run properly in any environment. The small performance benefit that you might gain from windowless activation in one browser is probably not worth the additional development and testing time.

D. ASYNCHRONOUS DOWNLOAD OF PROPERTIES

1. Your ActiveX controls may require large pieces of data from the Internet. For example, a movie control might need to download the 5 Megabyte AVI file that it is to play. You want the control to become active as soon as possible and the page to be displayed without waiting for the download. The user may never actually play it, especially if he's on a 28.8 kbaud phone line. You would like the download to proceed asynchronously in background without gumming up the viewer. The source code examples in this section are from a very simple text control which downloads its text asynchronously. The source files may be found in the directory \CHAP11\ATEXT, and instructions for it are at the end of this chapter.

2.When you check the box on the previous page, Control Wizard adds to your control a property called "ReadyState", which tells the container the state of your control's asynchronous download, and also adds an event called "ReadyStateChange", which the control fires when its ReadyState property changes. For example, the control might set the property and fire the event when it finishes its download, and the container might respond by enabling the "Play" button. Thus:

```
[ uuid(8B159891-0429-11D0-B8A1-00608C876FB3),
  helpstring("Dispatch interface for Atext Control"), hidden ]
dispinterface _DAtext
{
    properties:
      //{{AFX_ODL_PROP(CAtextCtrl)
      [id(DISPID_READYSTATE), readonly] long ReadyState;
      //}}AFX_ODL_PROP
    methods:
      //{{AFX_ODL_METHOD(CAtextCtrl)
      //}}AFX_ODL_METHOD
      [id(DISPID_ABOUTBOX)] void AboutBox();
};


//  Event dispatch interface for CAtextCtrl

[ uuid(8B159892-0429-11D0-B8A1-00608C876FB3),
  helpstring("Event interface for Atext Control") ]
dispinterface _DAtextEvents
{
    properties:
     //  Event interface has no properties
    methods:
     //{{AFX_ODL_EVENT(CAtextCtrl)
     [id(DISPID_READYSTATECHANGE)] void ReadyStateChange(long NewState);
     //}}AFX_ODL_EVENT
};
```

WARNING: At the time of this writing, MFC version 4.2A contains a bug that causes the ReadyStateChange( ) event entry in the ODL file to contain no parameters, even though the code in COleControl actually passes the new ready state. The type library generated in this case will not match the actual code. I had to add the "long NewState" parameter shown in italics above by hand. You must do this for your apps as well until Microsoft fixes this.

Note: If you forget to check the box in Control Wizard, or want to add asynchronous downloading to an existing control, you can easily add this property and event by hand. Make sure you get the names and dispatch IDs right.

342

3. You don't want your movie control hard-wired to one specific movie; you want your customers to be able to place it on their pages and specify any AVI file anywhere on the Web that contains the flick they want to play. You do this by making the desired URL a standard synchronous property of your control, which the page designer can set. The name of this property can be anything you think the human Web page designer will recognize. The type of the property should be OLE_DATAPATH, which is typedefed as a BSTR. Thus:

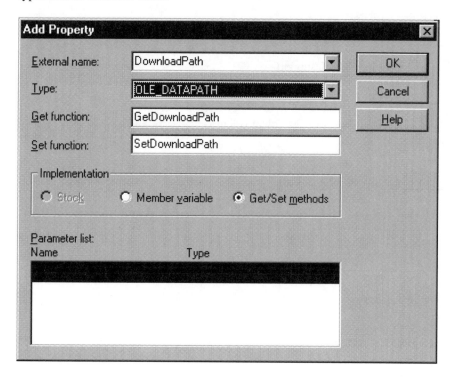

Note: At the time of this writing, the property type OLE_DATAPATH only appears in the drop-down list when you check the Get/Set methods radio button as shown above. Also, this type is not defined in the standard header files, so I had to #define it myself.

4. As discussed in Chapter 8, asynchronous downloading of data from the Internet is accomplished via the URL moniker and the IBindStatusCallback interface. The MFC provides a class encapsulating this functionality called *CAsyncMonikerFile*. Derived from it is the class *CDataPathProperty*, which connects an asynchronous downloading file to an ActiveX control. The class *CCachedDataPathProperty*, derived from CDataPathProperty, adds the functionality of automatically storing the downloaded data in a memory file, so you don't have to worry about reading it in. The hierarchy is:

CFile	File base class
COleStreamFile	Adds IStream support
CMonikerFile	Adds binding via a moniker
CAsyncMonikerFile	Adds asynchronous downloading via URL moniker
CDataPathProperty	Adds connection to a control
CCachedDataPathProperty	Adds automatic reading and storage of data in a memory file

For each separate URL that you want to download, you need to derive a class from one of these. Thus:

```
/*
This class supports automatic asynchronous download of text from the
Internet.
*/

class CAsynchText : public CCachedDataPathProperty
{
    DECLARE_DYNAMIC(CAsynchText)

    < rest of class definition>
}
```

After deriving your asynchronous file class, add an object of that class to your control. Thus:

```
/*
This control contains an object of class CAsynchText to provide
asynchronous download of its property.
*/

class CAtextCtrl : public COleControl
{
    DECLARE_DYNCREATE(CAtextCtrl)

// Constructor
public:
    CAtextCtrl();
    CAsynchText            m_AsynchText ;

    < rest of class declaration >
}
```

5. In the control, you must make the download path property persistent via the method **PX_DataPath( )**. When the control is loading its property set, use the method **CDataPathProperty::Open( )** to begin the binding process. The data path needs to know which control it is attached to, so we pass the method our `this` pointer. Thus:

```
void CAtextCtrl::DoPropExchange(CPropExchange* pPX)
{
    ExchangeVersion(pPX, MAKELONG(_wVerMinor, _wVerMajor));
    COleControl::DoPropExchange(pPX);

/*
Load or save download path property.
*/

    PX_DataPath (pPX, "DownloadPath", m_AsynchText) ;

/*
If we are loading the property set, then start the binding process for
the asynchronous moniker.
*/
    if (pPX->IsLoading( ))
    {
      BOOL bOK = m_AsynchText.Open (this) ;

      if (!bOK)
      {
          AfxMessageBox ("Couldn't start download") ;
      }
    }
}
```

6. In the derived class, you have to override the method **CDataPathProperty::GetBindInfo( )**, in which you return the flags that control the asynchronous moniker binding operation. At the time of this writing, the data-push model specified as the default does not work. You need to override this method and add the flag **BINDF_PULLDATA**, thereby using the data-pull model which does work. Thus:

```
DWORD CAsynchText::GetBindInfo() const
{
    return BINDF_ASYNCHRONOUS | BINDF_ASYNCSTORAGE | BINDF_PULLDATA ;
}
```

7. As the downloaded data is received, the moniker will call the method **CDataPathProperty::OnDataAvailable( )**. The default implementation of the CCachedDataPathProperty base class automatically reads the data into a memory file. You should override this method if you want to invalidate the control so as to render its data as it arrives. If you do this, make sure you call the base class as shown below, otherwise the data will not be read from the incoming stream and the download operation will hang.

The method **CDataPathProperty::GetControl( )** returns a pointer to the control to which the asynchronous download object is attached. In the example below, we use this to invalidate the control to force a repaint. When the last OnDataAvailable( ) notification arrives, as indicated by the flags, the method **COleControl::InternalSetReadyState( )** both changes the ReadyState property and fires the ReadyStateChange event. Thus:

```
void CAsynchText::OnDataAvailable(DWORD dwSize, DWORD bscfFlag) {

/*
Call the base class which actually reads the data into a memory file.
*/
    CCachedDataPathProperty::OnDataAvailable(dwSize, bscfFlag);

/*
Invalidate the control to which we belong to force a repaint. This
provides progressive rendering, with the data appearing on the screen as
it arrives.
*/
    GetControl( )->Invalidate( ) ;

/*
If this is the last OnDataAvailable( ) notification, set the ready state
flag and trigger the event.
*/
    if (bscfFlag & BSCF_LASTDATANOTIFICATION)
    {
      GetControl()->InternalSetReadyState(READYSTATE_COMPLETE);
    }
}
```

8. When the control's properties are reset in the method COleControl::OnResetState( ), you must stop any current download via the method **CDataPathProperty::ResetData( )**. Thus:

```
void CAtextCtrl::OnResetState()
{
    m_AsynchText.ResetData( ) ;

    COleControl::OnResetState();   // Resets defaults in DoPropExchange
}
```

9. The data path's Set( ) and Get( ) methods are shown below. When the download path property is set, calling the method **COleControl::Load( )** starts the download process. When a container wants to read the property, the method **CDataPathProperty::GetPath( )** returns the current value. Thus:

```
void CAtextCtrl::SetDownloadPath(LPCTSTR lpszNewValue)
{
    Load(lpszNewValue, m_AsynchText);

    SetModifiedFlag();
}

OLE_DATAPATH CAtextCtrl::GetDownloadPath()
{
    CString strResult;

    strResult = m_AsynchText.GetPath();

    return strResult.AllocSysString();
}
```

ActiveX Controls for the Internet

Directory: \EssenceofOLE\chap11\Download

This app uses the API function CoGetClassObjectFromURL( ) to download the control of your choice from the Internet. Run the app "client.exe" and select "Control – Create" from the main menu. When the dialog box appears, type in the class ID and URL of the control you want to download and install. The default points to a timer control on my Web site. If you have the timer control from Chapter 5 installed on your machine, it will give you a local copy of that. Unregister this control if you do not want this. You will see a progress bar as the control is downloaded from the Internet, and a security dialog box before the control is installed. If you like, type in the name and value of a property into the specified edit controls and the app will set the property to the specified value when the control is created. The default sets the background color, which most controls support, to yellow.

Directory: \EssenceofOLE\chap11\Atext

This is an extremely simple control that demonstrates asynchronous download of properties from the Internet. The control contains a property called "DownloadPath" which specifies the URL which it displays. Use the DLL Registering Tool app from Appendix A to invoke the self-registration code in "atext.ocx". After doing this, open the file "atextdemo.htm" using IE3. When IE3 runs the script, you should see the text of my home page appear. When the download is complete, the control will fire the "ReadyStateChanged" event and the "Ready" button will become enabled. It doesn't do anything if you click on it. Use the ActiveX control pad to set the "DownloadPath" property to point to different locations.

Directory: \EssenceofOLE\chap11\SignedTimer

This directory contains a timer control that has been signed with the Code Signing Wizard demonstrated in this chapter. Examine it with a binary editor and note the differences between it and the timer control from Chapter 5.

Chapter 12
ActiveX Scripting

A. CONCEPTS AND DEFINITIONS

1. Sitting on a page looking pretty is fine for a clock or a picture control. However, to use the full power of controls, you must be able to dynamically call their methods, set and get their properties, and respond to their events. A movie control, for example, is much more useful if it can be started, stopped, or positioned in response to commands from the user. Forms become much more convenient to use if you can validate their information on the client before submitting them to the server.

2. ActiveX makes this possible by means of *scripting*. A *script host* app, such as a web browser, reads a series of statements, the *script*, written in some interpreted language, such as Java or VB. The script host loads a *script engine*, a server provided by a vendor that knows how to read, interpret, and execute the script. While originally developed for and very useful on HTML pages, you can use ActiveX scripting any place and any time you want scripting capability.

3. The architecture of ActiveX scripting is independent of the script language. The script host and engine communicate via OLE interfaces, as described on page 355. Anyone who already has an interpreted language can make more money by packaging it into an ActiveX script engine, thereby allowing any host app that speaks ActiveX script to use it.

4. Microsoft provides the scripting engines VBScript and JavaScript, which provide the Visual Basic and Java languages, respectively. These are automatically installed when you install Internet Explorer, and are also available on Microsoft's Web site. The actual server files are VBSCRIPT.DLL and JSCRIPT.DLL. Their binary files are fully redistributable in accordance with Microsoft's license agreement.

B. SCRIPTING IN HTML

1. A script on an HTML page is indicated by the tag **<SCRIPT>**. Since scripts can use any interpreted language for which a script engine server is available, the value **"LANGUAGE"** tells the client app which script engine to load in order to interpret the script which follows. The tags **<!--** and **-->** keep the script's text from being displayed on browser apps that do not recognize the <SCRIPT> tag.

When the browser encounters the <SCRIPT> tag, it loads the specified script engine and sends it the script text that follows the tag. Code that is outside any procedure, such as the call to MsgBox( ) in the example below, is executed immediately upon page entry. Code in procedures is executed only when the procedure is called. In the example below, the subroutine Timer1_DblClick( ) is executed when the Timer1 object signals a double-click event.

The script shown below can be found in the directory \CHAP12\SCRIPTHOST\SIMPLE.HTM. You must have installed the timer control from Chapter 5 for it to work. If you open it with Internet Explorer 3.0 (IE3), you will see the message box. You will see the timer's About box when you double-click the mouse on it. Thus:

```
<HTML>
<HEAD>
<TITLE>New Page</TITLE>
</HEAD>
<BODY>
    <SCRIPT LANGUAGE="VBScript">
<!--

MsgBox ("Hello, World")

Sub Timer1_DblClick()
    call Timer1.AboutBox()
end sub

-->
    </SCRIPT>

    <OBJECT ID="Timer1" WIDTH=100 HEIGHT=51
     CLASSID="CLSID:69999373-BD40-11CF-8A6C-00AA00A58097">
        <PARAM NAME="_Version" VALUE="65536">
        <PARAM NAME="_ExtentX" VALUE="2646">
        <PARAM NAME="_ExtentY" VALUE="1323">
        <PARAM NAME="_StockProps" VALUE="1">
        <PARAM NAME="ShowSeconds" VALUE="1">
    </OBJECT>
</BODY>
</HTML>
```

2. The ActiveX Control Pad is a pretty good script editor. I used it to create the script on the previous page. Thus:

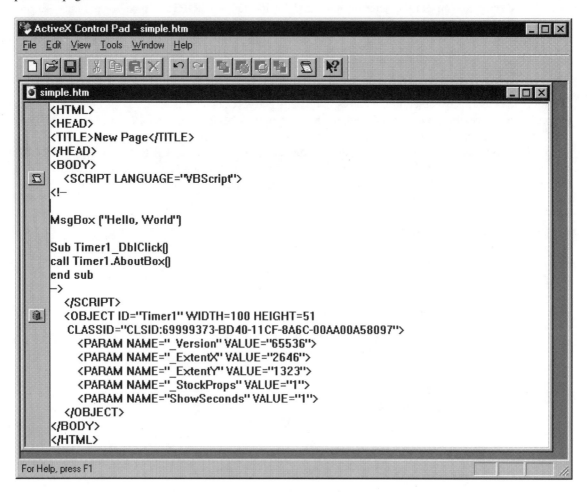

3. Selecting "Tools — Script Wizard..." from the menu brings up the Script Wizard dialog box, which allows you to easily choose events and specify the actions to be taken when they fire. In the example on the previous page, the event `Timer1_DblClick` was added using the Script Wizard, but the `MsgBox( )` line was added by hand. Thus:

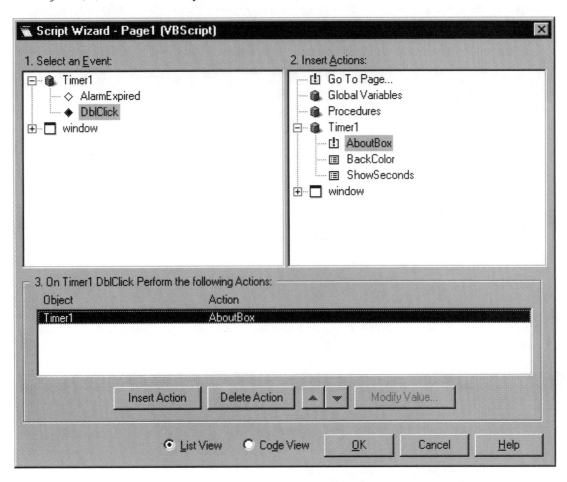

C. OLE ARCHITECTURE OF SCRIPTING

1. The connection between the script host and its engine is accomplished via standard OLE mechanisms. The "Language" value in the <SCRIPT> tag specifies the name of the script engine to use for interpreting the script that follows. That name must be registered with the "CLSID" key underneath it, exactly as is done with the name of any other OLE server. The key "OLEScript" designates that ID as belonging to an ActiveX script engine server, and is required for proper operation of IE3. Thus:

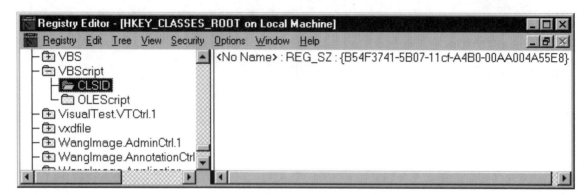

2. Under the registry key HKEY_CLASSES_ROOT\CLSID, the script engine makes the standard InProcServer32 entry, pointing to the DLL in which the server's code resides. A script engine also must add the key "OLEScript" as shown below, thereby identifying the server as an ActiveX script engine, similar to the way the presence of the "Control" key marked that entry as belonging to a full-featured OLE control. Thus:

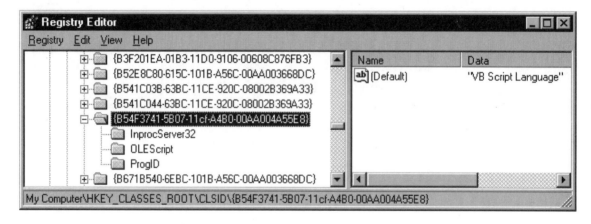

3. A script host and its engine communicate as shown in the following diagram:

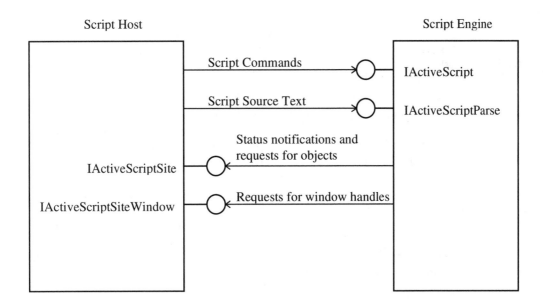

The script host must implement the *IActiveScriptSite* interface. The script engine uses this interface to communicate with the host while the script is executing, signaling such events as its entry, exit, and errors. This interface also provides the engine with pointers to automation objects required by the script. The methods of this interface are:

IActiveScriptSite::GetLCID	*// get locale of script, if other than default*
IActiveScriptSite::GetItemInfo	*// get IDispatch or ITypeInfo of an object in a script*
IActiveScriptSite::GetDocVersionString	*// get version string of document*
IActiveScriptSite::OnScriptTerminate	*// notify host that script has terminated*
IActiveScriptSite::OnStateChange	*// notify host that script has changed state*
IActiveScriptSite::OnScriptError	*// notify host of an error in the script*
IActiveScriptSite::OnEnterScript	*// notify script that execution has entered script*
IActiveScriptSite::OnLeaveScript	*// notify host that execution has left script*

If the host wants to allow the script any access to the Windows user interface, which is optional but customary, it must also implement the *IActiveScriptSiteWindow* interface. This provides the script engine with a window handle which it can use as a parent window for such things as message boxes. The methods of this interface are:

IActiveScriptSiteWindow::GetWindow	*// get hWnd to use as parent for script's dlg boxes*
IActiveScriptSiteWindow::EnableModeless	*// tell host to show or remove modeless dialog boxes*

4. A script engine is a DLL server that implements the *IActiveScript* interface. This interface allows the host to control execution of the script, for example, starting and stopping it. Its methods are:

IActiveScript::SetScriptSite   *// provide engine with IActiveScriptSite object*
IActiveScript::GetScriptSite   *// get current IActiveScriptSite used by engine*
IActiveScript::SetScriptState   *// set current execution state of script engine*
IActiveScript::GetScriptState   *// get current execution state of script engine*
IActiveScript::Close   *// politely shut down script engine*
IActiveScript::AddNamedItem   *// tell engine of existence of an object in the script*
IActiveScript::AddTypeLib   *// add new type library to script's name space*
IActiveScript::GetScriptDispatch   *// get IDispatch of object in currently running script*
IActiveScript::GetCurrentScriptThreadID   *// get ID of currently executing script thread*
IActiveScript::GetScriptThreadID   *// get ID of specified script thread*
IActiveScript::GetScriptThreadState   *// get state of specified script thread*
IActiveScript::InterruptScriptThread   *// stop an executing script thread*
IActiveScript::Clone   *// create clone of current script engine*

It is optional but customary for the script engine to also support the *IActiveScriptParse* interface. This allows the host to send the script to the engine in standard text format. The methods of this interface are:

IActiveScriptParse::InitNew   *// start new script*
IActiveScriptParse::AddScriptlet   *// add new piece to current script*
IActiveScriptParse::ParseScriptText *// send script in text format to engine for execution*

If the host does not support this interface, then it must support the IPersistStream interface to allow the host to provide its script.

D. SCRIPT HOSTS

1. The examples shown in this section come from the sample script host app shown below. The code may be found in the directory \CHAP12\SCRIPTHOST, and full directions are at the end of this chapter. The app searches your registry for all registered script engines and makes an entry for each one on the "Engine" menu popup. The left-hand pane is a CEditView which allows you to open, edit, and save scripts. The right-hand pane contains a single ActiveX control which you can select using the "Control – Replace Existing" menu item. The scripts that you write may refer to the control by the name "Control1".

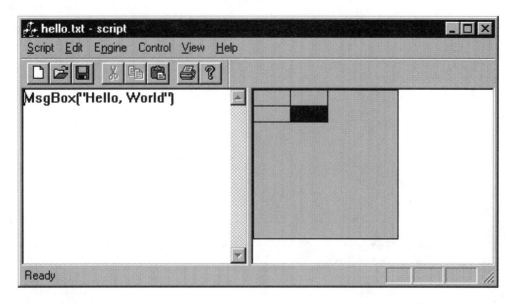

Note: Most Java apps require the host to provide a number of different objects, such as a window object and a document object. This host app does not support the object model, so don't be surprised if you can't do anything fancy with JavaScript.

2. When the user picks the menu command telling the sample app to run a script, we must first create the script engine object via our old friend CoCreateInstance( ). We ask the newly created object for the interface **IID_IActiveScript**, which we need to run the script. Note that the class ID that we pass to this function is the only difference between operating one script engine and another. The text in the script will probably vary, but the operation of the host need not.

Once we have this interface pointer to the script engine, we need to tell the engine about the site in which it runs. We do this by calling the method **IActiveScript::SetScriptSite( )**, passing a pointer to the IActiveScriptSite interface provided by the host. Our view contains a member variable of this class, whose implementation is shown beginning on page 363. Thus:

```
extern CLSID g_EngineClsid ;

void CScriptView::OnScriptRun()
{
    HRESULT hr;
/*
Create the active script engine to be used for the script in this
window.
*/

    hr = CoCreateInstance (
      g_EngineClsid,              // clsid of script engine server
      NULL,
      CLSCTX_INPROC_SERVER,
      IID_IActiveScript,          // need this interface to run a script
      (void **)&m_pActiveScriptEngine);

    if (hr != S_OK)
    {
      AfxMessageBox ("Couldn't create script engine object") ;
      return ;
    }

/*
Tell the IActiveScript about the site it lives in.
*/

    hr = m_pActiveScriptEngine->SetScriptSite(&m_ActiveSite);
```

3. Now that we have connected the circuitry between the host and the script engine, we need to feed the script to the engine. Most script engines will support the interface IActiveScriptParse, which allows the host to feed the script in text format directly to the engine. If the engine does not support this interface, it must support IPersistStream and allow the script to be fed in that way. Once we have this interface pointer, we initialize the script engine's parser via the method **IActiveScriptParse::InitNew( )**, then send the script to the engine via the method **IActiveScriptParse::ParseScriptText( )**. Thus:

<continued from previous page>
```
/*
We need the IActiveScriptParse interface to send the script to the
script engine.
*/
    hr = m_pActiveScriptEngine->QueryInterface (IID_IActiveScriptParse,
      (void **)&m_pActiveParse);

    if (hr != S_OK)
    {
      AfxMessageBox ("Couldn't get IActiveScriptParse") ;
      m_pActiveScriptEngine->Release( ) ;
      return ;
    }


/*
Initialize the script engine's parser.
*/


    hr = m_pActiveParse->InitNew( ) ;


/*
Fetch our text from our view's edit control.
*/


    char TextBuf [4096] ;
    GetEditCtrl( ).GetWindowText (TextBuf, sizeof(TextBuf)) ;


/*
Send it to the script engine in wide character format.
*/


    USES_CONVERSION

    hr = m_pActiveParse->ParseScriptText (
      A2W(TextBuf),        // text to parse, in wide chars
      NULL,                // item name
      NULL,                // debugging context
      NULL,                // end delimiter
      0,                   // cookie
      0,                   // start line number
      0,                   // flags
      NULL,                // buffer for processing results
      NULL) ;              // ptr to EXECEPINFO structure for results
```

<continued on next page>

4. Scripts will frequently need to access automation objects such as controls. The whole point of a script is to tie one object to another. A script engine needs to know what objects the script contains. You tell it by calling the method **IActiveScript::AddNamedItem( )** once for each top-level object in the script, passing the object's name. This will cause the script engine to call the host's method IActiveScriptSite::GetItemInfo( ) to get the IDispatch and type info that it needs to use the object, as shown on page 364. The provided sample app contains a single control whose name is always "Control1".

Once all the objects have been named, you can run the script via the method **IActiveScript::SetScriptState( )**, passing it the somewhat obtusely named state SCRIPTSTATE_CONNECTED. Thus:

```
<continued from previous page>

/*
Tell the script that the control exists.
*/

    hr = m_pActiveScriptEngine->AddNamedItem (
      L"Control1",                                    // object name in script
      SCRIPTITEM_ISSOURCE | SCRIPTITEM_ISVISIBLE) ;   // flags

/*
Tell script engine to run the script.
*/
    hr = m_pActiveScriptEngine->SetScriptState (SCRIPTSTATE_CONNECTED) ;


    if (hr != S_OK)
    {
      AfxMessageBox ("Script wouldn't run") ;
    }
    else
    {
      m_bIsRunning = TRUE ;
    }
}
```

5. Stopping a script is fairly simple; you call the method **IActiveScript::SetScriptState( )**, telling the script engine to go into the disconnected state. The method **IActiveScript::Close( )** tells the script engine to empty its buffers and release all the interface pointers that it holds to the host, including the IActiveScriptSite and IActiveScriptSiteWindow. Finally, the host releases the engine. Thus:

```
void CScriptView::OnScriptStop()
{
    HRESULT hr ;

/*
Put script into disconnected state.
*/

    hr = m_pActiveScriptEngine->SetScriptState (
      SCRIPTSTATE_DISCONNECTED) ;

/*
Close the script engine. This causes the engine to release its pointers
to the host.
*/

    hr = m_pActiveScriptEngine->Close ( ) ;

/*
Release all pointers.
*/

    hr = m_pActiveParse->Release ( ) ;
    hr = m_pActiveScriptEngine->Release( ) ;
    m_pActiveScriptEngine = NULL ;

    m_bIsRunning = FALSE ;
}
```

6. The host must implement the IActiveScriptSiteWindow interface in conjunction with the IActiveScriptSite interface. This is probably most easily done via multiple inheritance. Thus :

```
class CActiveScriptSite: public IActiveScriptSite,
    public IActiveScriptSiteWindow
{

    <rest of class declaration>

}
```

7. The IActiveScriptSiteWindow interface is trivial, so I'll knock it out of the way now. If the script engine needs a window handle for any reason, such to use as the parent of a dialog box required by the script code, it will query the script site for this interface and call the method **IActiveScriptSiteWindow::GetWindow( )**. If you omit this interface from the host app, the VBScript engine will never be able to show a message box. The method **IActiveScriptSiteWindow::EnableModeless( )** tells the host app to show or remove its modeless dialog boxes in the event that the script is about to show a modal dialog box. Both of the implementations are trivial. Thus:

```
/*
Engine asking for window to use as a parent for a message box.  Respond
with main frame window.
*/

STDMETHODIMP CActiveScriptSite::GetWindow(HWND *phWnd)
{
    if (phWnd)
    {
      *phWnd = AfxGetApp( )->m_pMainWnd->m_hWnd ;
    }
    return S_OK ;
}


/*
Engine telling us to show/hide modeless dialog boxes.  We don't have
any, so ignore it.
*/

STDMETHODIMP CActiveScriptSite::EnableModeless (BOOL bModeless)
{
    return S_OK ;
}
```

8. When the host tells the engine that an object exists via IActiveScript::AddNamedItem( ), the engine will obtain the object's interface pointers via the method **IActiveScriptSite::GetItemInfo( )**. The engine might ask for the object's IUnknown method providing access to its IDispatch, or it might ask for the type info describing the methods and properties which the object supports and the events that it might signal. In the case of the type info, you must provide the type info describing the object's entire CoClass, not just the properties and methods IDispatch. In this example, the base class CCtrlHolder, which wraps the control, contains helper methods for providing these pointers. You can view them in the sample source code. Thus:

```
extern        CCtrlHolder*        g_pControl1 ;

STDMETHODIMP CActiveScriptSite::GetItemInfo(LPCOLESTR    pName,
    DWORD         dwReturnMask,  IUnknown**  ppDispOut,
    ITypeInfo** ppTypeInfoOut)
{
    HRESULT hr;
    USES_CONVERSION

/*
See if the script engine is asking for our single control object.
*/

    if (wcsicmp (pName, L"Control1") == 0)
    {
/*
If they are asking for the object's IUnknown pointer, provide that.
GetDispatch( ) helper function provided in CCtrlHolder class.
*/

        if (dwReturnMask & SCRIPTINFO_IUNKNOWN)
        {
            hr = g_pControl1->GetDispatch ((IDispatch **)ppDispOut) ;
        }

/*
If they are also/otherwise asking for the type info, provide that. Make
sure it is the type info of the entire CoClass. GetTypeInfo( ) helper
function provided in CCtrlHolder class. See sample source code.
*/
        if (dwReturnMask & SCRIPTINFO_ITYPEINFO)
        {
            hr = g_pControl1->GetTypeInfo (ppTypeInfoOut) ;
        }
        return hr ;
    }

/*
Otherwise signal error.
*/
    MessageBox (NULL, W2A(pName), "Unknown object", 0) ;
    return TYPE_E_ELEMENTNOTFOUND;
}
```

9. If the script engine detects an error in the execution of the script, the engine will call the method **IActiveScriptSite::OnScriptError( )**, passing a pointer to an object which implements the *IActiveScriptError* interface. Its methods are: :

    IActiveScriptError::GetExceptionInfo   *// get EXCEPINFO structure describing error*
    IActiveScriptError::GetSourcePosition   *// get line number and character position of error*
    IActiveScriptError::GetSourceLineText   *// get text of script source code line causing error*

In the sample program, all we do is pop up a dialog box telling the user about the error.

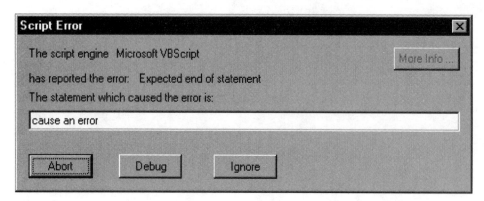

The code returned from this method by the host tells the script engine what to do in response to the error. Thus:

```
STDMETHODIMP CActiveScriptSite::OnScriptError(IActiveScriptError *pse)
{
    HRESULT    hr;

/*
Get the EXCEPINFO structure describing the error.
*/
    EXCEPINFO ei;
    hr = pse->GetExceptionInfo(&ei) ;

/*
Get the position in the source code at which the error took place.
*/

    DWORD context,line ;
    LONG CharPos ;

    hr = pse->GetSourcePosition(&context, &line, &CharPos) ;

/*
Get the text of the source line that failed.
*/

    BSTR bstrLine ;
    hr = pse->GetSourceLineText(&bstrLine);

    <continued on next page>
```

364

```
/*
Format and display error for user.
*/
    CScriptErrorDlg dlg ;

    dlg.m_ErrorName = ei.bstrDescription ;
    dlg.m_AppName = ei.bstrSource ;
    dlg.m_ErrorStatement = bstrLine ;
    dlg.m_HelpFile = ei.bstrHelpFile ;
    dlg.m_HelpContext = ei.dwHelpContext ;

    int i = dlg.DoModal( ) ;

/*
Clean up BSTRS.
*/

    SysFreeString (ei.bstrDescription) ;
    SysFreeString (ei.bstrSource) ;
    SysFreeString (ei.bstrHelpFile) ;
    SysFreeString (bstrLine) ;


/*
Return codes to tell the script engine what to do based on user's choice
of the Ignore, Debug, or Quit buttons.
*/

/*
Abort button clicked, abort execution of script.
*/
    if (i == IDC_ABORT)
    {
      return E_FAIL ;
    }
/*
Tell engine to run script in a debugger if available, otherwise handle
as if aborted.
*/
    else if (i == IDC_DEBUG)
    {
      return S_FALSE ;
    }
/*
This tells the engine to ignore the error and keep trying to run.
*/
    else
    {
      return S_OK ;
    }
}
```

E. SCRIPT ENGINES

1.   As previously stated, a script engine is an OLE server that exposes the IActiveScript and IActiveScriptParse interface. Writing the OLE wrapper of a script engine is several orders of magnitude less involved than writing the script interpreter itself. If you already have a scripting language, you can make it available to many more potential paying customers by packaging ActiveX script engine.

2. To make this happen, you simply write a standard in-proc OLE server that implements the IActiveScript interface. Microsoft says that IActiveScriptParse is optional, but support for it in other apps is so widespread that you ought to consider it mandatory as well. This section uses the sample app in the directory \CHAPTER12\SCRIPTENGINE. This is an extremely simple DLL that pops up a message box containing the script when you put it into the connected state. Instructions are given at the end of this chapter.

```
class  CScriptEngine : public IActiveScript, public IActiveScriptParse
{
     public:
       ULONG              m_RefCount;

       IActiveScriptSite *      m_pActiveSite ;
       SCRIPTSTATE              m_ss ;
       char *                   m_pScriptText ;
       DWORD                    m_ThreadId

        CScriptEngine  (void) ;
        ~CScriptEngine (void);

     < rest of class declaration >
}
```

3. As usual in OLE, many of the methods are trivial. For example, the **IActiveScript::GetSite( )** and **SetSite( )** methods work exactly like every other set and get in all of OLE. Thus:

```
STDMETHODIMP CScriptEngine::SetScriptSite(IActiveScriptSite *pass)
{

/*
Host is providing us with a pointer to the IActiveScriptSite interface.
Keep a copy of it, which means we have to AddRef( ) it.
*/

    if (pass)
    {
      m_pActiveSite = pass ;
      m_pActiveSite->AddRef ( ) ;
    }
    return S_OK ;
}


/*
Host is asking for the specified interface on the IActiveScriptSite
pointer that we are currently using. If it supports the specified
interface, AddRef( ) it and return a pointer to it. Otherwise return an
error code.
*/

STDMETHODIMP CScriptEngine::GetScriptSite(REFIID riid, void **ppv)
{
    if (m_pActiveSite)
    {
      return m_pActiveSite->QueryInterface (riid, ppv) ;
    }
    else
    {
      *ppv = NULL ;
      return E_NOINTERFACE ;
    }
}
```

4. The host puts our engine into the connected state by calling the method **IActiveScript::SetScriptState( )**. When this happens, we need to spin off a new thread to execute the script, thereby allowing the call to return and the script to stay active. In this example, the thread function ScriptThreadFunc( ) simply pops up a dialog box containing the script's text so you can see it. Thus:

```
extern DWORD WINAPI ScriptThreadFunc (LPVOID) ;

STDMETHODIMP CScriptEngine::SetScriptState(SCRIPTSTATE ss)
{

/*
Save script state in a member variable.
*/
    m_ss = ss ;

/*
If host has told us to connect the script, spin off a thread to execute
it. The thread function in this simple example does nothing but pop up a
box containing the script text.
*/
    if (m_ss == SCRIPTSTATE_CONNECTED)
    {
     DWORD dwId ;

     HANDLE hThread = CreateThread (NULL, 0, ScriptThreadFunc,
            this, 0, &m_ThreadId) ;

     CloseHandle (hThread) ;
    }

    return S_OK ;
}
```

5. To get the sample script engine to work with IE3, it was necessary to implement the methods **IActiveScript::GetCurrentScriptThreadID( )**. This returns an integer that identifies the thread to the script engine. It might as well be the thread's ID from the operating system, stored when we created the thread.

```
STDMETHODIMP CScriptEngine::GetCurrentScriptThreadID(
    SCRIPTTHREADID *pstidThread)
{
    if (pstidThread)
    {
      *pstidThread = m_ThreadId ;
    }
    return S_OK  ;
}
```

6. When the host calls the method **IActiveScript::Close( )**, the engine must release the pointers that it holds to the host's interfaces. Thus:

```
STDMETHODIMP CScriptEngine::Close(void)
{

/*
Script  engine  closing  down.  Release  pointer  to  IActiveScriptSite
interface if we have been given one by the host.
*/
    if (m_pActiveSite)
    {
      m_pActiveSite->Release ( ) ;
      m_pActiveSite = NULL ;
    }
    return S_OK ;
}
```

7. The IActiveScriptParse interface is conceptually quite simple. All we do is remember the script code provided by the host. In the sample app, we use a simple character array. Thus:

```
/*
Host telling us to initialize a new script.  Release memory holding
previous script, if any.
*/

STDMETHODIMP CScriptEngine::InitNew( void)
{
    if (m_pScriptText)
    {
      free (m_pScriptText) ;
      m_pScriptText = NULL ;
    }

    return S_OK ;
}


/*
Host is providing us with a new script.  Allocate memory to hold it and
copy the script into that memory.
*/

STDMETHODIMP CScriptEngine::ParseScriptText(LPCOLESTR pstrCode,
    LPCOLESTR pstrItemName, IUnknown *punkContext,
    LPCOLESTR pstrDelimiter, DWORD dwSourceContextCookie,
    ULONG ulStartingLineNumber, DWORD dwFlags, VARIANT *pvarResult,
    EXCEPINFO *pexcepinfo)
{
/*
Get length of script string.
*/
    int length = wcslen (pstrCode) ;

/*
Allocate buffer of that size.
*/
    m_pScriptText = (char *)malloc (length + 1) ;

    if (m_pScriptText == NULL)
    {
      return E_OUTOFMEMORY ;
    }

/*
Copy script text into script engine's storage, converting it to ANSI.
*/
    WideCharToMultiByte (CP_ACP, 0, pstrCode, length+1, m_pScriptText,
      length+1, NULL, NULL) ;
    return S_OK ;
}
```

F. SCRIPT SECURITY

1. Using HTML pages containing scripts poses a far greater security risk than using a control from the Internet in your own apps. You can reliably know who wrote a control and that the control hasn't been tampered with, and decide to trust it or not. But there is currently no way of identifying and deciding to trust the author of a script.

Think about the WinWord macro viruses that exist today. WinWord is a relatively benign app, written by a relatively reputable vendor. Because of WinWord's power, a malicious macro can do essentially anything to your system. A control in a script has the same problem.

2. When IE3 is running in its medium security level and opens a page that contains a script, it shows the following dialog box, allowing the user to choose whether to run the script or not. This doesn't help much if the script is malicious, but at least the user won't be able to curse Microsoft when the script formats his hard drive.

IE3 also contains a higher level of security which will not run scripts at all, and a lower one that always runs scripts without asking first. You probably want to build in some similar security feature into your script-aware apps.

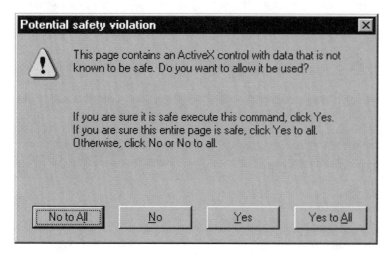

3. While today it is impossible to put trust certificates on Web pages, a control vendor can mark a control as being guaranteed safe in all situations. Consider the timer control that we developed in Chapter 5. It doesn't do anything except set a timer and draw on the screen. It can't possibly harm anyone or anything, no matter what methods a script calls or what properties are set to what values.

A control promises its complete harmlessness by making entries in the registry. A browser app that creates such a control may read the registry, check for the presence of these keys, and omit the security warning if they are present.

What if the control is lying about its harmlessness? There is no need for it to do so. If a control wanted to be malicious, it could trash your hard drive as soon as it passed WinTrustVerify( ). What if the control says it's harmless and honestly believes it, but some malicious Web page author finds a hole in it? You're scrod. See the previous chapter for ways to set up a sandbox for your apps.

4. In order to mark your control as safe, you must make entries under the new "Component Categories" registry key. This key was added to organize the entries that OLE servers make to identify the capabilities they promise to provide. It holds zero or more *category IDs*, 16-byte GUIDs, each of which identifies a particular capability that a registered class promises to support. It is conceptually similar to the "Control" or "OLEScript" registry keys, which promise specific, relatively large levels of functionality. Each category ID represents a similar promise, generally of a smaller level of functionality.

In the case of scripting, the category ID `CATID_SafeForScripting` indicates that a control is safe for using in scripts if no data is provided to it. The category ID `CATID_SafeForInitializing` indicates that the specified control is safe no matter what initialization data the script provides to it. If both of these category IDs are present in all controls used in a script, IE3 allows a script to run without a warning, even in the high-security mode that doesn't normally allow scripts at all. I don't know if I like to take a control's word for it, especially in the latter case, but that's how they wrote IE3. Thus:

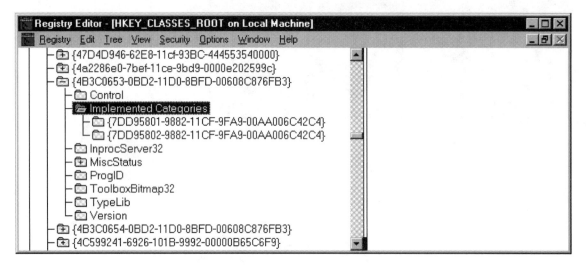

5. You can make category ID entries in the registry by using the *component category manager* provided by the operating system. This is an OLE server that provides the *ICatRegister* interface, a set of methods used for manipulating categories. Its methods are:

ICatRegister::RegisterCategories   *// register human-readable category name*
ICatRegister::UnRegisterCategories   *// unregister human-readable category name*
ICatRegister::RegisterClassImplCategories   *// register a class as implementing a category*
ICatRegister::UnRegisterClassImplCategories   *// unregister a class as implementing a category*
ICatRegister::RegisterClassReqCategories   *// register a class as requiring a category*
ICatRegister::UnRegisterClassReqCategories   *// unregister a class as requiring a category*

You instantiate an object of this class via our old friend CoCreateInstance( ), creating an object whose GUID is **CLSID_StdComponentCategoriesMgr**, asking for the ICatRegister interface. You must include the header file **"comcat.h"**. The method **ICatRegister::RegisterClassImplCategories( )** actually places the category IDs in the registry. The IDs for the safety-related categories are in the file **"objsafe.h"**. Thus:

```
#include <objsafe.h>
#include <comcat.h>
extern GUID guid ;

STDAPI DllRegisterServer(void)
{
    <standard App Wizard registration code omitted>
/*
Register control component categories. First, open category manager
object.
*/
    ICatRegister* pcr ;
    HRESULT hr = CoCreateInstance(
      CLSID_StdComponentCategoriesMgr,
      NULL, CLSCTX_INPROC_SERVER,
      IID_ICatRegister, (void**)&pcr);
  /*
Use category manager to place entries in the registry.
*/
    if (SUCCEEDED(hr))
    {
      CATID catid[2] ;
      catid[0] = CATID_SafeForScripting ;
      catid[1] = CATID_SafeForInitializing ;

      hr = pcr->RegisterClassImplCategories(
            guid,       // GUID of control to make entries for
            2,          // number of CATIDs being added
            catid);     // array of CATIDs to add
    }
    if (pcr != NULL)
    {
        pcr->Release();
    }
    return NOERROR;
}
```

ActiveX Scripting

Directory: \EssenceofOLE\chap12\scripthost

This app is a simple script host. It searches your registry for all registered script engines and makes an entry for each one on the "Engine" menu popup. If it can't find any, it complains and exits. The left-hand pane is a CEditView which allows you to open, edit, and save scripts. The right-hand pane contains a single ActiveX control which you can select using the "Control – Replace Existing" menu item. The scripts that you write may refer to the control by the name "Control1". Several text files containing scripts are provided for you to use. Try the simplest one first, "Hello.txt". Commands for starting and stopping the script are found on the "File" menu.

Directory: \EssenceofOLE\chap12\scriptengine

This is an extremely simple script engine. Use the DLL Registering Tool app from Appendix A to invoke the self-registration code in "scriptengine.dll". After doing this, open the file "enginetest.htm" using IE3. When IE2 runs the script, you should see a dialog box appear containing the script text found on the HTML page. You may also see various message boxes informing you of the different methods of the script engine's interface being called by the host. After registering the engine, you will also see it appear on the menu of the host sample app discussed above.

Directory: \EssenceofOLE\chap12\safecntrl

This control makes entries in the registry that identify it as safe for use in scripts under all conditions. Use the DLL Registering Tool app from Appendix A to invoke the self-registration code in "safecntrl.ocx". After doing this, open the file "safecntrl.htm" using IE3. You will see a control appear on the page with the word "Safe" inside it. IE3 will not show you any warning messages regardless of the security setting, because it trusts the control's declaration that the control is safe at all times.

Appendix A
Self-Registering Servers

This page intentionally contains no text other than this sentence.

1. As we have seen throughout this book, OLE servers need to place entries in the system registry so that OLE can locate the server when asked by a client app to create an object. For the sake of transparency the example code in this book has primarily provided this capability through a .REG file which the user must edit to contain the server's exact path and explicitly place into the registry. This need for user intervention is inconvenient and prone to error. How many times in the course of using this book have you mistakenly set the wrong path to a server? It would be very convenient if somehow the servers knew how to register themselves. For OCX and ActiveX controls, it isn't just convenient, it is required.

2. An in-proc (DLL) server provides self-registration capability by exporting the named function DllRegisterServer( ). An example of this is shown on the next page. When an external app wants to register the server, it loads the DLL, queries for this function, and calls it as shown on page 381. The code in this sample uses the registry API to make all the entries required by the server. The server should also provide a mechanism for unregistering itself by exporting the named function DllUnregisterServer( ) as shown on page 380. The sample code for a self-registering in-proc server can be found in the directory \chapAppendixA\SelfRegisteringDll.

3. A local server can perform self-registration in a slightly different manner. Since it cannot export functions by name, a local server should look on its command line for the switches /RegServer and /UnregServer, which should cause it to register or unregister itself accordingly. The local server should make API calls to register itself in a manner similar to the source code example for the DLL.

4. When used for OLE automation or controls, App Wizard automatically attaches the MFC's own self-registration functions. When you are writing custom interfaces, you can provide this functionality by tapping into the MFC object method COleObjectFactory::UpdateRegistryAll( ), as discussed at the end of Chapter 9. In an in-proc server, the MFC exports the named registration functions as described above. In a local server, as far as I can tell, the MFC ignores the command line flags described in the previous paragraph. An MFC local server simply registers itself every time it is launched as a standalone app (i.e., not by OLE), which is not a bad idea. That way, if a server gets moved, it will automatically patch up the registry the next time it is run, even if the user doesn't know about the /RegServer flag. An MFC local server does not seem to support the /UnregServer flag or any other form of unregistration, which is a bad idea.

```
static char *pGuidString = "{351D1CE0-DCAA-11cf-B85F-00608C876FB3}" ;
HINSTANCE hDllInst ;

STDAPI DllRegisterServer( )
{
    HKEY hClsidKey, hMyKey, hNameKey ;
    char FileName [256] ; int length ; LONG retval ;
/*
Open key to HKEY_CLASSES_ROOT\Clsid.
*/

    RegOpenKey (HKEY_CLASSES_ROOT, "CLSID", &hClsidKey) ;

/*
Create subkey using object's GUID
*/

    RegCreateKey (hClsidKey, pGuidString, &hMyKey) ;

/*
Get file name of the DLL.  Create the InProcServer32 key based on it.
*/

    length = GetModuleFileName (hDllInst, FileName, sizeof(FileName)) ;
    retval = RegSetValue (hMyKey, "InProcServer32", REG_SZ, FileName,
       length) ;

/*
Create human-readable name keys.
*/

    RegCreateKey (HKEY_CLASSES_ROOT, "EssenceOfOLE.Data5", &hNameKey) ;
    RegSetValue (hNameKey, "Clsid", REG_SZ, pGuidString,
       lstrlen(pGuidString)) ;


/*
Close keys and return success or failure code.
*/
    RegCloseKey (hMyKey) ;
    RegCloseKey (hClsidKey) ;
    RegCloseKey (hNameKey) ;

    if (retval == ERROR_SUCCESS)
    {
      return S_OK ;
    }
    else
    {
      return E_UNEXPECTED ;
    }
}
```

5. To be a good citizen, your DLL also wants to provide a mechanism for unregistering itself, which it does by exporting the function **DllUnregisterServer ( )** in a similar manner. Thus:

```
STDAPI DllUnregisterServer( )
{
    HKEY hClsidKey, hMyKey, hNameKey ; LONG retval ;

/*
Open top-level key and our object's guid key.
*/
    RegOpenKey (HKEY_CLASSES_ROOT, "CLSID", &hClsidKey) ;
    RegOpenKey (hClsidKey, pGuidString, &hMyKey) ;

/*
Delete our InProcServer32 server key.
*/
    retval = RegDeleteKey (hMyKey, "InProcServer32") ;

/*
Delete our object's guid key.  Under NT, this will fail if there are
other subkeys, which is the behavior we want.  Under Windows 95, it will
succeed and delete any subkeys, which isn't.  See note below.
*/
    RegDeleteKey (hClsidKey, pGuidString) ;

/*
Remove human-readable name entries.
*/
    RegOpenKey (HKEY_CLASSES_ROOT, "EssenceOfOLE.Data5", &hNameKey) ;
    RegDeleteKey (hNameKey, "Clsid") ;
    RegDeleteKey (HKEY_CLASSES_ROOT, "EssenceOfOLE.Data5") ;
/*
Close registry keys, signal success or failure.
*/
    RegCloseKey (hMyKey) ;
    RegCloseKey (hClsidKey) ;
    RegCloseKey (hNameKey) ;
    if (retval == ERROR_SUCCESS)
    {
      return S_OK ;
    }
    else
    {
      return E_UNEXPECTED ;
    }
}
```

Note: Self-unregistration is only supposed to remove keys that the server itself placed in the registry. If another app added a key to this CLSID, such as a LocalServer32 key or a TreatAs key, the DLL should not remove it and therefore must not remove its guid key either. In Windows NT, the above sample complies with this requirement, as the function RegDeleteKey( ) will not remove a key which contains subkeys. If another key has been placed under the object's key, the call will fail. Windows 95 does not provide this extra security, however. If you run this code under Windows 95, the key will be removed even if there are subkeys, so you must do more extensive checking before you call it.

6. A DLL needs the assistance of an app to register itself. VC++ contains a command line utility called REGSVR32.EXE. I have written a GUI version and supplied it to you in the sample directory \chapAppendixA\DllRegisteringTool. The active portion of the code looks something like this:

```
void CRegdllDlg::OnDoitnow()
{
/*
Get file name selected by user in edit control.  Load specified library.
Signal error if unable to do so.
*/
    char FileName [256] ;
    GetDlgItemText (IDC_EDIT1, FileName, sizeof(FileName)) ;

    HINSTANCE hLib = LoadLibrary (FileName) ;

    if (!hLib)
    {
      AfxMessageBox ("Specified file could not be loaded.") ;
      return ;
    }


/*
Based on selection of Register/Unregister radio button, query for the
address of the named function DllRegisterServer. If unable to find it,
signal error.
*/

    FARPROC pRegisterProc ;
    if (IsDlgButtonChecked (IDC_RADIO1))
    {
      pRegisterProc = GetProcAddress (hLib, "DllRegisterServer") ;

      if (!pRegisterProc)
      {
            AfxMessageBox ("Specified DLL does not export the
                  function DllRegisterServer( )") ;
            return ;
      }

/*
Call registration function exported by the DLL. Signal success or
failure.
*/
      if ((*pRegisterProc) ( ) == S_OK)
      {
            AfxMessageBox ("DLL server successfully registered") ;
      }
      else
      {
            AfxMessageBox ("DLL register unsuccessful") ;
      }
    }
}
```

Appendix B
The ANSI-Unicode Problem

1. You will by now have noticed that every string parameter to every OLE API function or interface method is defined as the type LPOLESTR. In the 16-bit world, this was just a regular ANSI character string, so you could ignore the entire issue, but in the 32-bit world, an OLESTR is of type WCHAR. This is a wide character string, a string made up of 16-bit characters using the Unicode character set. For anyone who has to provide Far Eastern character sets that require Kanji and doesn't mind restricting himself to Windows NT, Unicode is an incredible advantage. For anyone who doesn't care about non-Western character sets or who needs to support Windows 95, it's nothing but a pain in the ass. For a complete discussion of exactly what Unicode is and how it works, see Chapter 11 of *Advanced Windows NT* by Jeffrey Richter (Microsoft Press).

2. Regardless of your philosophy, OLE demands to be fed Unicode, so if we want to make an OLE app run, that's what we have to feed it. The easiest solution is to build your app to be Unicode-only. It's quite simple to do, you just #define the constant **UNICODE** in your system header files. This was done on some of the more involved sample apps, such as the Eliza local server in Chapter 9. The entire app is compiled to use Unicode strings. Windows NT uses Unicode internally, and your app will actually get slightly faster if you do this. But Windows 95 does not speak Unicode, so your Unicode app will not run on it at all. Very few markets, and no large ones, are willing to restrict themselves to NT at the time of this writing. Too bad.

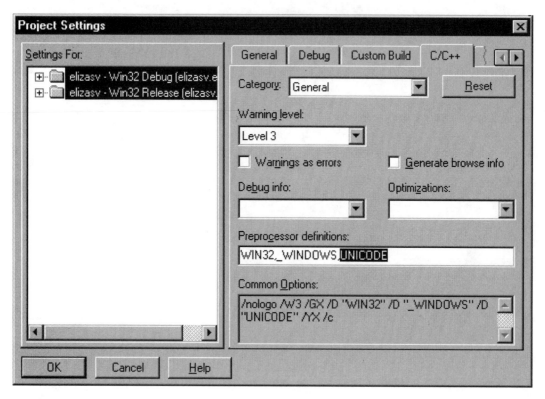

3. In the absence of a Unicode app, you have to handle all strings on a case-by-case basis. In places where strings are hardwired into code, prepending the capital letter 'L' (as in Long) onto a string causes the compiler to make it Unicode, even if the app around it isn't. Thus:

```
case ID_DATAOBJECT_CREATEDLL:
{
    HRESULT hr ;

/*
Read class ID from registry key. Must pass a Unicode string to this
function, so prepend 'L' to the string.
*/

    CLSID clsid ;
    hr = CLSIDFromProgID (L"EssenceofOLE.Data3", &clsid) ;

/*
Create object based on class ID read from registry.
*/

    hr = CoCreateInstance (clsid, ...) ;

    <rest of creation case>
}
```

4. To convert ANSI characters into Unicode, use the API function **MultiByteToWideChar( )**. In the example below from Chapter 8, we need a Unicode string to pass to the API function CreateItemMoniker( ). We assemble it in ANSI and convert it to Unicode. Thus:

```
extern WCHAR WideFileName ;

case ID_EDIT_COPYFILEITEMLINK:
{
    LPMONIKER pFileMoniker, pItemMoniker, pCompositeMoniker ;
    LPDATAOBJECT pData ;  char out [256] ; WCHAR wout [80] ;

/*
Create moniker for currently open file.
*/
    CreateFileMoniker (WideFileName, &pFileMoniker) ;

/*
Get selection of text, convert to wide chars, and create item moniker
naming it.
*/
    DWORD dwSel = SendMessage (hEdit, EM_GETSEL, 0, 0) ;
    wsprintf (out, "%d:%d", LOWORD(dwSel), HIWORD(dwSel)) ;

    MultiByteToWideChar (CP_ACP,        // code page
            0,                          // flags,
            out,                        // ANSI string to convert
            -1,                         // string is null-terminated
            wout,                       // output buffer for Unicode string
            sizeof(wout)) ;             // max # of characters to convert

    CreateItemMoniker (L"!",  // delimiter character
      wout,                   // object name
      &pItemMoniker) ;        // output variable

<rest of code omitted>
```

5. When OLE passes a string to one of your object's methods, the string is always in Unicode. In the following example, also from Chapter 8, OLE calls the method IOleItemContainer::GetObject( ), passing the name of the object which it has parsed from a moniker. We need to convert from the Unicode OLE gives us to the ANSI that we use internally. The API function **WideCharToMultiByte( )** performs this conversion for us. Thus:

```
STDMETHODIMP CFileTextData::GetObject(LPOLESTR pWideItemName,
    DWORD dwSpeed, LPBINDCTX pbc, REFIID riid, VOID **ppv)
{

    HRESULT hr ;
    char ItemName [256] ;

/*
Convert item name from wide to the ANSI that we use internally.
*/

    WideCharToMultiByte (CP_ACP,          // code page
            0,                            // flags
            pWideItemName,                // Unicode char string to convert
            -1,                           // string is null-terminated
            ItemName,                     // output buffer for ANSI string
            sizeof(ItemName),             // size of buffer
            NULL, NULL) ;                 // not used

    <rest of function>
```

6. In an MFC app, the MFC handles most of the conversions for you. For example, when you specify the name of a method or property in OLE automation, the MFC implementation of IDispatch::GetIDsofNames( ) knows to convert the string from ANSI to Unicode. But you will occasionally have to convert manually. In the following example, also from Chapter 8, we need to pass a Unicode string to the API function CreateURLMoniker( ). The MFC macro **A2W( )** performs this conversion in place for us. The macro **W2A( )** performs the opposite conversion (not shown). Both macros requires that you include the MFC macro **USES_CONVERSION** within the scope of their functions. All of these macros are defined in the MFC header file "**afxpriv.h**", which must be included as well. Thus:

```
#include <afxpriv.h>

void CUrlmonikerDlg::OnBind()
{
    char name [256] ;
    HRESULT hr ;

/*
Get name from combo box control. It is in ANSI characters.
*/

    m_URLCombo.GetWindowText (name, sizeof(name)) ;


/*
Use name to create an URL moniker. Store moniker in a member variable.
This function, as do all OLE functions, requires a wide character
string. The macro A2W( ) is an MFC macro that performs this conversion.
The macro USES_CONVERSION must be inserted prior to it as shown.
*/

    USES_CONVERSION ;
    hr = CreateURLMoniker (NULL, A2W(name), &m_pUrlMoniker) ;

    <remainder of code omitted>
```

MFC and, 114
registration, 113
Visual Basic, used in, 106
TYPEATTR structure, 128

U

UnmarshalInterface( ), IMarshal interface method, 306

V

VARDESC structure, 130

VARIANT structure, 72
VariantChangeType( ) function, 94
VariantInit( ) function, 74
Visual Basic
automation example, 98
Type libraries, used in, 106

W

WinVerifyTrust( ) function, 347
Write( ), IStream interface method, 228
WriteClassStm( ) function, 230

LICENSE AGREEMENT AND LIMITED WARRANTY

READ THE FOLLOWING TERMS AND CONDITIONS CAREFULLY BEFORE OPENING THIS SOFTWARE PACKAGE. THIS LEGAL DOCUMENT IS AN AGREEMENT BETWEEN YOU AND PRENTICE-HALL, INC. (THE "COMPANY"). BY OPENING THIS SEALED DISK PACKAGE, YOU ARE AGREEING TO BE BOUND BY THESE TERMS AND CONDITIONS. IF YOU DO NOT AGREE WITH THESE TERMS AND CONDITIONS, DO NOT OPEN THE PACKAGE. PROMPTLY RETURN THE UNOPENED SOFTWARE PACKAGE AND ALL ACCOMPANYING ITEMS TO THE PLACE YOU OBTAINED THEM FOR A FULL REFUND OF ANY SUMS YOU HAVE PAID.

1.   **GRANT OF LICENSE:** In consideration of your payment of the license fee, which is part of the price you paid for this product, and your agreement to abide by the terms and conditions of this Agreement, the Company grants to you a nonexclusive right to use and display the copy of the enclosed software program (hereinafter the "SOFTWARE") on a single computer (i.e., with a single CPU) at a single location so long as you comply with the terms of this Agreement. The Company reserves all rights not expressly granted to you under this Agreement.

2.   **OWNERSHIP OF SOFTWARE:** You own only the magnetic or physical media (the enclosed disks) on which the SOFTWARE is recorded or fixed, but the Company retains all the rights, title, and ownership to the SOFTWARE recorded on the original disk copy(ies) and all subsequent copies of the SOFTWARE, regardless of the form or media on which the original or other copies may exist. This license is not a sale of the original SOFTWARE or any copy to you.

3.   **COPY RESTRICTIONS:** This SOFTWARE and the accompanying printed materials and user manual (the "Documentation") are the subject of copyright. You may not copy the Documentation or the SOFTWARE, except that you may make a single copy of the SOFTWARE for backup or archival purposes only. You may be held legally responsible for any copying or copyright infringement which is caused or encouraged by your failure to abide by the terms of this restriction.

4.   **USE RESTRICTIONS:** You may not network the SOFTWARE or otherwise use it on more than one computer or computer terminal at the same time. You may physically transfer the SOFTWARE from one computer to another provided that the SOFTWARE is used on only one computer at a time. You may not distribute copies of the SOFTWARE or Documentation to others. You may not reverse engineer, disassemble, decompile, modify, adapt, translate, or create derivative works based on the SOFTWARE or the Documentation without the prior written consent of the Company.

5.   **TRANSFER RESTRICTIONS:** The enclosed SOFTWARE is licensed only to you and may not be transferred to any one else without the prior written consent of the Company. Any unauthorized transfer of the SOFTWARE shall result in the immediate termination of this Agreement.

6.   **TERMINATION:** This license is effective until terminated. This license will terminate automatically without notice from the Company and become null and void if you fail to comply with any provisions or limitations of this license. Upon termination, you shall destroy the Documentation and all copies of the SOFTWARE. All provisions of this Agreement as to warranties, limitation of liability, remedies or damages, and our ownership rights shall survive termination.

7.   **MISCELLANEOUS:** This Agreement shall be construed in accordance with the laws of the United States of America and the State of New York and shall benefit the Company, its affiliates, and assignees.

8.   **LIMITED WARRANTY AND DISCLAIMER OF WARRANTY:** The Company warrants that the SOFTWARE, when properly used in accordance with the Documentation, will operate in substantial conformity with the description of the SOFTWARE set forth in the Documentation. The Company does not warrant that the SOFTWARE will meet your requirements or that the operation of the SOFTWARE will be uninterrupted or error-free. The Company warrants that the media on which the SOFTWARE is delivered shall be free from defects in materials and workmanship under normal use for a period of thirty (30) days from the date of your purchase. Your only remedy and the Company's

only obligation under these limited warranties is, at the Company's option, return of the warranted item for a refund of any amounts paid by you or replacement of the item. Any replacement of SOFTWARE or media under the warranties shall not extend the original warranty period. The limited warranty set forth above shall not apply to any SOFTWARE which the Company determines in good faith has been subject to misuse, neglect, improper installation, repair, alteration, or damage by you. EXCEPT FOR THE EXPRESSED WARRANTIES SET FORTH ABOVE, THE COMPANY DIS-CLAIMS ALL WARRANTIES, EXPRESS OR IMPLIED, INCLUDING WITHOUT LIMITATION, THE IMPLIED WARRANTIES OF MERCHANTABILITY AND FITNESS FOR A PARTICULAR PURPOSE. EXCEPT FOR THE EXPRESS WARRANTY SET FORTH ABOVE, THE COMPANY DOES NOT WARRANT, GUARANTEE, OR MAKE ANY REPRESENTATION REGARDING THE USE OR THE RESULTS OF THE USE OF THE SOFT-WARE IN TERMS OF ITS CORRECTNESS, ACCURACY, RELIABILITY, CURRENTNESS, OR OTHERWISE.

IN NO EVENT, SHALL THE COMPANY OR ITS EMPLOYEES, AGENTS, SUPPLIERS, OR CON-TRACTORS BE LIABLE FOR ANY INCIDENTAL, INDIRECT, SPECIAL, OR CONSEQUENTIAL DAMAGES ARISING OUT OF OR IN CONNECTION WITH THE LICENSE GRANTED UNDER THIS AGREEMENT, OR FOR LOSS OF USE, LOSS OF DATA, LOSS OF INCOME OR PROFIT, OR OTHER LOSSES, SUSTAINED AS A RESULT OF INJURY TO ANY PERSON, OR LOSS OF OR DAMAGE TO PROPERTY, OR CLAIMS OF THIRD PARTIES, EVEN IF THE COMPANY OR AN AUTHORIZED REPRESENTATIVE OF THE COMPANY HAS BEEN ADVISED OF THE POSSIBILITY OF SUCH DAMAGES. IN NO EVENT SHALL LIABILITY OF THE COMPANY FOR DAMAGES WITH RESPECT TO THE SOFTWARE EXCEED THE AMOUNTS ACTU-ALLY PAID BY YOU, IF ANY, FOR THE SOFTWARE.

SOME JURISDICTIONS DO NOT ALLOW THE LIMITATION OF IMPLIED WARRANTIES OR LIABILITY FOR INCIDENTAL, INDIRECT, SPECIAL, OR CONSEQUENTIAL DAMAGES, SO THE ABOVE LIMITATIONS MAY NOT ALWAYS APPLY. THE WARRANTIES IN THIS AGREEMENT GIVE YOU SPECIFIC LEGAL RIGHTS AND YOU MAY ALSO HAVE OTHER RIGHTS WHICH VARY IN ACCORDANCE WITH LOCAL LAW.

ACKNOWLEDGMENT

YOU ACKNOWLEDGE THAT YOU HAVE READ THIS AGREEMENT, UNDERSTAND IT, AND AGREE TO BE BOUND BY ITS TERMS AND CONDITIONS. YOU ALSO AGREE THAT THIS AGREEMENT IS THE COMPLETE AND EXCLUSIVE STATEMENT OF THE AGREEMENT BETWEEN YOU AND THE COMPANY AND SUPERSEDES ALL PROPOSALS OR PRIOR AGREEMENTS, ORAL, OR WRITTEN, AND ANY OTHER COMMUNICATIONS BETWEEN YOU AND THE COMPANY OR ANY REPRESENTATIVE OF THE COMPANY RELATING TO THE SUBJECT MATTER OF THIS AGREEMENT.

Should you have any questions concerning this Agreement or if you wish to contact the Company for any reason, please contact in writing at the address below.

Robin Short
Prentice Hall PTR
One Lake Street
Upper Saddle River, New Jersey 07458